# AN EASY OUT

# AN EASY OUT

## Corporate America's Addiction to Outsourcing

*Jack Buffington*

PRAEGER

**Westport, Connecticut**
**London**

**Library of Congress Cataloging-in-Publication Data**

Buffington, Jack.
    An easy out : corporate America's addiction to outsourcing / Jack Buffington.
        p.  cm.
    Includes bibliographical references and index.
    ISBN 978–0–313–34502–9 (alk. paper)
    1. Contracting out—United States.   I. Title.
    HD2365.B84    2007
    338.6′3–dc22        2007027851

British Library Cataloguing in Publication Data is available.

Library of Congress Catalog Card Number: 2007027851
ISBN-13: 978–0–313–34502–9

First published in 2007

Praeger Publishers, 88 Post Road West, Westport, CT 06881
An imprint of Greenwood Publishing Group, Inc.
www.praeger.com

Printed in the United States of America

The paper used in this book complies with the
Permanent Paper Standard issued by the National
Information Standards Organization (Z39.48–1984).

10  9  8  7  6  5  4  3  2  1

*This is for Mom and Dad, who brought me up right,*
*my beautiful wife, Kari, who loves me even when I'm up at 1:00 A.M.*
*writing every night, and my wonderful daughters, Kaitlin and Marin, who*
*remind me every day of the importance of the future.*

# Contents

# Illustrations

# CHAPTER ONE

# The Need for Productivity

During the early nineties when I was a graduate student, America became obsessed with fear of the exploding Japanese economy. Japan's economic growth rates of 10% in the sixties, 5% in the seventies, and 4% in the eighties were viewed as a threat to our economic well-being. Manufacturing centers in America became rust belts, and coming from a family with roots in blue-collar labor, I paid attention to what was happening. Even though I was taught in school that it was America's destiny to evolve from an industrial to an information-based economy, I thought there was something wrong with this theory. Not until I joined the corporate ranks did I begin to understand how important the concept of productivity was to large corporations, achieved or not. When I accepted my first professional position in 1990, I was three months away from having to survive massive waves of layoffs at the company, the first layoffs in the company's history. I wondered, sometimes aloud, why the leaders who were being forced from power never thought through the need for productivity, and whether there was a realization that the result was that thousands of employees would need to lose their jobs. For the next seven years, I learned how to survive within the company that continuously laid off people, *Black Friday* after *Black Friday*, year after year. I eventually became a manager, and as a rite of passage, had to lay off four managers reporting to me, each old enough to be my father, with twenty to thirty years of experience. Was productivity the same thing as laying people off, I began to wonder?

Having become disenchanted with the manner in which the corporate world viewed productivity, I sought to fully understand the concept of productivity through the application of academic research. I conducted work on a doctoral dissertation, seeking to determine how U.S. corporations could become more productive and competitive. Armed with this knowledge, and now being the late 1990s, I went in the direction of Big Five consulting as an avenue in which to apply my passion and newfound knowledge. Instead of becoming the productivity guru that I longed to become, I was forced to be an agent of the firm, seeking primarily to find better ways to increase revenue billing at the client site. In many cases, clients weren't interested in difficult solutions that involved hard work, but rather ready-made, instant answers. This is not a critique on the consulting firms, but rather a statement regarding Corporate America's reluctance to do what is required to fix their own problems. It became clear to me that most U.S. corporations were not willing to do the heavy lifting that it would take to become more productive.

Shortly thereafter, I distanced myself from the cottage industry of Big Five consulting and moved on to the next big thing in American business: the dot-com craze. What better way to perfect the concept of productivity in the corporate setting than to lead dot-com initiatives within a traditional company? I became the first Director of e-Business for a 200-year-old organization, and thereafter for a 125-year-old organization. Many of my colleagues laughed at me for seeking to apply e-business principles at old, traditional companies rather than dynamic new-age ones. In the end, some of my best productivity achievements were in preventing departments at the corporations from wasting resources of e-business ventures with no value. From these lessons, I learned that some of the best productivity decisions that a company can make are the ones that avoid poor decisions.

My next step in the journey in search of productivity was back to where it all started: in a manufacturing setting. With dreams of Henry Ford, Frederick Taylor, and engineered standards dancing in my head, I felt relieved to finally be back at the last bastion of hard work where my passion for productivity improvements could be launched. And yet once again, my dream turned into a mirage. Instead of being a productivity guru, I became the *henchman of outsourcing*, seeking cost reduction only by making problems go away. As in consulting, outsourcing has become a cottage industry, with the promise to the customer that productivity can be achieved through simply handing the keys to the car over to a third party with supposed core competency expertise and/or lower labor cost. At this stage of the journey, I realized that the typical American corporation would do just about anything to avoid facing up to and addressing its problems and the concept of outsourcing was now the best way to prevent it from ever having to do that. It is an *easy out*. Today, it is difficult for the American executive to suggest otherwise.

In just fifteen years of my career, I have seen massive waves of layoffs, happening year over year over year. I have seen the "wizards" of consulting develop services and products aimed at improving a company's performance, and I have seen the dot-com craze take off like a rocket, and then pathetically crumple to the ground like an injured bird. And just lately, I have seen and taken part in the latest alternative to good old-fashioned productivity focus within a corporation in the efforts of outsourcing and offshoring. Certainly, some companies have focused energy on productivity, and there are strong methodologies being used that support such efforts, such as Six Sigma and Kaizen, when applied appropriately. But for sure, these efforts have not achieved the passion and rage within American business as have layoffs, the consulting craze, dot-comism, and now outsourcing and offshoring. My premise is that while achieving true productivity improvement within a large corporation is very hard and often-contentious work, these alternatives are often the *easy out*. In this book, you'll learn how badly taking *easy outs* has, and will, hurt U.S. corporations in the global economy. There are certainly alternatives to *easy outs* that corporate executives, workers, labor unions, academics, consulting firms, and politicians must consider if they wish to be a part of *win–win* solutions that assist our corporations as well as our workforce. Yet for this to occur, everyone must be willing to reform and think through the problems without the buzzwords of the current day. To use an often-overused corporate phrase, we must *think out of the box*. If we don't, we will not be competitive with the growing economies of China and India in the future.

Estimating job losses due to outsourcing varies from source to source, and nobody really knows the true impact. In 2004, The Center for American Progress noted a range of 300,000–995,000 of net lost jobs to date (2004), projected job losses in the future of 3.3–6 million, and jobs at risk of 14.1 million, all on a base of 140 million American workers.[1] In a longitudinal study on the use of third party logistics providers (3PLs), it was reported that 70–75% of all companies in the United States use 3PLs for some or all of their functions.[2] I suspect that if all types of outsourcing services are considered, almost every Fortune 500 company outsources some function or another within the United States, and offshores quite a bit more. But we must be clear: there is traditional outsourcing, which essentially is tied to the definition of a core competency and is primarily domestic, and there is offshoring, which is typically tied to globalization, and low-cost-country sourcing. The distinction between these two types of services will be important for the reader to understand throughout the chapters of this book.

So what does America outsource/offshore? A better question might be, What doesn't America outsource/offshore? Let's begin with Wal-Mart, the world's largest retailer. It's not only the world's largest retailer, but also the world's largest toy store, and the largest grocery retailer in the United States. It is estimated that a staggering 93% of all households shop at Wal-Mart at least once a year. In 1995, Wal-Mart imported 6% of its merchandise versus 60% in 2004, and over 70% in 2007! As well, Wal-Mart itself accounts for one eighth of all exports from China to the United States, and 80% of its worldwide factory suppliers are in China.[3] The Wal-Mart model is the perfect fit for outsourcing/offshoring because its very raison d'etre is lower prices on mainly simple manufactured products. That bike that you bought your daughter for her birthday at such a good price? You may have bought it at Wal-Mart (No. 1 retailer of bikes), and it's 98% likely that the bike was built in a place like China or Mexico.[4] There is story after story of Wal-Mart squeezing American-based manufacturers to either lose a contract or to have to source their production from out of China, Mexico, Vietnam, or elsewhere. We assume that the Wal-Mart model of "lowest prices, always" must lead the labor of manufacturing to continually cheaper alternatives, but is this necessarily true? Can American corporations compete against the *China Price* through process improvements and greater technological innovation? Before we respond negatively, we must understand the new definition of productivity.

Today, it is not a stretch to suggest that Wal-Mart is engaged in a joint venture with China. If Wal-Mart were a separate nation, it alone would be China's #5 trading partner, ahead of Britain and Germany.[5] But are Wal-Mart and China the villains in this story, or are U.S. corporations, their workforces, consumers, and American society in general to blame? We owe it to ourselves to think through this, from more than just a keep-jobs-in-America perspective. Let me clearly state my disagreement with the protectionist objective of keeping jobs in America: that model has not and cannot make sense in a global, wired economy. But on the other hand, the professed globalists appear to be mesmerized solely by the $1.00-an-hour labor rates in Chinese factories (compared to $23.00 in the United States), or $20 an hour for educated software engineers in India (compared to $125–$150 in the United States). Can our nation's outsourcing policy afford to be simply yes or no, black or white?

Some economists suggest that old, traditional economic tenets are tumbling down given the dual emergence of China and India, and technological innovations like the Internet. Back in the nineties, no less than the world's most famous management theorist, the late (and definitely great) Peter Drucker advised us that it was acceptable for us to transform ourselves into this new Information Age and leave the manufacturing to developing nations.[6] Yet today, emerging economies like India and China are capturing sophisticated Information Age functions that should be a competitive advantage to the United States. China is becoming increasingly efficient and sophisticated in manufacturing, and India is winning the battle of white-collar business process outsourcing (BPO). The patriarch of modern-day economics, Paul Samuelson, now questions whether the emergence of China and India will be good for the United States, which is a radical shift in thinking. Three million gross manufacturing jobs have been lost to China during the six years of the Bush administration. Per Meta Group, an IT consulting research firm, big U.S. companies are eliminating 500 to 2,000 IT employees at a time. Future trends indicate that job losses will continue toward higher-educated, white-collar work, which flies in the face of conventional economics. We must begin to look at outsourcing much differently than we have in the past.

Ironically, the U.S. Government has recently reported our nation's strong productivity growth rates. The third quarter 2006 report from the Bureau of Labor Statistics (BLS) indicates that productivity keeps increasing in the United States, up 5.9% for manufacturing. The *Economic Report of the President*, in February 2006, showed that productivity had grown at a faster pace for any 4.5-year period (2001–2005) since 1948, and a strong rate in 2006 as well.[7] The paradigm has changed: productivity success stories of the past won't do, as the result of an emerging China and India. The past is irrelevant. We need to understand the new definition of productivity in the hypercompetitive global economy.

It has and does continue to disappoint me how freely Corporate America is willing to outsource its problems without first understanding them. I have always believed that if a company wants to properly outsource or offshore, it needs to heal its wounds before the responsibility for this function is delegated to some third party to fix. This is my main problem with much of outsourcing and offshoring: not that it is not or cannot lead to strong productivity and financial results, but rather that it too often leads to the sweeping of the dirt underneath the rug. As a corporate manager, it has been relatively easy for me to get support for outsourcing/offshoring initiatives, but not for pure productivity, process-based solutions. No matter what the corporation outsources, it cannot outsource the fixing of its own managerial/operational problems. Very few in Corporate America are willing to open their closets and expose the skeletons. We need to face these harsh realities, and soon. Companies cannot achieve true productivity from outsourcing as a means to an end.

In a *Harvard Business Review* (*HBR*) article in 1990, C. K. Prahalad and Gary Hamel introduced the term *core competency* as "an area of specialized expertise that is the result of harmonizing complex streams of technology and work activity."[8] For example, Volvo's core competency has been shown to be safety, while Honda's has been in the efficiency of its engines. With this theory becoming popular in business circles in the late eighties, corporations began to think about what they had expertise in, and what they did not. Almost at the same time (some think 1989?), outsourcing really began to take off as a business strategy. Coincidence? Maybe not. The concept of the core competency became the U.S. Corporations' next reason for avoiding what was too painful to face, and allowed them to find the *easy out*. After all, what is easier than saying, "We make good widgets; we don't need to focus on customer service." As a result, specialists companies were born: customer service companies, IT companies, human resource companies, payroll companies, and every other possible company. All great concepts, but in practicality too often, *easy outs*. Corporate managers should proudly proclaim, "We're inefficient in that function because it's not our core competency." Everyone could point to the *HBR* article, and nod affirmatively. Another excuse for poor corporate productivity is enabled.

It is definitely true that the concepts of core competency and specialization have led to productivity enhancements for both the customer of the services and the new specialized supplier. Classical vertical companies, such as General Motors, did get improvements through outsourcing. The Coors Brewing Company, another classic vertically integrated company, has achieved productivity through outsourcing. The outsourcing of less-sophisticated manufacturing and assembly has also been a win. But I wager that these solid examples pale in comparison to the poor decisions that will be made within corporations as a result of a failure to face their own productivity issues, and an overeagerness to join the herd. Furthermore, as these benefactor-outsourcing companies achieve revenue as a result, the blood is in the water, and specialization evolves into the development of a cottage industry. Just as when consulting firms were making money hand over fist to take over the problems from the corporate sector, now the outsourcing companies are doing it as well. Everything is outsourced, and corporations can ignore their own problems by turning it over to a specialist or a low-labor-rate provider. The *easy out* personified.

Lately, the trick of the trade has been for outsourcers to focus on labor-rate reduction instead of achieving productivity through process improvement and innovation. Why is this? The answer is that it is easier to compel the customer to achieve savings through lower labor rates than promoting more difficult improvements that require customer involvement. Ridiculous labor-rate differences via offshoring are the ultimate *easy out*. And when the customer company is either unwilling or unable to heal itself, the outsourcer is left only with a lower labor rate as an opportunity to save money. Obviously, this labor-rate differential is a sucker's bet for two reasons: first, a lower labor rate doesn't mean the cost will be lower; cheaper resources may be less productive. Second, for the third party outsourcer to make a profit, the company must find labor/productivity that is at least lower than their profit margin in the deal. If its labor is 10% lower, and its margin is 15%, the customer loses money on the deal. Third, there are often unexpected, or hidden costs associated with outsourcing and offshoring that companies fail to consider; these hidden costs will be addressed later in the book. In the absence of a policy to focus on productivity first, most company and specialty outsourced relationships cannot create sustained efficiencies because the initial effort was based on rate savings reduction, and not cost efficiencies. Rework costs can erode the cost savings associated with a lower labor rate. In the end, outsourcing or offshoring solely on labor-cost reduction can never be sustainable, as labor-rate reduction without productivity will in many cases lower *rates* but not improve *costs*. The labor-rate savings tactic is a mirage, whether it is the chief reason noted for third party outsourcing, onshore or off. Unfortunately, too many third party outsourcers either deliberately or not so make money off corporations through the confusion of these terms.

This *easy out* story can become more about perceived cost reduction, and less about productivity. A company has outsourced the management of its transportation, and actually seen its costs increase, while the rates per shipping lane appear to go down. Another company has offshored an IT operation to India, and now has five times the number of programmers at the lower labor rate. Is this cost-effective? A Boston Logistics Group (BLG) study from 2005 suggests that companies, on the average, achieve a 13% net savings when using a low-cost country, such as India or China; this is much lower expected savings than conventional estimates (stated typically between 40 and 50%) because of the difference between gross and net savings.[9] Outsourcing within the United States has not achieved its promise in many occasions. Given the BLG study, one must wonder whether we can automatically assume that the China/India model will always work, in every industry. Perhaps if we dig in and figure out specifics, maybe we can learn how to out-produce India and China through our own competitiveness.

Many consider the differential between gross and net saving when outsourcing/offshoring as a hidden cost. The outsourcers from both America and abroad present a very persuasive yet somewhat academic response to why a company should outsource its operations. When the business case is presented to the company's decision makers, a gross savings estimation is made, with the caveat of not having sufficient information to finalize pricing. When the outsourcer signs the deal, and then gets full access to the operations, many assumptions can change, and then the savings are net of these changes. Some of the hidden costs associated with offshoring are as follows:

1. Higher freight costs (expediting to make up lost time, unreal assumptions, etc.)
2. Higher testing costs (software and manufacturing)
3. Interpreter services costing more
4. More and costly third-party audits needed
5. More return costs due to quality issues
6. Greater currency fluctuations
7. Draconian government inspection processes
8. Higher recruiting costs (a lot of opportunity in China/India, so more job hopping)

In many cases, the differential is due to the client company not understanding its own processes and culture well enough to demonstrate to the third party an accurate story. In any event, many outsourcing firms use this as an opportunity to play the game on pricing. Whether intentional or not, many third party outsourcers have made a lot of money through this approach, both onshore and off.

Can lower labor rates really provide sustainable productivity improvements? According to BLS data, the answer is clearly *yes*. Yet in Corporate America, the answer cannot be a sustainable yes given lower labor rates is a one-time opportunity to improve productivity through the reduction of cost. Even labor-cost reductions plus technology implementations cannot achieve sustainable productivity improvements alone. True productivity, coupled with innovation, must be sought and achieved. In the past, productivity could be defined as a function of labor alone; today it must be redefined as a function of innovation in a global marketplace. America cannot possibly win the "labor rate" game with the likes of China, India, and others. However, we can win through the redefinition of productivity to focus on true efficiencies and innovations, as no country is better at this than us. Our business and public leaders must focus on this new definition for us to win.

Today, it appears as if America has concluded that light and sometimes heavy manufacturing are not *core competencies*, or even important to the American corporation and society. Today, only about 10% of our labor pool is dedicated to manufacturing. Will white-collar organizations follow the same unintended path, and if so, what's next for us? Today, one dysfunctional white-collar operation is outsourced and traded for another inefficient operation as an outsourcing play. When the savings to achieve do not materialize, other options have to be considered. Lowering cost through labor rate was the *easy out*, but the jury is out regarding its effectiveness. The company must look at itself in the mirror and determine why it isn't productive, no matter where its labor pool resides. Accounting and financial systems must recognize true differences between rate and cost reductions, and treat them as sufficiently distinct so that managers are encouraged to make the correct decisions.

As an American, how does this unfolding story sound to you? If you are a corporate manager, you likely view this outsourcing/offshoring story as inevitable. Why? Because many corporate managers do not understand this new definition of productivity in the competitive global economy; they only understand what rate reduction means within the old definition. They also don't understand the differences between outsourcing and offshoring. As is illustrated in the example earlier, a corporate manager may believe that a lower labor rate always means a lower cost. Of course, there are many cases to present (and will be presented in this book) showing that this is not true. The other problem is that the corporate manager will sometimes accept a short-term win for a longer-term problem in most cases. Like many corporate leaders, I am often faced with a difficult annual budget to achieve. If a third party outsourcer proposes a short-term band-aid to a severe productivity issue, many corporate managers will accept this as taking action. Many third party outsourcers have become very good at showing first-year savings to the client in five-year deals, taking advantage through their own understanding of the corporate budgeting game. Unfortunately for the corporate manager who does not know what he got himself into, the honeymoon can end on the second year or earlier, and turn the savings inside out.

But don't place the entire blame on the corporate manager. While the corporate manager can often achieve a higher annual bonus as a result of taking the *easy out*, the American financial system is also at fault. The role of accounting principles in business is to fairly and accurately represent the business results, as well as to incent the right behaviors through rules. Whether it is an extreme case like Jeffrey Skilling of Enron and Bernie Ebbers of Worldcom, or a typical case like a manager trying to make his or her budget, the right behaviors are not being rewarded.

Another contributor to the problem is that of the worker. Often, the undertaking of a corporate initiative to improve productivity is an exercise in futility. A what's-in-it-for-me mentality of workers can often kill an idea that helps the company, which enables poor worker behavior. There is little loyalty left between the worker and the manager. And when things go entirely wrong, the ineffective manager has nothing left in his arsenal other than outsourcing or offshoring the workforce to a lower-paying provider. The worker loses in this circumstance, and must take at least partial responsibility for the environment that led up to the outsourcing. The workforce and management keeps spiraling the situation into the *easy out* that leads to a worse situation relative to our competitive situation in the world economy, and fewer good jobs. It is time that we do something about it.

Meanwhile, while American workers and managements are ignoring the relative benefits of increased productivity, India and China are becoming less about lower rates and more about better quality and innovation. If we think of India and China as backroom operations, and only textile workers, we are making a fatal error in judgment. Indian professionals are becoming our financial, legal, engineering, marketing, and even medical professionals; they are more than low-level programmers and customer service reps. China may produce 50% of the garments sold in the United States, but high-tech exports have grown to 28% of the total.

If we continue to ignore the signs of our own inefficiencies, China and India will overtake us on labor cost, efficiency, quality, and innovation. These nations are emerging faster than any nation in history; today, they account for 6% of global output, but midcentury, it could be 50%! We cannot wait any longer to respond.

Yet, America must let the rules of the global market apply, and not try to subvert them with any sort of protectionism. This book is not yet another protectionist book professing to focus on keeping American jobs in America. It is also not a view of the blinded globalist who sees these new economic rules as an acceptable *easy out*. Instead, the intention of this book is to determine how American businesses and workers can become more competitive within the corporate walls in order to make the right outsourcing and offshoring decisions, which, it should be emphasized, may mean not making this decision at all. If we allow ourselves to do this, more jobs will stay in the United States through an appetite for competition, bringing back the golden age of the Industrial Revolution, when America was the most competitive nation on earth. Having chased the productivity dream myself, I know that there's something better for us Americans. Unlike the protectionists, I know that while offshoring can negatively affect U.S. jobs, there needs to be an offset through new sectors of employment. This book will explain why outsourcing/offshoring isn't really the problem, but rather the existence of poor productivity leading to bad outsourcing/offshoring decisions. The problem stems from how U.S. businesses are being run, and an inadequate focus being placed on productivity and innovation that made our companies so great in the nineteenth and early twentieth centuries. There is a lot that can be done by the politicians, media, consultants, and the like, but the focus of this book is the relationships between the worker and the manager at the corporation. This is where productivity and competitiveness needs to start. America's rejuvenation needs to start at the corporation, with all of us.

Politicians and the media must not stoke the fires of protectionism. They cannot give the impression that outsourcing/offshoring is a new phenomenon or evil sweeping our nation. Instead, outsourcing/offshoring is essentially what founded our nation, and has made us a very prosperous society. Our culture has been exported throughout the world, and the United States has been a significant benefactor of this for decades, if not centuries. The brand names of McDonald's, Disney, Coca Cola, Pepsi, Nike, and Starbucks, to name a few, are among the most widely recognized in the world. We have been abundantly blessed as the primary offshore provider in the world for decades. Why don't the media and politicians recognize that our nation has been more blessed than cursed when it comes to being competitive in a global economy? Should these pundits be allowed to scare off competition, after decades of success that has arisen from it? That's not fair. Instead of wishing competition away, let's prepare for it, because being fearful of it in a global economy will never work. Americans are better than this.

Statistics can be damning and confusing as well. During the 2004 election, outsourcing and, more important, offshoring was seen as a key battleground topic of discussion. One media survey indicated that outsourcing was the cause of 9% of all mass layoffs, which led to a lot of finger pointing and blame. Yet BLS data indicate that less than 2% of the problem is due to offshoring, and the balance due to domestic outsourcing. Some politicians felt that these statistics were more due to inaccurate or incomplete data. On the other hand, Daniel Drezner, a renowned author on the subject of outsourcing/offshoring, notes that domestic outsourcing is a bigger chunk of the pie, and often leads to a relocation of the job from one company to another, not job losses overseas. He also notes that the financial benefits from domestic outsourcing, or even offshoring, leads to a quasi-multiplier effect, allowing companies to spend on other goods and services.[10] In my opinion, both the pro and anti-outsourcing/offshoring advocates are not being entirely truthful or accurate. Outsourcing is a symptom, not a problem or a benefit. Having a debate to determine whether outsourcing/offshoring is good or bad for a corporation is to not understand what makes a corporation effective or ineffective. Productivity and innovation makes a company efficient, and having it or not having it is more important than whether its IT or transportation resources reside at the company's headquarters, two hundred miles away in Ohio, or six thousand miles away in Bangalore, India.

In my view, considering domestic outsourcing as more palatable than offshoring may be confusing our nation. If outsourcing in the United States creates lower-paying jobs without benefits to American workers, is this better or worse than shipping jobs overseas? Truly, both scenarios can hurt the labor market in the United States, and if one is to be addressed, so should the other. Most U.S.-based outsourcing contracts have some sort of labor-rate reduction as a primary reason for the decision. Therefore, both U.S.-based outsourcing and foreign offshoring can often be symptoms to the much larger problem of poor productivity. Again, it becomes obvious as both symptoms provide the *easy out* for the corporation.

America's inconsistent view within outsourcing and globalism/offshoring is hypocritical as well. I don't hear many negative views associated with harvesting bananas in Honduras, but we've all heard a lot about IT programmers in India. Likewise, migrant labor in the United States may have greater negative impacts than Chinese manufacturing labor, but is not nearly as much of an issue. Since America became the world's largest economy through globalization and outsourcing/offshoring without any constraints, can we dare seek to make rules that only apply for us? Probably not. Instead of business leaders, politicians, labor unions, and the rest demonstrating hypocrisy on the world stage, they could place their efforts in making America competitive again. This is the only language that the global market understands, or even should understand.

Speaking of rhetoric, politicians, and the media, why isn't America upset with the trend toward a temporary workforce? This trend, starting in the 1990s, places the focus on short-term profits over long-term growth. Management thinkers in the 1990s such as Peter Drucker and W. Edwards Deming considered this short-term thinking as a major culprit for the declining U.S. position in world markets. This view was that "by declining or manipulating expenditures needed for future business success, businesses may make the bottom line look better now, but such practices may ultimately jeopardize the organization's future." This quote, from an *HBR* journal, was written twelve years ago. Today, the presence of temporary labor on any kind of permanent basis is both inefficient and ineffective to both the corporation and the employee. I have been responsible for both manufacturing and white-collar operations that have had a higher percentage of temporary workforce than a permanent workforce in some situations. The creation of a *permanent temporary workforce* leads to what is almost a caste structure that significantly hampers productivity, at least in the longer term.

Today, the temporary workforce is growing faster than the 2.5% growth in 2003, and the 1% growth from ten years ago.[11] The reason? Today, every position can be a temp one, from a day laborer to a CEO. The financial insecurity that is often the result may be worse than sending jobs overseas, without the attendant publicity. The employment agency typically receives 30–40% less than what the company would have paid a full-time employee (in gross revenue). The temporary employee, depending on his or her role, and skillset, will receive a percentage of that already lower rate from the agency, perhaps as little as 50%. This clearly is not a healthy worker/management scenario created to achieve rate reduction as an *easy out* to achieving productivity. How is this situation not recognized to be at least as dangerous as sending jobs overseas? A dysfunctional workforce situation is just as much of a symptomatic result as is shipping jobs overseas. Both are direct results of competitiveness problems that America has in the global economy that force us to undertake short-term stopgaps that create more dissension between the workers and the managers. To the workers, this is an example of corporate managers making money by destabilizing their earning potential. To the corporate manager, this is an example of seeking to remain competitive, by market means. Both parties are right, and both are wrong. And both parties lose when they choose to not work together.

This book does not promote protectionism, in any sense. This book also does not promote a corporate manager's setting an irrational path toward globalization without regard to productivity. Instead, this book promotes productivity as a solution to the problem, and outsourcing and offshoring as sensible solutions when implemented in a rational manner. Today, outsourcing and offshoring typically are not being handled rationally, and it makes no difference whether it happens in Indiana or India. Why must management and workers be contentious toward one another? Must it be the case that the Wal-Mart retail model can only work well with foreign suppliers? Did it make sense for U.S. programmers in the 90s and early 00s to be overpaid with no backlash, while hiring Indian programmers causes such alarm? Why is it that some blue-collar workers make $90,000 a year, while others are essentially day laborers without benefits? Clearly, all situations bring dysfunctionality to our economy, and must be addressed. Business leaders need to be responsible for fully understanding the dynamics that cause problems and opportunities.

The reader of this book might find it hard to believe that rational options exist as alternatives to the corporate addiction to outsourcing. Statistical data, qualitative surveys, and my experiences with outsourcing all indicate that outsourcing cannot be judged as an effective or ineffective solution. Therefore, the rational alternative to outsourcing as a means to an end is seeking true productivity. Opportunities to improve labor relations are a solid alternative to outsourcing as well. The problems today between managers, workers, and productivity are not much different than those that Frederick Taylor faced in America in 1912 when he sought to eliminate much of the contention between workers and managers. There is precedent in the past regarding this problem, and certainly for the solution on how to fix it.

Our government leaders, the media, and other interested parties also have a vested interest in breaking this addiction that corporations have with outsourcing. Although I don't believe that the solution is a macroeconomic one that can be dispensed from news reports and policy writings, I believe we can focus policy on the need for greater competitiveness and productivity and better worker–manager relations. I really believe that America's workers and managers can devise a better plan, one that takes into account how America can become more competitive, and not need to always send jobs overseas. A scenario where U.S. workers aren't being turned into blue-collar and white-collar migrant workers, wandering from one site to the other, without benefits. A scenario where corporate managers are not forced to make the wrong decision owing to short-term, bookkeeping pressures. There are better options, and we must embrace them, and give them a chance. What we need are *new ideas that are old*. The framers of the Industrial Revolution have something to offer us when it comes to world competition. I hope that this book becomes the foundation for a grassroots effort to transform our corporations in a way that seeks credible solutions and not *easy outs*.

Our government needs to think through economic statistics that show our productivity levels at the highest in the world. Definitions of what productivity is must be updated to reflect the emerging world economy, and the impact of superstar developing nations. America may be very competitive in economic statistics relative to the developed nations of the world, but what about against countries like India, China, and Vietnam? In many government statistical reports, China and India aren't even used as data points in comparison to the United States. We wake up to these new world rules that are impacting our economy.

The second chapter in this book lays out the various views and perspectives on outsourcing and offshoring, and what's fact and myth. As the topic of outsourcing is very diverse and complex, a thorough understanding is necessary to start the book. Chapter 3 discusses the "Opportunists of Outsourcing," the entities that have prospered because of outsourcing. It is important to understand that the term *opportunist* is not intended to infer that these parties are acting fraudulent, but rather to address how and why these parties have profited through the corporation's addiction to it. Chapter 4 reviews America's accounting policies to better understand how these principles fuel our addiction to outsourcing. The media often turns the corporate manager into a mindless, heartless monster to explain how and why these individuals make decisions to outsource and offshore. Yet instead, the media and others should understand these decisions within the financial structure that these corporate managers face. I myself have made outsourcing decisions for what ultimately were the wrong reasons, but which appeared to be the right reasons at the time. In Chapter 5, I discuss how the pressures of the accounting system and the financial markets enable corporate executives to make poor decisions on outsourcing. I discuss the difference between economic and accounting performance, and how this difference allows corporate executives to justify decisions that are more short-term than viable for the health of the company and employees. If the reader understands the constraints of the financial accounting system, he will better understand how and why these contentious situations occur. In many cases, well-educated and experienced managers with strong personal ethics will be forced into positions that the workforce doesn't understand. If the corporate manager doesn't respond to the situation, and makes the courageous decision, he may be at odds with his company and be terminated. The corporate manager faces the kill-or-be-killed scenario that can naturally create contention, with no other choice. Luckily for all of us, the answers to this contentious situation between workers and managers have historical precedent to guide us. Chapter 6 discusses the lost art or science of corporate productivity, allowing the reader to begin to understand what transformation must take shape in the corporate setting. From this chapter, the reader should start to understand that better days are possible if all parties take responsibility. Yet if the need for increased productivity is so obvious, why isn't America addressing it now? The answer to this question lies in Chapter 6, which explains why productivity is not sought or achieved at a corporate level (not at a macroeconomic level, where it is typically studied).

Chapter 7 introduces the antithesis of the *easy out*, which is the *difficult in*. This concept of the *difficult in* provides some fundamentals for how America can become more competitive in the global economy, and make the right policy decisions. In too many cases, our corporations in particular make bad decisions for the wrong reasons. Much of this has to do with the prevailing nature and culture of our corporations, but a lot of it as well has to do with regulatory controls, draconian accounting rules, rhetorical policy makers, and inaccurate fantasy statistics. Laying out the *difficult in* after a lengthy discussion on the *easy out* begins to lay a roadmap of action for the reader.

Chapter 8 asks how well we understand nations like India and China in the emerging world market. In spite of the rhetoric of our media, China and India are growing by understanding the new rules of the global economy. But what is China and India's strategy on outsourcing? Everything is brought together in Chapter 9, in a nightmarish scenario; on our current state track, how does it all play out for the United States? Using assumptions from earlier chapters, it is clear that our future isn't bright unless things change. Chapter 10 brings forth a future of optimism based on things changing and the productivity dream being enabled. This chapter gives the reader hope if we choose to act. And we must act for our collective futures.

This book is an activist book, and the book concludes giving the reader ideas of how he or she can act and make things better for our nation. The chapter gives ideas to the corporate executive, the management consultant, the academic, economist, and politician. Americans have choices, and the opportunity to build their individual and our collective destinies. Therefore, we can start moving away from the *easy out*.

Having worked in Corporate America for fifteen years, I know that there are no perfect concepts or ideas, but there are solutions. Such solutions often begin as idyllic dreams in need of hard work. It is very likely that this book will be viewed with suspicion from many parties, notably managers, economists, and, most important, third party outsourcing and offshoring providers. That's okay, but I ask those who raise suspicions to think aloud about our trade deficit with China in 2006 of $233 billion that surpassed 2005s $202 billion record (and will be surpassed again in 2007). I ask them to think about our growing temporary workforce, many of them without adequate benefits, such as health insurance. I ask them to wonder why American companies are being increasingly nixed from supplying products to the nation's, and the world's, largest retailer. I ask them to think about why our corporate managers are not allowed to make the effective decisions that they were taught to do in business school. I also ask you to think about what sort of work Americans should do, or not do? Once we think about these questions, we should understand whether our current business framework is conducive toward success. And we'll understand that our willingness to take the *easy out* too often has and will lead to us losing in a global economy.

I invite the reader to seek America's need for productivity through www.iaprod.org, or the Institute for American Productivity. It's time for us to get involved and make a difference before it's too late.

## CHAPTER TWO

# The History and Myths of Outsourcing

Research indicates that as far back as the thirteenth century, outsourcing was raising the ire of European guild workers. Fast forward to 1602 when the formation of the Dutch East India Company (VOC for short) created the first multinational corporation in the world, and the first to issue stocks. (As a point of trivia, this first stock certificate issued by the VOC was the focused heist by the burglars of *Oceans Twelve*, the 2004 movie starring George Clooney.) It was not the Dutch, nor the British, but rather the Portuguese that dominated India first, with colonies there as early as 1498. However, in 1594, a group of Dutch merchants sought to break this Portuguese monopoly with their own expedition (it failed) to India. Eventually, the Dutch merchants succeeded, and the VOC was successful in India and elsewhere in Asia and the rest of the world. It got silver from Peru, copper from Japan, and traded them in India and China for textiles. Among its other responsibilities, the VOC company assisted in the Dutch control of the all-important spice trade. Interestingly enough, the company's headquarters was eventually located in Jakarta, Indonesia; how's that for globalization and outsourcing in the sixteenth century?

Similar to the Dutch difficulties breaking through the Portuguese stronghold in India, the British struggled mightily in encountering the Dutch in the early seventeenth century. Eventually, though, the British East India Company presided over the British Raj in India, established Hong Kong and Singapore, employed Captain Kidd to stop piracy, and cultivated tea in India, the same tea incidentally that was the subject of the Boston Tea Party. This company laid claim as the administrative arm for India for the British for centuries, seeking to make profit, and having to restore order. While the legacy from this period is one of harsh imperialism, the British Raj has been responsible for providing many important contributions to the subcontinent, such as a railroad infrastructure, the English language (the language of government and administration), medical and engineering expertise, and a rule of law.

But outsourcing history was not restricted solely to European powers. The ancient Chinese empire and the Japanese were adept at outsourcing to their conquered nations. Perhaps as early as 5000 B.C., farmers were growing crops in northern and southern China. The Chinese learned to rely on agriculture as a means of self-reliance, but, as all cultures have learned, progress and advancement cannot occur without contact and trade with other nations. During the reign of the Han dynasty (206 B.C.–A.D. 220), China extended its political and cultural influence over Korea, Mongolia, Vietnam, and Central Asia, and even had several Roman embassies during this period. During this period, the famous passageway to Southeast Asia, the Silk Road, commenced, and expanded for military and economic reasons. It is interesting to note that while China wasn't a part of the Roman Empire during this period, it had a friendly relationship, much of which was based on trade.

Back and forth the Chinese rulers opened and closed trade. Another example of trade as a political issue was the commerce in opium. Opium was used and produced in China for medicinal purposes but not smoked as a drug until the eighteenth century. As the Chinese government sought to stop the consumption and trade of opium within its borders, the British were taking control of the trade from their European rivals. The British East Indian Company waged war for three years in order to secure the right to sell opium in China. The production of opium in India was very profitable for the East Indian Company, and was used to trade for manufactured goods and tea. Because of the social impacts of these opium dens, the Chinese government made opium illegal in 1836, and sought to close down these facilities. The British refused the request to stop exporting opium, even though it was illegal in its own native land. When the Qing government sought to pressure Queen Victoria by threatening to cut off all trade in response, the Opium War began, and the British triumphed, ending with the Treaty of Nanking in 1842. This treaty gave Britain unfair trade provisions, and allowed them to keep Hong Kong as a British Colony (it was a barren island at the time). To this day, the legacy of this war provides a history of Chinese resentment and concern in its dealings with the West. Certainly, outsourcing and globalization have deep roots in history, often ugly, deep roots.

Many outsourcing experts may disagree, but I believe that it's impossible to separate the historical aspects of colonization from that of outsourcing. In Thomas Friedman's best-selling book *The World Is Flat*, the author illustrates this by describing the evolution of globalization through three phases: Globalization 1.0, 2.0, and 3.0.[1] To Friedman, Globalization 1.0 started with Christopher Columbus, and countries; Globalization 2.0 proceeded with companies; and Globalization 3.0 evolved to individuals. If one analyzes some of the Globalization 1.0 hotspots, it will be clear that they are consistent with those that exist in today's Globalization 3.0. Is this coincidental? Absolutely not. India is as popular of a Globalization 1.0 spot as it is for Globalization 3.0, as will be discussed in this book. Globablization 1.0 provides our foundation for the new definition of productivity today in the world economy.

I want to propose a new definition of outsourcing to you, one that is different than what you're used to. My need to define outsourcing much differently for you is to give you a basis for the future; we must properly understand the past and present to predict the future. Using this approach, I will outline the ten myths of outsourcing to start you off with my new definitions as a foundation for this book.

## MYTH 1: OUTSOURCING IS A RECENT PHENOMENON IN AMERICA

America's history belies this notion. Our country began, of course, as a British colony, providing raw materials (crops, iron ore, timber, furs, cotton, tobacco, etc.) to its mother country for production into goods that would be shipped back to America to be sold for high prices with high taxes. As a British colony, America was founded from the very concept of outsourcing. Why is the harnessing of raw materials from an American colony different from the harnessing of cheap labor for production of toys to China, or the use of cheaper labor in India for call centers? It is most certainly not.

In 1790, the brand-new American nation had a population just under 4 million, and 90% of the population were farmers. There was plenty of land to homestead and farm, with slavery, but not enough labor. In the mid–nineteenth century, the population of the United States began to grow following revolutions and famines in Europe; however, more immigrants were living in cities, or seeking gold mines in the frontier. The farm population fell to 69% during this initial stage of industrialism. Immigrants started to pour into the nation, slavery was replaced with sharecropping, and the percentage of the population involved in farming continued to fall. With the start of the twentieth century, immigration continued at a rapid pace, industrialization moved workers to the cities, and provided greater efficiency in the farms, using less labor. In 1900, the farming population in the United States fell to 38%. With the Second World War, more workers were diverted to the cities and the war, and farmers made up 18% of the workforce. In the 1990s, this percentage went down to 3% of the total workforce.

Why is this history of American agriculture important to understand relative to the subject of outsourcing? We need to understand the historical impact, or creative destruction (destroying one industry but creating another) of the farm industry, as we analyze what has and is happening in manufacturing and the service industries. During the Napoleonic Wars, America was gaining wealth, as a neutral shipper for both Britain and France, yet wanted to free itself from commercial arrangements made by both nations that were too restrictive. The newly formed American nation passed the Embargo Act of 1807 that intended to prohibit exports from American ports, thereby rescinding the restrictions that Britain had placed on its trade. In the end, President Jefferson's efforts turned against the new nation regarding its trade, and the Embargo Act was repealed in 1809. It was one of the contributing events that led our nation into the War of 1812, and as a result of this, our nation had an incentive to improve its transportation system, as well as more manufacturing independence from Britain in order to establish its autonomy and power. Manufacturing in the United States expanded as a result, and the Industrial Revolution was born. Productivity and outsourcing went hand in hand.

Three important elements led the Industrial Revolution in the United States. One was that the transportation system was expanded, much like what is happening in China today. Second, electricity was harnessed. And lastly, production processes became more effective, and led to a productivity acceleration. These points provide historical relevance to events within our global economy even today.

Through the path of the Industrial Revolution in the United States, creative destruction played a large part, with innovation, technology, and better manufacturing processes leading our nation from one definition of labor and management to another. Cotton farms in the South produced raw materials to be sent to the North's factories for finished product fulfillment, much like what happens today in manufacturing, but on a global playing field. Back then, the "China" of our industry was the South, providing cheap labor through slavery, and then through lower standards of living than in the more urban North.

Creative destruction, in both product design and manufacturing processes, led to the remarkable growth of a past agricultural British colony, to the most powerful economic nation in the world.[2] Every step in our economic development was formed through innovation, specialization, and productivity. For anyone to suggest that outsourcing is a novel term in our American lexicon is an ignorant assumption; we became powerful as a result of outsourcing! In fact, there is some commonality between our economic growth history and that of China today; for decades, China's growth as an industrial power has been predominantly near seaports, given its lack of a strong transportation infrastructure in the nation. Much like America's push to improve its transportation system after the War of 1812, China understands that it must improve its transportation network within its inland area for continued economic growth. History is repeating itself! Despite the historical relevance of outsourcing in our history and our present, the process of creative destruction has been the key within our economy. Today, we must create new industries for what is being destroyed with outsourcing, we must learn from our past. We have been successful outsourcers and insourcers, but only as a function of productivity!

## MYTH 2: OUTSOURCING HURTS WORKERS BY MOVING JOBS OVERSEAS

What does losing jobs mean when considered in a global sense? From one perspective, when jobs are shipped from the United States to India or China, this can be viewed as a nominal job loss. However, if such trade leads to U.S. economic growth, and since our economy is so large, this can actually lead to a net job gain. In 2002, China surpassed Mexico as the second largest exporter to the United States, and for the first month of 2007, China was the largest exporter, overtaking Canada. Per the Trade Partnership Worldwide, LLP, an international trade and consulting firm, imports from China has a net positive impact of 1 million jobs to our economy.[3] Per this point of view, America is trading lower-paying manufacturing jobs for higher-paying professional jobs like business services, consulting, accounting, legal, and computer programming, etc. This is creative destruction at work.

The future can be brighter than it is today in our relationship with China, our fastest-growing trading partner. As this country gains GDP and wealth growth, its middle class will continue to grow, as will its demand for imported goods and services. In 2004, China became the fifth largest market for U.S. imports, and today, it is number four (behind Canada, Mexico, and Japan). Out of these top four, China represents the largest opportunity for growth of U.S. goods and services for the future. Per the IMF Outlook of September 2006, China's economy will grow by 8% annually in the next ten years, and have a larger GDP than the United States.[4] Some of my counterparts in industry tell me that they are manufacturing in China primarily as an entrée into a very important future market. China is already the world's largest cellular market, and number three in the auto market.[5] It won't be long before it's the largest consumer market in just about everything.

Wal-Mart is a good example of how wealth and jobs can be transferred from China as much as it can be transferred to it. According to the consulting firm Bain and Company, China's retail market is growing at a pace of 15%, and will hit $860 million by 2009. Yet the world's largest retailer, which alone would be the tenth largest world economy, has only a 3.1% market share in China. In 2006, Wal-Mart purchased Trust Mart, a Taiwanese chain of hundred big box stores in twenty Chinese provinces. And the Wal-Marts in China are starting to become localized in order to not offend Chinese customers (having live or unpackaged meat as a local cultural way). As China is opened more to foreign retailers in the future, its growth capacity could be enormous.

In the ten years from 1996 to 2006, American exports to China and India grew faster than with America's other largest trading partners. During this period, American exports to China grew 360%, India 254%, Mexico 136%, Canada 72%, the EU 48%, and Japan shrunk by 12%.[6] India's population is well educated, and despite a large swell of poverty and unemployment (could be as high as 20%, and over 100 million people), there is a great potential for rapid middle class growth. America will continue to need to be patient with India, and there are many economists who believe that the same multiplier effect happening with Chinese imports is happening with Indian ones as well. With an economy so much larger than both China and India, America may feel like it's losing when in fact it may be building economic growth through stronger economies in such large, developing nations. Figures 2.1 and 2.2 show the growth of imports and exports between the United States and India/China. While most Americans may focus on the trade imbalances, we must remember that it is in our best interest to grow our trade with these hyper-emerging economies.

The largest benefactors of outsourcing from American companies are American companies. Starting the discussion with manufacturing, American domestic third

**Figure 2.1**
**India Trade with United States**

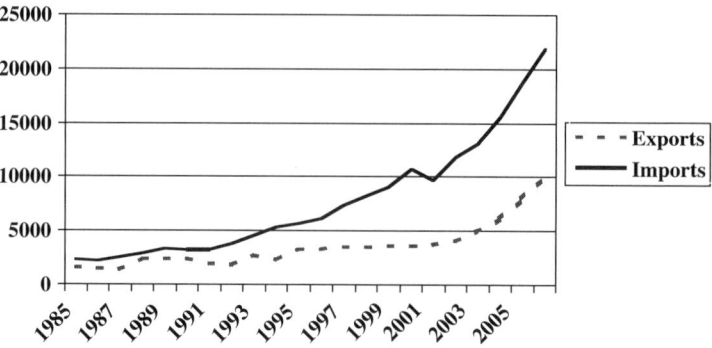

*Source:* U.S. Census Bureau (all data in million dollars).

parties are growing when it comes to third party services. In industries such as consumer products, third party manufacturing and packaging is becoming very large, with almost every company taking part. In this industry, over 50% of the largest companies use contract copackers, and the industry is expected to grow by 10–15% per year. Today, if you peered through the true operations of many of our large companies, you will see interesting relationships relative to making, packaging, and shipping of products. Through the concept of core competencies, companies make decisions as to what they should retain, and what should be outsourced. Some of these many outsourcing conditions may lead to Americans staying employed.

What about automotive? In 2005, Toyota manufactured over 1.5 million cars, and over 1.2 million engines in America, a new record, with targets to further increase production by 2008.[7] As well, Toyota invested capital and hired more workers/paid more overtime in many of its facilities in 2005 and early 2006,

**Figure 2.2**
**China Trade with United States**

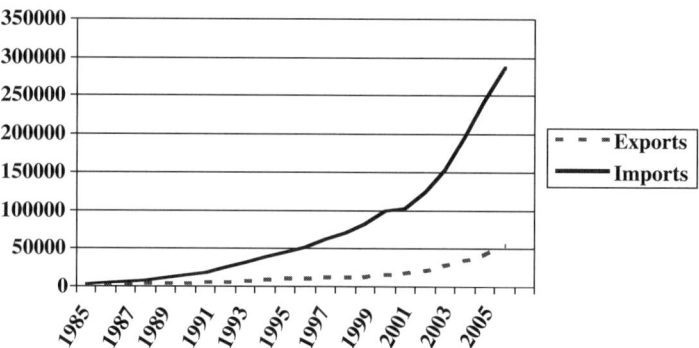

*Source:* U.S. Census Bureau (all data in million dollars).

making many wonder whether globalism and outsourcing is as bad idea of an idea as many of the politicians say that it is.

## MYTH 3: OUTSOURCING DOESN'T HURT WORKERS

No, this Myth isn't contrary to Myth 2, so read on! In the discussion of Myth 2, I demonstrated that outsourcing can be a good thing when it provides our economy with in-roads to fast-growing markets, but much smaller economies that are developing middle classes that will be future customers of American goods and services. Given the relative size of their economies, and the American jobs associated with fueling their growth, the trading relationship between China/India and the United States should be a good thing, given traditional economics.

Myth 3 is an interesting one because it is true what our politicians and business leaders have stated about outsourcing, but for all the wrong reasons. Indeed, some American workers are being hurt by outsourcing. But the pain is not being caused solely from India or China, or even Mexico, as Ross Perot suggested a while back, but rather more so from us. Our country has created a dreadful lack of understanding toward outsourcing that has and is paralyzing our middle or lower classes. Much of domestic outsourcing is painful to workers for the following reasons. First, much of the outsourcing from one company to another often has no corresponding benefit to our economy other than the reduction of labor cost; it does not render increased trade between countries, like offshoring. Second, much of this outsourcing is done in lieu of true achievement of productivity, instead of as a function of it. It is questionable whether "labor rate productivity" is sustainable past the first year. Third, this type of outsourcing has a negative impact on the social fabric of our country. And of course, fourth, unproductive domestic and foreign outsourcing can hurt workers.

The working poor are defined as those where work has failed to meet their families' basic needs. These individuals are on an economic treadmill that is virtually impossible to get off in lower-paying jobs, with often little or no benefits. There is no question in my mind that outsourcing has had a distinct negative impact on turning more of the middle and lower classes into working poor. Corporations that have not achieved the necessary levels of productivity required to compete in their industries often outsource to companies that can get away with paying lower wages, and no benefits, but offer little productivity. Some of these companies use legal and illegal immigrants, who will often work for much lower wages. In his book *Fast Food Nation*, Eric Schlosser calls the current workforce in our nation's slaughterhouses "the new industrial migrants."[8] Two-thirds of these workers cannot speak English, earn a lower wage of $9.25 an hour, don't get benefits, have a turnover rate of 80% a year, in a dangerous, disgusting job. Yet, the meatpacking industry is hardly alone. Fortune 500 companies in the logistics field outsource to 3PLs in order to reduce our fully loaded labor costs by 30–50%. Maintaining a healthy middle class will be critical to success in the world economy!

To understand the temporary workforce, let's segment temporary workers into three categories: one, the seasonal worker; two, the prototypical temporary worker; and three, those unable to attain full-time, stable work.

The first category, the seasonal worker, is a legitimate category for temporary work. Profiles of these types of workers include college students seeking to earn a little money during breaks and housewives seeking to earn higher pay at a time when the company will pay more given the busiest time of its year. An example of this is a seasonal worker for UPS during the Christmas season. This is a very traditional definition of temporary work that is legitimate to its title, and doesn't pose any direct impact on the labor market as a rule.

The second category, the prototypical temporary worker, is a legitimate use of temporary work as well. This work can occur during any time of the year, and is frequently associated with some specific task, such as a special promotion within a company. Usually a little different from part-time work that may pay lower wages, this work can be classified as requiring full-time skill but not with an ongoing need. The demographics of this group can again include students and housewives, and also can include those seeking to make money while trying to make it in another field (like a band, or some other labor of love). This again is a good match between supply and demand; however, this category of temporary labor has opened the door for the third, and very dangerous, category of the growing temp workforce.

The temporary worker sector is growing 11% annually for a reason. It isn't due to seasonal and project-type assignments growing, but rather a growing, reclassification of what can constitute as a temp worker. No longer is temp work restricted to blue-collar and clerical, but can now include all categories of work, and typically a function of cost cutting versus a true classification of temp labor. I once had an employee who was a temporary worker for almost five years before I was able to push, and offer her a permanent job. While the official driving forces of why temp labor is on the rise is due to "the need for flexibility," "specialists not needed long-term," and "core competency," I believe the reasons are much more unfortunate, both from a cause-and-effect standpoint. The cause for the rise of temporary workers is due to the lack of true productivity achieved within the corporation; therefore, the *easy out* in reducing cost is through temporary labor. The effect for the increasing use of temporary workers is the reduction of the social contract between management and its workforce, leading to haves and have-nots in each type of work. Beyond any sort of laws surrounding fair labor practices, a company cannot achieve Six Sigma–type levels of productivity and quality with an ever-turning, or disenchanted, noncommitted workforce. The growth of the temporary worker structure in traditionally nontemporary settings is not good for business, in too many cases.

There is no question that domestic outsourcing has a high correlation to temporary work. Beyond this association, outsourcing is tied to the definition of *underemployment* where a worker is either doing work that he or she is overqualified to do, or is not paid enough to do the job. There is no question that trends in domestic outsourcing led to such dysfunctional relationships. This type of outsourcing has little productivity benefit to the American economy. It is time for America to understand the truth that domestic outsourcing can be just as dangerous or as effective as offshoring. Outsourcing without production is a problem in the United States, and elsewhere.

What hurts workers isn't when outsourcing causes jobs to be lost in the economy, but rather when creative destruction doesn't occur, and new industries/jobs aren't formed. In the past, America always migrated employment to the next evolving industry. Today, the new global economic realities have placed both traditional and emerging jobs under attack. Therefore, outsourcing will hurt workers when there are no comparable jobs to move on to in a new economic model. Without creative destruction, outsourcing can negatively impact our workers and our economy.

## MYTH 4: OUTSOURCING IS DONE TO PEOPLE BY COMPANIES

In the thirteenth century, nations began to outsource. As early as 1440, chartered companies such as Hudson Bay and East India Company moved capitalism from being country capitalism to commercial capitalism. Today, the world is changing again. Thomas Friedman's Globalization 3.0 reflects that the world continues to get smaller and smaller.[9] In the first stage, nations like the Netherlands and Britain tried to control the seas in order to control their outsourcing, and they failed. Britain sought to control its colonies, but in the end, it could not. Labor groups and government agencies have sought to control a company's ability to globalize, and this has failed as companies have become multinational. The final frontier, that of the individual consumer and worker, has sought to be controlled, but it won't be. Americans can direct their purchase of products and services over the Internet directly with foreign companies, or even individuals. They can outsource practically any service, real time, without any regulation from the government. Online casinos, recently declared illegal in the United States, can be accessed without control. Students can have term papers produced in other nations by companies or individuals. This concept of Globalization 3.0 allows everyone to be an outsourcer, and an insourcer. Outsourcing is not restricted to countries and companies anymore.

Why should we limit our thinking to Globalization 2.0? The world was global, and is now becoming micro-global. Globalism is not restricted to the nation or company, but extends to the individual. I can establish a Web site that allows me to conduct commerce with people from all over the world. I can become an exporter or an importer. The outsourcing world knows no bounds.

The conventional thinker must understand the past to understand the future, and be a part of the present. Conventional outsourcing theory focuses on the company, and that's why it's limiting America's capabilities. This lack of imaginative thinking can never guide America toward the future of business, and outsourcing.

Creative destruction needs to find new ways for the economy to evolve, and new ways for our nation to succeed within these new economic realities. The power of Globalization 3.0 is the power of the individual, and it could swing the momentum back to our nation. China and India are nations of groups; we are a nation of individuals. How does this not give us the advantage in the future? America can leverage our culture of innovation and creativity, in comparison to India and China, who don't have such characteristics.

When we think of Globalization 2.0, what do we think about? We think naturally about the structure of the worker and the company, a relationship of management and workers at a factory, or in an office setting. It is centered on the structural, physical nature of a gathering site when people work and make money. We may feel a sense of loss when we no longer are able to gather and make money as structured workers, and we definitely get upset when our gathering has been taken over by other nations. Much of the physical and concrete Globalization 2.0 will be replaced with peer to peer, across the globe Globalization 3.0; are we ready?

The younger generation in developing nations understands the concept of Globalization 3.0. While it may not be called microglobal by them, I assure you that the young in developing nations understand the need to succeed without assistance from government and company resources that have failed them in the past. I have been to India five times and, each time, I have attempted to reach out to the people beyond my corporate hosts. Indians are surrounded by the limitations of what their government can do to solve its nation's problems. With streets lined with poor, and a lack of government creativity to get past red tape and old ways of thinking, the new-age Indian sees himself as someone needing to connect to the world in spite of his surroundings. It's an amazing contrast to be speaking to a young student surrounded by abject poverty who speaks of a successful future. So if young Indians can rise above their environments, shouldn't we ensure that our youth can do so as well?

### MYTH 5: OUTSOURCING ALWAYS RESULTS IN LOWER COSTS

It is natural to ask that if outsourcing doesn't always lower cost, why should we be doing it? The answer to this question is that assuming that outsourcing lowers cost is an obvious leap of faith; expected to happen, but not always (or even often) the case.

Figure 2.3 is the most glowing example of how outsourcing provides the low costs that everyone wants. Certainly, these wage differentials are staggering, and even more staggering when comparing Chinese versus U.S. manufacturing rates. But is overseas outsourcing (offshoring) and domestic outsourcing always efficient? My experiences have led me to suggest the answer to be no. Almost always, whether outsourcing within the United States or shipping the work overseas, the wage rate is lower. I have outsourced IT services to India, and logistics services in the United States, and the potential for savings was always favorable on the surface due to labor differentials. For IT, I was able to avoid paying $250 an hour

**Figure 2.3**
**U.S. vs. Indian Wages (Hourly Wages, 2002–2003)**

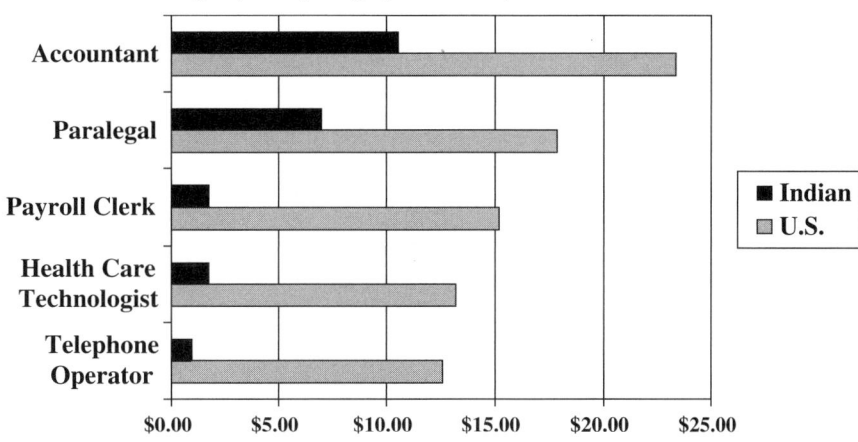

*Source:* outsourcing.com survey.

for a software developer, and pay $35 an hour for a software engineer in India. For logistics, I have been able to replace $40-an-hour employees with $25-an-hour outsourced. The *China Price* typically promises 30–50% savings.[10]

An efficient company may save money when outsourcing, but an inefficient one rarely does, no matter the labor-rate savings. This seems counterintuitive, doesn't it? Shouldn't an efficient company have less cost savings to achieve than an inefficient one? Shouldn't the opportunity of rescuing a really bad company be too easy, and therefore a win–win for both the outsourcer and the outsourcing customer? My experience is that it just doesn't work that way. For domestic outsourcing, a 30% labor savings can be eaten away when the third party's profit margin, hidden costs, and a lack of productivity are greater than the labor differential. The gross labor savings on a deal can quickly evaporate when hidden costs and poor productivity are heaped upon profit margins and bad assumptions. Then, if the customer company is ineffective in managing the third party provider's performance, the customer could actually lose money on this endeavor. In my career, I have seen more customers lose money than gain money on third party contracts. An effective company will save money when they choose the right goods and services to outsource, and processes and contracts are executed properly.

Any economist worth his pipe would never consider a lower wage to be directly correlated to lower costs. And yet frequently in America, we choose to attack costs solely through wages. From a foreign outsourcing standpoint, this can make sense, as paying a lower wage for a good or a service leads to creative destruction through creating trade channels that may not have existed in the past. When we outsource, we need to really look for reverse business opportunities in the other countries market. China is becoming that market for us, and we must be patient. Lower wages in the United States create an opposite effect on our economy: a lower standard of living. Offshoring can lead to productivity through market growth (in a developing market), while domestic outsourcing may only reduce cost, which may not lead to productivity. How can we let corporations forgo productivity and competitiveness at the expense of our workers and our future domestic growth? It makes no sense. Bad outsourcing is an arm of harm for our workers and our economy in so many cases. We can't just focus on lowering wages as a solution.

## MYTH 6: POLITICIANS CAN'T INFLUENCE OUTSOURCING

You heard it before; politicians like Ross Perot and John Kerry noting the evils of offshoring. These politicians have it wrong, and need to articulate the alternatives in an increasingly dynamic global market. What they should be focusing on is the worrisome trend of the underemployment of Americans as a function of poor management discipline within our largest corporations.

Let me make myself very clear; I am not proposing that our politicians legislate and regulate our country toward better domestic practices of productivity and competitiveness. However, our politicians are our policy leaders, and should exercise leadership over the formation of a much-needed domestic policy for competitiveness. Underemployment and declining competitiveness are the issues here, not outsourcing. America has gained economic growth through various forms of outsourcing that have made economic sense to our economy, and to our workers. When campaign season happens, too many potential leaders focus on *easy out* targets, such as the Indian call center employee who annoys us when we want to book an airline flight, or the endless list of products manufactured in China. This sort of approach is irresponsible, and one that turns a deaf ear toward the true problem, that of underemployment and poor competitiveness.

There are many examples of how our politicians should and should not steer public opinion in the way of the issues surrounding outsourcing, underemployment, and world competitiveness. Take, for instance, what's happening in Europe today. Unemployment in Europe has been almost 10% for the last few years, and in the United States is around 4.6%.[11] It is clear from research that European policy toward the welfare state has hurt the competitive nature of business in a global economy. France is the best example of the battle between the welfare state and a global economy. In March of 2006, French Prime Minister Dominique de Villepin introduced employment reform that provoked Unions and youth to cripple the nation by means of strikes. However, De Villepin started to introduce employment reform that would effectively make its labor market more competitive and lower youth unemployment, which is over 20%. With his approval ratings in the thirties, De Villepin abandoned the reforms that were in the eyes of most to be in the best interests of the French economy. The French example is one of government policy influencing unemployment through the perpetuation of the welfare state, and the inability to articulate rational policies in the face of public pressure. However, of late, courageous policy changes enacted in France have reduced unemployment from 9.9% in October 2005 to 8.8% just a year later, and 8.3% in March 2007 (a 24-year low!); policy, not rhetoric, can make a difference.

The U.S. government and its leaders play a large role in influencing outsourcing as an effective economic tool within our economy. There is clearly a correlation between economic growth in developing nations like China and India, and its government policies versus those of mature economic markets, such as France and Britain. The lesson to be learned for future John Kerry/Ross Perot types is to not exploit a populist, yet irrational, political stance that will result in job losses. By focusing on creative destruction, and seeking to create industries as a function of destroying others (through outsourcing), our leaders will be promoting responsible economic policies that create good employment. Politicians can make a difference through policy, not rhetoric.

## MYTH 7: COMPANIES UNDERSTAND OUTSOURCING AND MAKE RATIONAL DECISIONS

Many companies outsource before understanding it as a strategy. First, the client company doing the outsourcing requires more, not less, management responsibility over the third party. Second, companies must only outsource after having cleaned up their problems not as a substitution for doing so. Third, many companies outsource without having determined what is strategic, or core to their operations, and what is not. I will discuss each in detail for the reader to understand my view that most companies don't understand outsourcing very well before adapting the strategy.

Why does a company need more, or better management when outsourcing than when the function is insourced? The answer to this question is remarkably simple: out of sight cannot require out of mind. Out of sight means that you as a manager have less control responsibility and yet greater leadership responsibility. Companies that outsource and consider the operation out of mind are practically always (as a rule) disappointed with the results. Companies that outsource and stay close to the operation from a leadership standpoint are typically satisfied with the results. And yet, there's another story to be told; the client company management that stays closer to the third party does so because they are more familiar with the operation. Companies that don't stay close typically don't because they don't understand the function that they are outsourcing. This is corporate incompetence at its worst.

Another problem exists when a client company doesn't understand the function that it is outsourcing; it tends to attract many irresponsible and advantageous third parties who profit from the client's lack of understanding. I have worked for companies that have outsourced IT, logistics, marketing, and many other services. The companies that are honest and successful third parties are ones that understand the scope and nature of their responsibility, and choose not to overstep these boundaries. However, other third parties take advantage of the leadership gap from the client company, and take on more responsibility in the relationship than it should. Why do they do this? Obviously, the more functions that the third party takes over, the more revenue that is generated for their company. This dysfunctional relationship between the third party and the client is the real reason why most in business have a bad taste in their mouths regarding third parties; many have experienced these bad relationships.

Interestingly enough, the blame for these dysfunctional relationships typically points to the third party instead of the client, but shouldn't the customer look in the mirror as well? Both the naïve client and the third party who took advantage of the situation are responsible.

The second point of this myth is that the client company must clean up its mess before it outsources. Not so, say some of the world's largest outsourcing companies. To them, outsourcing a function not understood is a function that isn't a core competency. And as many noted consultants have proclaimed, it is fine to outsource functions that aren't core competencies. But can a company outsource transportation without first understanding what is working, and what is not working within its transportation system? Isn't this transportation system also a function of how the company makes and packages its products? The consulting firm that leans on the client company and tells it that it doesn't need to fix its processes first before outsourcing is an irresponsible partner. Some of the most famous Fortune 500 companies have stumbled when they chose to put outsourcing in front of process improvement. And yet many companies, when faced with both options, will outsource before, and instead of, improving critical business processes.

How do companies determine whether they should outsource a function? According to outsourcing lore, anything that isn't core to your business can be outsourced. But what is truly core, and how do companies determine this? Can anything be considered core, or can anything be considered not core? Within industries, there isn't a clear definition of what should be outsourced, and what should not. We must really question this concept of a core competency in business today, and how corporations all too willingly use it as a reason for not addressing its core problems.

## MYTH 8: OUTSOURCING IS A BETRAYAL BY CORPORATIONS OF THE AMERICAN WORKER

When politicians like John Kerry call American CEOs who outsource "Benedict Arnolds," the facts become less important to the storyline than the emotion that is evoked from these sorts of statements. Aren't those same American workers the American consumers who are demanding low prices at Wal-Mart, or dirt-cheap income tax returns from H&R Block and Jackson Hewitt? Shouldn't consumers look for the lowest prices, as a matter of fact in a capitalist economy? Consumers will demand what the corporation must provide, and if this is not the case, the corporation will lose. Simply look at the auto industry as an example of the success story of Toyota versus the nightmare being faced today by General Motors and

Ford Motor Company. Any politician who asserts that the CEOs of these American car companies shouldn't do everything legal within their willful powers to save the financial states of these famous U.S. landmark corporations doesn't understand the gravity of the situation. These companies more so than others sought to protect American workers with "America First" type slogans of patriotism, partnered with the strong union foothold within their operations. As their market shares tumble, how many would consider the necessary actions for survival as anything but mandatory?

The politicians and unions must get on the correct side of this issue; the side toward productivity versus some sort of perceived employee/manager loyalty. Myth 8 sounds very French in its loyalty factor, and yet would the American workforce trade its circumstance with that facing France today? An American economy with about half of the unemployment in France, and a U.S. economy that is growing in an ever-increasingly competitive global marketplace. Our politicians must be more responsible in addressing the foreign offshoring issue in order to lead toward policies of economic growth, as opposed to the fear and protectionism that is gripping France and, to a lesser extent, some historic U.S. corporations.

If there is a betrayal to be addressed, and yes, I think that there might be, it should be directed toward the corporate CEO and the politician in a different sense. How about the fact that CEO pay sometimes does not often correlate to company performance? As an example, in 2003 Schering-Plough's top five executives made over $28 million while the company lost $93 million.[12] I am definitely a fan of paying the CEO a whole ton of money when the company's financial performance is strong, but what about when it is not? When things aren't going well, many of these companies will reduce costs through layoffs, and foreign and domestic outsourcing practices that lower the wages of the individuals performing the tasks. The betrayal is through a lack of leadership in attacking the problem in a way to protect the worker, at the same time being competitive to the consumer. When the corporate executive gets a bonus for losing the shareholder's money, and doesn't deliver productivity benefits that in turn become savings for the consumer, the CEO has failed, and in effect, has betrayed our competitive position.

After working so many years in Corporate America, I really still don't understand the dysfunctional relationship among our consumers, workers, leaders, and investors. In a rational economic equation, optimization occurs when the benefit of each are maximized without severely impacting the needs of the others. Politicians are playing the class warfare card when they suggest otherwise, and the leaders of our companies are enabling such political behavior when they demand and get ridiculous compensation packages without producing appropriate results.

## MYTH 9: OUTSOURCING AND GLOBALIZATION ARE DIFFERENT PHENOMENONS

When a company considers either domestic or foreign outsourcing in an optimal manner, there is little difference between outsourcing and globalization. The nature of a capitalistic economy is to gain innovation through new ideas, and new ideas are best spurred within an open, global mega-society. Outsourcing, whether domestic or foreign, is an optimization scheme, just as is globalization. Both have in some instances been dismal failures within a market economy, and both have in other situations been unbridled success stories. Neither is separate from the other in definition; both are functions within a competitive market economy. And both are dependent variables based on productivity, whether it is the productivity of a successful company or country.

Outsourcing and globalization take on different meanings in India than they do in China, and than they do in the United States. With a growing, vibrant economy and a low worker wage, the opening of globalization opens up new possibilities for burgeoning economic powers. In India, outsourcing is a source of pride, yet globalization can be seen as a threat as much as it is a promise. On the world stage, with these new economic rules, outsourcing will become prominent and permanent. With capital flowing freely from market to market, with a few exceptions, what is to stop the fluid nature of outsourcing? Cannot contract manufacturing be temporary and global? What about tax returns via the Internet? In 1492, globalization was limited to those who would play, country by country. Today, with a few exceptions such as countries like North Korea, all nations must play on the global stage because outsourcing will become an individual-level initiative, and not a national one. Companies will be powerless in the face of outsourcing and globalization, and must succumb to its forces in order to generate positive, not negative, repercussions.

## MYTH 10: AMERICA DOESN'T NEED TO BE A MANUFACTURING POWER

In his famous book *The New Realities* (1989), Peter Drucker noted that manu-facturing is becoming increasingly uncoupled from labor.[13] In Drucker's model, the "sweat of the brow" work would move to developed countries, and developed societies like America will become "knowledge workers." In the past, very few jobs required any sort of knowledge, including some leaders of companies. Today, in Drucker's view, knowledge has become the true capital.

Yesterday's steel workers in America aren't by definition becoming today's knowledge workers. But with today's global rules, who's to say that all Americans should be knowledge workers, and all Chinese should work in a sweatshop? If America is wise to what's happening, we will all understand that this myth is a very dangerous one. Since the Great Leap Forward, China has lifted millions of its people to literacy, rising from 60% back then to 96% today. Since 2000, India's school enrollment for six- to fourteen-year-olds has grown from 75 to 90%, and its famous Indian Institute of Technology (IIT) is widely considered one of the best universities in the world.[14] With such sweeping reforms to educate its masses of people, why would Americans think that Indians and Chinese want to continue to do the jobs that we no longer want to do? Such thinking would represent a very naïve interpretation of what's happening in the world today.

Perhaps with the new rules of the global economy making it open game for developing nations to take on targeted functions of the developed world, developed nations can now be innovative and focused on becoming more productive in areas typically reserved for developing nations, like manufacturing. Through process innovations, Indian companies like Tata are finding creative ways to make manufacturing affordable to serve the consumer market of the masses of Indian poor. If this sort of innovation is possible, perhaps Americans can develop innovative manufacturing techniques to make manufacturing viable to serve the depressed areas of our inner cities. We should not expect a majority of our inner-city and rural poor to become knowledge workers for the world, as China and India (among others) want to compete in this arena. How about making manufacturing matter, in innovative ways, for some of the poorer in America? We can't give up on manufacturing when knowledge work is being attacked within these new economic rules.

## MYTHS AND HISTORY

The fables and distortions surrounding outsourcing have become symptoms that cloud our collective thinking as a nation. What can we learn from Globalization 1.0 or the American Industrial Revolution that can teach us to be more competitive with China and India? What should be the role of the U.S. CEO, the politician, the American worker, and others? Is it too late for America to turn to a different path for economic success?

The answer is no, and the remainder of this book will lead the reader down the course needed for success.

# CHAPTER THREE

# Strange Bedfellows—The Opportunists of Outsourcing

By now, you've probably gathered that the concept of the *easy out* is one that is bad for the U.S. economy. But do economic data support this theory? Since the start of the outsourcing trend around 1970, Gross Domestic Product (GDP) growth has averaged 3.16% per year, after inflation.[1] Compared to other mature developed countries, and given that our economy has been the world's largest for the entire period, by far, such growth should be viewed as a solid achievement. Since 2001, our GDP growth has been double of that of Europe! So, as even the casual observer might note, the *easy outs* being employed in American business over the last thirty to forty years could not have been so bad if such a solid story of economic growth transpired within the world's largest economy.

Can we assume that our economic growth has been a function of the *easy out*? Should we assume that such economic growth will continue now that the political shackles have been loosened in India and China? Never before in the history of capitalism have the two most populous nations' economies taken off at the same time! True, use of the *easy outs* haven't yet harmed our economy, but that doesn't mean that our future won't be impacted, and that we should wait to find out if it does.

It is also clear that the average American worker hasn't believed that U.S. economic growth has been such a miracle of late. If the worker is an hourly employee, he is increasingly under the threat of being outsourced, or turned into a temporary worker. According to a recent report by Staffing Industry Analysts, temporary staffing grew by 7% for all of 2006, and projected 5% in 2007.[2] For many companies, a role of the corporate manager is to find opportunities to convert workers into temporaries in order to reduce its overall labor cost; this is not a secret across corporations today. But the disposable worker option is not restricted to blue-collar workers in today's market. Increasingly, it is the case that management and professional employees are becoming disposable. As a corporate manager myself, I am required to seek options for labor-cost reduction within the hourly ranks, but also in the indirect labor and the management ranks as well. Today's executive herself must also be warned that her employment situation is not necessarily stable. I consider myself to be a mercenary, someone who must hunt for productivity and cost reductions, and am potentially always under the gun myself. One of my managers once told me that in corporate America, you either "make the product, sell the product, or are going along for the ride." The phrase "going along for the ride" is of course just another way of saying someone is ripe for termination. As a corporate leader, I must take action myself, or be eliminated in the process.

Who are the benefactors of outsourcing? These are the individuals and entities that I will call the *opportunists*. In this definition, the opportunist should not be viewed as an abuser, but rather someone or some entity wise to the rules of the game. These benefactors can consume within the economy by creating wealth without a great need for corporate productivity. In addition, corporate productivity cannot be achieved simply through moving cost to the third party without any value proposition. In simple economic terms, the corporation hasn't achieved greater output as a result, but the opportunist has. Through understanding who these opportunists are, how they are able to prosper, and whether it is beneficial or not to the average worker and manager, we can have an insight regarding how to fix whatever the problems might be. We must look deeper into the economic data to understand what's happening through these third party relationships and to identify the net impact on our national economy.

While the 1950s can be considered a period of U.S. economic domination, the 1960s and 1970s were truly the years of a rebounding world economic presence. Things began to spiral out of control in the seventies as oil prices rose, trade deficits rose, and the massive flood of imports from low-cost countries really start to take effect. After being the world's breadbasket, the world's automotive manufacturer, and so on, America finally started to face more intense competition on the commercial front. The perceived postmanufacturing economy started to emerge.

The origin of the outsourcing of services began with the onset of consulting as a business. In 1890, the father of management thinking (at least in my mind) Frederick Taylor took his developed theory of Scientific Management and became the first management consultant.[3] The development of time studies allowed his customers to better understand the productivity of their own operations. Taylor had been forced to become a management consultant after being kicked out of his company for ideas that were before his time. After Taylor, consulting firms took two different paths: one in accounting, with firms such as Coopers and Lybrand (now PriceWaterhouse Coopers) in 1898; and the other in engineering, with firms such as the Emerson Company in 1899. In 1910, H. L. Gantt (developer of the Gantt chart) published *Work, Wages, and Profits*, which was the first entrée into the field of project management. In 1927, the famous study in the Hawthorne factory showed a correlation between factory lighting and productivity and, in the end, such performance improvements were actually starting to be viewed as strategic and scientific. As the thirties came, and into the forties, the automotive industry drove the consulting industry to take notice, and professional consultant efforts to seek out productivity assisted America in the Second World War. Americans were no longer a dumb bunch of farmers, to paraphrase Hitler, and we emerged from the war completely victorious from a global standpoint.[4] Industrial engineering met war planning for the Americans, and many of these experts trained during the war became champions in industry during the forties and fifties, leading America to economic superpower status that would be unrivaled for the next thirty or so years. Our unprecedented economic growth was driven largely by scientific management principles.

During the late sixties and early seventies, these champions and partners of American industry transformed themselves into corporate entities by going public in the financial markets. A. D. Little went public in the sixties, but reversed course because of a fallen stock price. Booz Allen did the same in the 1970s, with the same course correction. However, the transformation had occurred: consulting firms had become true businesses in and of themselves, and a cottage industry was born. In 1969, consulting became a very popular industry, attracting the best and the brightest from schools such as Harvard with wages of $15,000 a year![5]

Economic growth in the U.S. economy began to slow in the 1970s, but consulting firms continued to prosper, primarily through globalization. With such gurus emerging in the eighties as Michael Porter, consulting continued to grow, fueled by a rising number of trained MBAs and the growth of the service sector. Perhaps the greatest boom for consultants came in 1982 from Tom Peters and Robert Waterman in their famous book *In Search of Excellence*, which became the mantra for consultants seeking to enable companies to be successful by being encouraged to do what they do best.[6] As well during the 1980s, corporate takeovers became prominent and consulting firms played a large role in these corporate transactions. General Motors (GM) purchased EDS in 1986, which really gave credibility to the entire IT third party services industry. In the 1990s, many significant events transpired: one, C. K. Prahahad and Gary Hamel coined the phrase *core competency*, which continues to drive consulting firms and other third parties inside the walls of the American corporation to take over work. With large reengineering and layoff efforts (Who could tell the difference?) occurring everywhere, consulting firms were called on to assist corporations in these efforts, with tidy profits as the result.

The late nineties and early twenty-first century really boomed with the advent of the Internet and the World Wide Web, and the threat of Y2K. Big Five Consulting, as it was back then, really flourished (I was a part of it back then), and client executives were all too willing to pay ridiculous rates in hopes of career-saving strategies. The Web and its development took a back seat in the late nineties owing to the threat of Y2K, and this was when India really came to the forefront because of the high price of American programmers, and the cost of Indian programmers at 10% of the cost. At the start of the offshore rise, Internet strategy firms started to take form, with names like Scient, Viant, and MarchFirst. In 2001 and later, all of these companies started to crash or become less important due to the overhype of what the Web truly was to our economy. The lesson learned was that Internet Strategy firms seeking to create wealth without productivity could not sustain their operations.

During the mid–2000s as offshore development became less of a fad, and more of a part of IT, business process, call center, legal, and accounting outsourcing (to name a few), domestic business process outsourcing (BPO), such as manufacturing and logistics, really had started to take off. Domestic outsourcing had become very dependent on labor rate plays, and the use of the temporary workforce. Contract manufacturing, much of it under private labels, has grown prominent under the big box retailers, led by Wal-Mart, to cut prices. Foreign manufacturing has been driven strongly over the past ten years through this Wal-Mart–China alliance, allowing Wal-Mart to become undisputedly the world's largest retailer. And BPO has turned India into the backroom for many of our white-collar industries while we sleep at night.

The last thirty years of business has been a crazy period in manufacturing, and white-collar work, particularly in consulting and professional services. Creative destruction has worked, with industries disappearing (farming) and waning, while others have emerged (third-party outsourcing, consulting, services). But has this creative destruction that has benefited these opportunists actually helped the health of the U.S. economy? More important, will such trends help us, given these new global economic rules? To determine the answer to this question, we must examine each of the opportunists and their impact on the U.S. economy.

## OPPORTUNIST 1: CONSULTING COMPANIES

Having worked as a Big Five consultant in my career, I can personally attest that consulting firms have profited handsomely over the years as a result of business outsourcing. The history of what can be perceived as consulting and business has been a legendary relationship back to the days of Frederick Taylor and W. Edwards Deming. Some of the proudest moments of innovation spurred in American industrial history have originated from the minds of consultants. The infrastructure of consulting and the M.B.A. programs to support and feed them has been a great model of success for a long time in American business. Today, consulting firms still do the thinking for many American businesses, but the model has changed, and old-school consulting firms are typically smaller and not well known by the average CEO. The prototype for this sort of practice is a small five- to ten-person firm, typically anchored by an experienced business grey-hair who was a leader at a large corporation in that expertise previously in his career. Usually, these types of practices can as a practical matter only support two to three clients as the clients want access to the experience of the grey-hair. I will call these the "old-school consulting firms," as they take on the feel of the consulting firm before most of them became more of corporate entities. I have worked with old-school firms, and have had a lot of success with them in utilizing the experience of the grey-hair.

In the beginning, the service provided by the consulting firm was thinking or experience. In the period before consulting became corporate in the seventies and eighties, the outsourcing of thinking from these firms was a very practical idea: to be able to utilize a brilliant, experienced mind in the industry without having to hire that individual who might be very expensive, or even unavailable for hire. Back to the legendary times of U.S. business, the outsourcing of thinking prompted a relationship between the client management and the experienced consultant that led to fabulous levels of efficiency and innovation. The consulting mind was one of the most effective tools in the U.S. economic model, increasing the value of innovation in the economic growth formula. Tying profit to innovative thinking is what has driven American business for decades.

Yet, something terribly wrong happened to this traditional consulting model, and I experienced it myself in Big Five consulting. As the traditional consulting firms grew, and became corporate, they started to sell firm concepts instead of legendary, experienced thinkers. Why? Because in a growth model, it is not possible for the consulting firm to grow through the recruitment and hiring of legendary thinkers, as the consulting firms' revenue growth objectives were greater than their capacity to hire a sufficient number of grey-hairs. So instead of slowing their potential for revenue growth, they simply had the grey-hairs of the firm develop the consulting firm concepts that could be administered by much less experienced resources. So the new formula for the consultant was an M.B.A. from a top echelon university, and firm training on the services that were being sold to the client. As a result of this, the consulting firm began to change the nature of the candidate that they could hire; instead of seeking an experienced, "been there, done that" type of person, the firm would hire a Harvard M.B.A. right out of business school who was smart enough to learn the firm concepts very quickly. The crème de la crème consulting firms tend to hire predominately from top schools in order to offset experience with intelligence. No longer was thinking and experience critical, but rather prepackaged concepts and ideas.

This was an unfortunate transformation of the consulting industry, but a necessary one in order to fuel its corporate growth objectives. So the match of strange bedfellows that I faced in Big Five Consulting was as follows: the CFO of the client company was good friends with our consulting partner, and the CFO needed our consulting firm to do an assignment for him. However, he wasn't asking for innovative, legendary solutions, as was from the glorious past, but rather save-my-butt quick solutions needed to save his job. The consulting partner would get the deal through his relationship with the CFO. The partner would assign the project to me as the senior consultant, or the consulting manager, and I would interview the CFO to determine the nature of his problem. The irony of this situation was that I was thirty-one years old, and the CFO was fifty-five. Why would a CFO with as many years business experience as I was alive seek me as his alleged expert? The CFO would get a prepackaged save-my-butt solution, all wrapped tidily within an impressive looking PowerPoint presentation. Our consulting firm would get our hefty fees, and the satisfaction of making a lot of money by giving the customer exactly what he wanted. It is no wonder that the Big Five concept came dysfunctionally crashing down upon itself in the early twenty-first century, as it was a cottage industry in service to itself.

A couple of the largest, most well-known consulting firms were notorious within the industry of "backing up the school bus" with large assignments. *Backing up the school bus* means dumping a bunch of young, inexperienced consultants onto a project, with one knowledgeable expert and/or a prepackaged solution. When I was in consulting, I was marginally experienced and, frequently, I was the one that our firm wanted to send out with a litany of others. On one occasion, the client told the partner that he just wanted me on his assignment, but the partner told the customer that one consultant can't be a solution; the solution included a team to implement our firm concepts. I often had to take the newbies with me to customer presentations, and held my breath hoping that none of our M.B.A.s would advance cliché-laden firm concepts that meant nothing to an experienced executive. Through the arrogance of these top consulting firms, the customer was often lost in the process and firm revenue was exalted as a means to an end.

Yet, many large-scale consulting firms realized that opportunities existed other than the outsourcing of thoughts that are large revenue opportunities. IT hardware and software services are big opportunities for companies. Other professional services like tax preparation, legal, and any other service that one can think of. Recently, the phenomenon of BPO has become very popular, but very tricky as well. In some cases, these efforts can become value-added in the throw-back sense through going back to the days of strategic thinkers working with tactical managers in order to improve performance. In other cases, these business offerings have become the *easy outs* for companies that, for example, don't understand their HR function, so the easiest option is to simply get rid of it. I also wonder how giving your operation to a third party without productivity improvements ever leads to reduced costs and improved service levels?

The general concept of consulting in today's corporate setting has often become an *easy out*, and as such, consultants have become the true opportunists in the outsourcing sector. Consulting as a practice has a legendary role in the development of America as an economic superpower. However, when old-school consulting lost its soul and became a corporate means-to-an-end function of revenue, it stopped being the creative thinking arm for American business at a time when it needs it the most. Can the consulting industry lead America through this next needed phase of creative destruction? For our sake, I hope the answer is yes, but for this to be the case, it needs to return to its roots, and stop being an opportunist in an *easy out* corporate setting.

## OPPORTUNIST 2: THIRD PARTY PROVIDERS (U.S.)

Today, you can outsource just about any function from a company simply by stating that it isn't a core competency of yours, and then finding someone who professes to have that core competency. Consider some of the functions available to be outsourced:

- Accounts payable outsourcing
- Manual labor
- Business process outsourcing
- Call center outsourcing
- Data entry outsourcing
- Finance and accounting outsourcing
- Graphic design outsourcing
- Human resource outsourcing
- IT outsourcing
- Logistics outsourcing
- Medical transcription outsourcing
- Strategic outsourcing

Some of the theoretical reasons for outsourcing can be very compelling:

- Renewed focus on core business
- Mitigation of risk by reliance on an expert
- Improved customer satisfaction owing to improved processes not a part of your culture
- Project enhancements
- Service improvements
- Skills upgrade
- Skills retention
- Skills access
- Technology infusion
- Cost reduction
- Asset conversion
- No capital investment outlay

Typically, poorly performing companies will outsource more frequently than top performing companies, and therefore, there are more opportunities for outsourcers with these poorly run operations. Probably with the best of intentions, these massive outsourcers seek to grow their clientele in the right manner, but can get addicted to the revenue stream associated with even troublesome business engagements. An outsourcing firm's growth opportunities are greater in pushing companies to outsource than to find optimal situations for companies to outsource. Pushing companies to outsource is quicker and easier than working through difficult situations with a company to determine if outsourcing is the right decision. The larger outsourcers needing more and more revenue to achieve growth targets can conflict with being opportunists to the easy out, or can watch their competitors do so. As long as client companies are too willing to outsource before they solve their own problems, outsourcers will be left with no other choice than to take such easy, vulnerable business. Very few outsourcers can turn away revenue opportunities, no matter how difficult the potential clients are.

And, oh, by the way, the offshore labor rates are much higher than they were in 1999.

No doubt about it, many of these Indian firms have taken advantage of our *easy out* corporate environment. Years ago, I would pick up the phone, and call one of the company's top executives in India when I had a problem. Today, I can face the same layers and attitude that I receive from American companies. The Americans taught the Indians how to market, how to penetrate new business, and how to always be selling. The typical offshore company has gone from charming and responsive to annoying and corporate.

Not only in IT, but what about call centers? When I was last in India, I visited a call center in Bombay of one of the largest corporate entities in India. After hearing all of the world dialects of English they can speak (to trick the caller into thinking that he's talking to someone he's comfortable with), I started to ask financial questions: beyond the labor rate cost differential, how much money was this operation saving its client? The general manager of the facility didn't quite know the answer to this question, but he cheerfully rebutted, "You understand our labor rates are lower, right? So you understand that our costs are lower." These companies have learned American sales techniques using Indian labor. Their comments regarding labor are generic, and sometimes can't be substantiated.

It is clear that lower labor rates don't necessarily translate into lower effective costs. India Inc.'s marketing program appears to be as follows lately: take on characteristics to sell and manage accounts in the United States, and market the obvious rate difference between India and the United States The problem with this logic is that lower rates don't always translate into lower costs. When I was in India last, my offshorer honored me by having me cut the ribbon for its new wing dedicated to my company. The allure of using consultants is being able to flex your labor up and down; having a large wing of dedicated programmers was not value add for me, regardless of the wage differential.

In some ways, India Inc. has lost its charm. Today, I receive many calls a week from offshore outsourcing companies offering me everything that I really don't need, but they want to explain to me that I do. Even some of my dearest colleagues from India from our past have become talking realization targets! I never would have heard that from these guys ten years ago. They have become American salespeople in an India location. Thus, the price of success!

Many businessmen, particularly from damaged domestic industries such as textiles and electronics bemoan the opportunist known as China Inc. This moniker, coined by Ted Fishman in his book titled *China Inc.*, illustrates how powerful the Chinese economy has become as a result of a tight-knit relationship between the government and industry. In my mind, China Inc. is a definition of how a government can use a company to achieve the economic results that is needed to advance its nation in a global marketplace. Take for instance the Chinese Yuan. This currency has traditionally been valued lower than its true value on the financial exchanges owing to Chinese government control. Many American businesses cry that keeping China's currency low is an unfair trade act as it makes its costs of goods to be artificially higher than those goods in China. Since 1995, Asian currencies have declined 28%, and this has hurt the textile industry mightily. The popular press has called this the "Asian Flu." During this same period, Asian imports have increased by 154%.

Not only have American businesses found China Inc.'s artificially low currency to be opportunistic, there are also concerns about Chinese subsidies. In a speech in July 2006, Daniel DiMicco, CEO of Nucor, a large steel company, noted, "Since 2000, we (America) has lost 3 million jobs to China (in the steel industry), directly related to these subsidies from China."[7] From 2000 to 2005, China's steel capacity grew 170%, with exports rising 140%. DiMicco concedes that China Inc. should have a large steel market share, due to market factors, but not to be able to grow to 31% of the world market so rapidly.

Look at China Inc.'s growing relationship with Wal-Mart. Wal-Mart, of course, is the world's largest company, and growing sales all over the world, including China. Do the math between Wal-Mart and China; Wal-Mart is a $200-billion company, and has doubled its imports from China in a five-year span. If Wal-Mart were a country, it would be China's eighth largest trading partner. Even with its economic growth rapidly escalating, Wal-Mart represents 10% of all China's exports. This is a powerful relationship between China Inc. and Wal-Mart that has the potential to be too cozy for America's liking. Why is this? Because more of Wal-Mart's future growth is in China, not the United States. Therefore, Wal-Mart has a lot of incentive in promoting Chinese exports as a way for growing its market share for retail in the country. This could be classified as an unfair opportunity for Wal-Mart.

Certainly, outsourcing firms located in China and India, to name a few, have become opportunists in American business. Good for India and China Inc. for their ability to learn the opportunity of the easy out in today's corporate environment. When it is noted that American companies are offshoring 500–2,000 IT employees at a time, it is clear to me that such actions are being taken without thinking through productivity first. Despite the glitz of offshore development, there are failures as well, despite the much lower labor rate. But don't blame the opportunists; learn from them.

## OPPORTUNISTS 4: "BODY SHOPS" (TEMPORARY LABOR)

Question: What is the definition of a "temporary"?
Answer: A worker who is permanently looking for a decent job.

There are two sides to every story, and certainly, there are two different views regarding the fairness of the temporary agency marketplace. Despite anyone's view whether this service is good or bad for the American worker, it is clear that it is a profitable business operation. Take Manpower Incorporated, the world's

Remember that the premise of this book is that outsourcing as a function is overused, and that there are some good arrangements for outsourcing that have been executed and make business sense for the company. However, just as in consulting, when the outsourcing firm needs revenue growth to sustain itself, it will make a choice that doesn't provide value over revenue. The top-line needs of the outsourcer forces the firm to develop *easy out* service offerings. All too often, there are companies looking for such *easy out* solutions for their businesses.

However, with the emergence of India and China as rate plays in the past decade, U.S. third party outsourcers who compete with global operations have sought to differentiate themselves on a quality and innovation basis, as they no longer are able to compete on price. These efforts, when taken, have come off with mixed results. Today, these firms must succeed at innovation and quality if they are to survive the Asian onslaught of competition. The rise and fall of the IT services industry is littered with American companies who are winners and losers, depending upon their ability to offer quality, efficiency, and innovation, and to not compete with India on price.

## OPPORTUNISTS 3: OFFSHORE PROVIDERS

During the nineties, India had a massive balance of payment crisis as a result of oil shocks, and thus economic reforms came about. In the late nineties, the Chinese Communists announced that state-owned industries were to be phased out, which began what was to become the fastest-growing economy in world history. For the Y2K scare, General Electric and other multinationals used India as a programming hub at a fraction of U.S. prices. China became an unleashed manufacturing power. Offshoring wasn't new, but during the 1990s and 2000s, the concept of offshoring was taken to a new level.

As a result of such astounding success, the Indian offshore software development firm has really changed since its general introduction to American business through the Year 2000 panic. Back then, your account manager was an Indian programmer who was typically a middle-aged man sloppily dressed with sneakers. There wasn't much interaction between you and his team, as the work to be done was essentially to correct lines of code with digits to allow for the Year 2000 to pass without crashing the mainframe. The work was simple, the business requirements given to the Indians were minimal, and the work output was cheap and well handled. A perfect scenario for the first stage of Indian offshore development.

Today, not even ten years later, the Indian software-consulting firm, in many cases, has lost its soul. Instead of being visited by a lead Indian programmer masquerading as an account manager, you'll be visited by a real salesperson; a true American sales guy, wearing a perfectly tailored suit, armed with all the latest buzzwords. Ralph, the sales guy, replaces Ravi. Glossy brochures and golf outings have replaced the no frills of before. Ralph may have never even been to India, but is fully versed on the always-be-selling approach, pestering you without fail.

second largest temporary staffing agency, with 4,000 offices worldwide, placing 2 million temporary jobs per year. Over a five-year period from November 11, 2001, to November 11, 2006, Manpower's stock increased from $30.90 a share to $69.82, a mind-boggling increase of 225%! There is no doubt that the business of temporary workers is a good business to be in, and we must understand how and why these opportunists are doing so well.

This survey shows why workers choose this work, as is noted in Figure 3.1.

**Figure 3.1**
**Reasons for Temporary Employment**

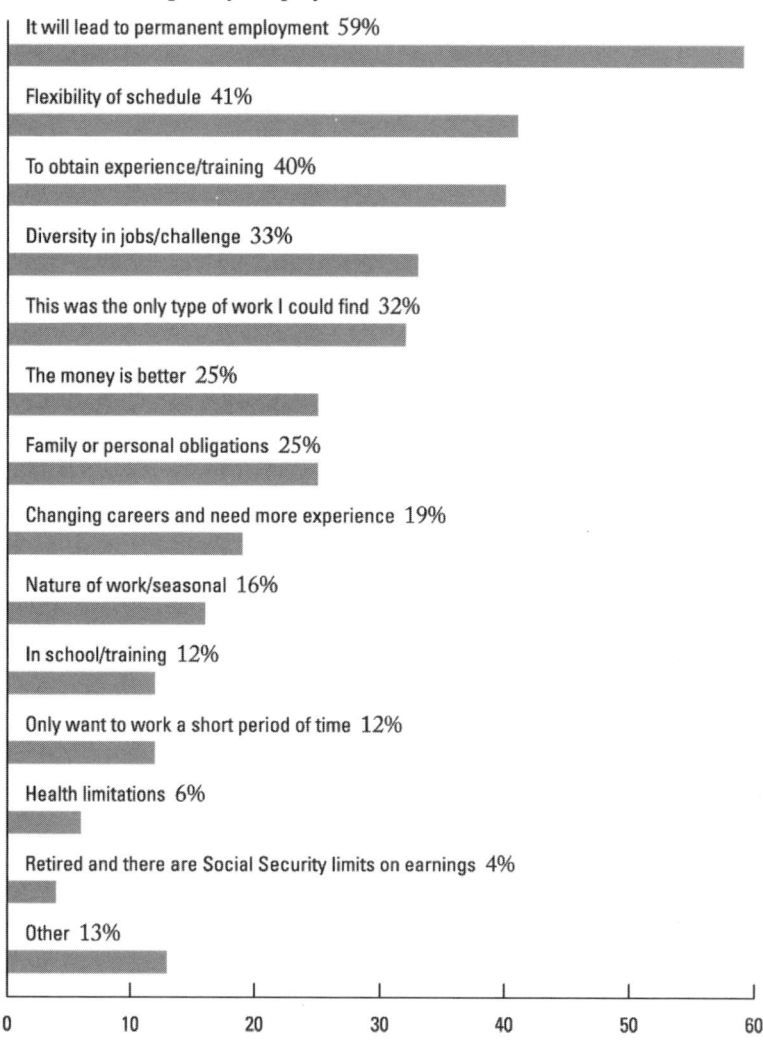

*Source:* American Staffing Association, 2006.

In another study that I found from 2001, 78% of temporary workers would prefer full-time, permanent employment, per the National Association of Temporary and Staffing Services.[8] The research seems to suggest quite clearly that while workers used to have different reasons for being temporary in the past to match their lifestyle, the trends of the twenty-first century indicate that a greater number of temps really wanting to be permanent employees. Today, the number is likely much higher.

Displacement rates by industry also provide a telling story: through the 1980s, 1990s, and the 2000s, more blue-collar workers have been displaced than white-collar workers. While blue-collar displacement rates may be falling, they still appear to be higher than that of white-collar jobs. Interestingly enough, all of the scuttlebutt about outsourcing and offshoring started when white-collar jobs started to go to India, but what about the permatemps of blue-collar and administrative work? A *permatemp* is a temporary worker who works alongside a regular employee doing similar work for a long period of time. From what I have seen, this type of employee has been the greatest growth trend for the temporary agencies. The other reasons for temporary labor (seasonality and revenue fluctuation) would appear to be the same situation as has existed in American business for quite a while. The permatemp is the reason for this amazing growth in the business of the temporary workforce. Large Fortune 500 companies have sought ways to reduce labor costs other than the traditional methods of innovation within an economic model. The famous Microsoft case in 2000 where thousands of employees were misclassified as contractors to illegally deny them benefits led to a $97 million settlement. To avoid such harsh penalties, corporations have partnered with the temporary agencies for cost-saving solutions. Often, it leads to the permatemp worker.

Unfortunately, temporary staffing becomes increasingly difficult and exploitative as it works its way down to the lower levels of the U.S. labor pool. For manual labor–type functions, the going rates from the customer are low to start with, with high administrative costs, such as worker's compensation (given manual labor) and hiring costs (large turnover). Even with this being the case, the agency may make 50–100% of what the laborers' gross wage is. For work that is more white collar in nature, the temporary agency may make only 20% margin. Typically, I have seen, on average, the temporary agency grossing 40–50% an hour, which, after their costs, should lead to 20–30% net profit from the transaction.

Companies like Manpower should not be blamed for their business model, even though they can take a healthy percentage from a worker who could be classified as "working poor." After all, they are in the business to make money for their shareholders, and, as is evident by their stock price, they are doing so. The real blame should be extended to the economic policies that allow companies to increase their number of temporary workers through a wider definition of what is a temporary versus a permanent position within the workforce. The concept of the permatemp has been a windfall for the temporary agencies, sometimes at the expense of the American worker. Addressing the issue of the permatemp is not a sociopolitical issue from my perspective, but rather a productivity one, as I will address in a later section.

## OPPORTUNISTS 5: CORPORATE EXECUTIVES

There is no question that outsourcing or offshoring has been a significant benefit to the corporate executive. In a typical economic equation, there is labor, capital, and technology. The combination of capital spending and technology of any sort should lead to higher levels of productivity and, therefore, greater profitability. Yet, when capital spending and technology or process improvements don't lead to increased productivity for the company, the chief executive officer and his or her staff have a big problem. What should they do? Spending more capital on technology may prove to be a perpetuation of earlier problems. The CEO may feel the need to find cost-reduction techniques that are possible without productivity. So what are these possibilities? Clearly, the labor play is the biggest one that many CEOs are counting on. Yet, the truth of the matter is that this sort of cost reduction without a corresponding productivity improvement is either short-lived or a fantasy. The company that can offer the CEO this labor play must develop an insight to that company's culture and operating environment that is completely special in order to deliver on the promise. And yet the CEO is often able to ride the short-term labor play to make a healthy bonus without really improving his or her operation.

Take what's happening in the auto industry today. In 2006, 30,000 hourly employees decided to leave GM in early buy-outs and retirement by January 1, 2007, which was two years ahead of its schedule. Yet given the large number of workers leaving GM and some of its suppliers, like Delphi, GM has had to scramble to find workers to keep the assembly lines working, and often has turned to temporary workers as a solution. For the five months since these large layoffs have been exercised to November 2006, GM's stock price has gone from $26 a share to almost $35, a healthy price increase for a company in the state that GM is in.[9] Taking a labor play without productivity has been a short-term win for GM, but will it be sustainable? I'm pretty sure that the answer will be a resounding no.

The problem in the CEO or executive compensation model for American businesses is that it is tightly tied to stock price, which doesn't necessarily tie to the value of the company. Frequently, CEOs make decisions that are good for the short-term stock price that can turn out to be fundamentally wrong for what's best for the company. Certainly, the use of outsourcing or temporary workers without fundamental process and productivity improvement within the company is an example of this. When the CEOs of these companies make massive bonuses or cash out stock–stock options based on productivity-less decisions, these executives are another group of opportunists in the world of outsourcing. Such actions must be controlled for America to focus on productivity again for our workers and our shareholders.

## OPPORTUNISTS 6: POLITICIANS

As has been previously been stated in this book, politicians who get elected through playing the India–China bogeymen card are not only opportunists but also irresponsible ones at that. If these politicians want to garner votes through associating with voters as to why they are losing their jobs, that's fine, so long as they get the story straight. And why should they create artificial bogeymen when real ones exist? It's always easier to conjure up villains that don't exist than it is to arrest and eliminate the villains that do. And that is precisely the point that will be addressed regarding the opportunist politician.

According to a congressional report dated June 18, 2004, only 2% of total U.S. employment might move overseas by 2015.[10] A 2% reduction in jobs occurring in the future hardly sounds like the epidemic, or "huge sucking sound," conveyed to voters by our politicians. Making a political case against offshoring is easy because the villain is not us. As well, politicians aren't addressing what America can receive back from such massively growing economies like China and India. And it doesn't address corresponding jobs associated with these jobs moving overseas. The current numbers, no matter how you slice them, don't support the existence of a massive wave of offshoring that will cripple the U.S. economy.

But there are some 400-pound gorillas in our midst that our politicians either can't see or choose not to; that is, the growing inability of our workers to be competitive in key sectors like manufacturing, the poor and declining state of our educational system, the eroding of our middle class, and the new rules of productivity. Economic policies must be enacted, like what is happening in China that is pro-growth for its own nation. Second, our youth are becoming a lost generation, unable to be productive, and not competitive with their counterparts in other parts of the world. We are moving away from having a prosperous middle class, and it's not due to too much competition. In fact, it's due to being unable to compete.

Yet there is only so much that legislation can do. The rest is up to our corporations and our cultural society. Corporations must become more competitive. Families and our society must sacrifice a bit for the sake of our educational system in order to avoid creating yet another lost generation. Politicians should lead us in these areas, but not overlegislate solutions.

## WHAT TO DO ABOUT OPPORTUNISTS?

Just to be very clear, I don't consider these opportunists in a negative sense; they are simply taking advantage of the current business environment in a legal, if not sometimes ethical, way. Consultants, domestic and foreign third parties, body shops, corporate executives, and politicians are simply working within a democratic, free-market socioeconomic setting in a successful manner. My only contention with these entities is that they are band aids for corporations that need real surgery. Consultants may be seeking productivity in American corporations, but it is not being done as efficiently as did the thinkers in our past. I have nothing against consulting firms making money in a private enterprise setting, but I would sure like them to play an important role in the next wave of creative destruction needed for our economy, instead of profiting from *easy out* solutions.

The domestic and foreign outsourcers, plus the body shops, are legal businesses seeking to make a profit in the business of people. There efforts often help American corporations, and they should be allowed to do so without exception. In too many cases, they are not in the business of process and productivity improvement, but rather people outsourcing. Interestingly enough, all of these entities are in the same business, yet the foreign offshorers are seen as the enemy, while the domestic outsourcers and body shops are not. Americans must understand that foreign offshorers have probably done less damage than have its domestic counterparts up to the present day. As much as I understand and appreciate the role of third-party outsourcers, I don't think that they can assist a client in understanding process improvement, productivity, and competitiveness if the company chooses to ignore these factors. That's an *easy out* for the corporation.

The final two opportunists, the corporate executives and the politicians, must be placed in a different category than the other consultants and third party providers because they have a civic responsibility to the public to do better for both its shareholders and citizens. Many corporate executives are making a lot of money personally without developing significant value for the corporation beyond short-term gains that the market allows (I will discuss the shortfalls with our accounting system that allows for this in the next chapter). And yet corporate executives should be doing better for their shareholders, and some executives have been doing so. Famous examples of CEOs who have raised the corporation's shareholder wealth beyond short-term gains are Jack Welch of General Electric, Steve Jobs of Apple, John Chambers of Cisco Systems, and Narayana Murthy of Infosys. More executives need to seek long-term wealth-building activities versus short-term efforts aimed at propping up a stock price.

Our politicians are to blame as well. These individuals are some of the most powerful and educated men and women in America, and aren't at the mercy of shareholders, who want solely short-term gains. They own the public trust, whether they like it or not. They must make our country choose the hard decisions for the good of our nation, and lately they have not. They are doing very little to make our nation competitive with India and China. Our school system is creating one lost generation after another. Our citizens are poorly informed as to what's happening in the global market, as they sink deeper toward underemployment. They need to become less politically oriented and more focused on implementing policy.

But the blame shouldn't stop there. What about us, the citizens? What responsibility do we have for America's lack of productivity? How many of our citizens think about this? Likely very few of us consider such heavy matters, but what about our educational system? How many of us think about whether our educational system is able to properly prepare our children to compete in a global marketplace? Without getting into any political overtones (as I don't think that there are differences in approach from one party to another), I believe that our citizens must understand what's happening in the world economy today, and act as citizens to avoid us from becoming the next France. We certainly own a piece of the problem, even if we are the victims, and not the opportunists, per se. We need to stand up and take action.

# CHAPTER FOUR

# Market Myopia, Enron, and Political Overreaction

Nearly ten years ago, I wrote a research paper titled "Measuring the Differential between Economic and Accounting Performance of a Public Corporation within the Global Economy" (sounds thrilling, doesn't it?).[1] Today, the main principles of this research are as relevant as they were back then, and they will be used as the foundation of the discussion of why accounting rules and the financial market valuations do not support appropriate decision making within a public corporation. Companies will often make inappropriate choices regarding outsourcing that they probably wouldn't have made otherwise.

In my research paper, I started by debunking the myth that many believe that financial data are objective; despite what we have been taught, data aren't necessarily objective. The accounting system in which these financial data reside is an inexact and subjective container, and, as such, financial data could be viewed differently depending on the nature of the accounting system. For instance, the same financial results will likely be stated differently in the United States than they would be in France or in Japan. Not only country-to-country, but results from company to company can be different. Therefore, there is a need for independent auditors to determine whether financial results are credible.

In my study, I compared two variables, one called economic performance of the company (ECONP) and the other accounting performance of the company (ACCTP). By definition, ECONP will never equal ACCTP, as ECONP is largely a theoretical variable, and ACCTP (however imperfect) is a practical one. Yet which of these variables more accurately reflects the value of the company? One big challenge that exists today within an ACCTP valuation is how to measure intangible assets and knowledge. Today's corporation is such a complex operation that it is difficult for even the most objective accounting system to place value. How does the market place value on Wal-Mart's intrinsic knowledge of its distribution system, and future potential to gain market share in China? For sure, we are talking about subjective values that must be measured in a very imprecise manner. Yet if we look at what happened with Enron, we understand that such difficulties can lead to disaster.

The conclusion from my research study is that while differentiating between ECONP and ACCTP is difficult, if not impossible to measure, it is very important for the stock market, regulatory bodies, and even the corporate executives to understand these differences as best and objectively as they can. The cries from critics such as myself have fallen on deaf ears. Since this time almost ten years ago, our nation has faced some of the greatest accounting scandals in our history: Enron, World-Com, Global Crossing, Imclone, etc. Each of these companies' experience represents a chapter in our nation's history of accounting scandals that rocked our financial markets, and decimated the lives and savings of millions of employees and investors. In an angry response to such scandals, the Congress enacted the Sarbanes–Oxley Act (SARBOX) in 2002, which, among other things, established the Public Accounting Oversight Board responsible for eliminating accounting abuses and improving auditing processes. While it is true that SARBOX has helped to control extreme cases of corporate accounting abuses, it will not catch more subtle examples of corporate accounting abuses, and will cause large costs for corporate compliance. Not only has SARBOX increased administrative costs for corporations that would never had the Enron or World-Com problems in the first place, it also has stymied much of the innovation and risk taking within corporations in fear of violating the provisions of this law. The leaders of Enron were magnificent risk takers who were in many ways ahead of their competitors; they were also unethical in concealing certain activities. Instead of preventing fraud, SARBOX has in some ways stifled creativity and risk taking at a time when our corporations really need it. And when corporate managers feel stymied from innovation and taking risks, they choose the *easy outs* as one of the few options in achieving their numbers. It appears as if SARBOX loves outsourcing!

The chronology of Enron to SARBOX is yet another shining example of how our politicians and corporate executives are continually promoting a business environment based on rules and rhetoric rather than economic policy. The three factors that often prevent corporate executives from creating productivity change are legislation, financial market myopia, and corporate culture. All executives have to face the first two impediments, and corporate cultures guide their approach. The risk-averse companies will choose options such as outsourcing, even if it isn't a good option, because it is a safe one from a market perspective. Companies choosing safe options in a competitive business environment will lose, as you can bet that the escalating global competitive environment in practically every industry will not allow for it. But what happens when these factors of legislation and market myopia make all American companies more risk averse? This has an obvious negative impact on the American companies' ability to compete in a global marketplace, to make innovation and efficiency happen.

Interestingly enough, the potential impediments of legislation and market my-opia tie nicely to the concepts of ACCTGP and ECONP. Much of the financial regulation/legislation makes its way in the form of accounting rules, and market myopia can distort the perception of economic value of the firm. Corporations respond largely to these factors in their operational decision making, such as whether or not to outsource. As this story unfolds in the chapter, the reader will truly get a sense for why some corporate executives act as they do, and real themes will appear for reform that is needed to improve American productivity.

To begin the discussion on American accounting rules, I would like to go back to the late eighties/early nineties when I lived in Baltimore, and was working on my M.B.A. The university that I attended had a business school full of younger professors who were activists regarding what was transpiring in business at the time; rising deficit spending, layoffs of blue-collar workers, and the threat from an economically powerful Japan. For me, these points resonated well, as I lived in this essentially blue-collar town and saw my relatives lose their jobs owing to what I was learning about in business school. One of the books that caught my attention during this period was *Short-Term America*, written by Michael T. Jacobs in 1991.[2] In his book, Jacobs notes many of the reasons why America was losing its competitiveness. The main reason, per the author, was "the distant relationship between the providers of capital (shareholders and lenders) and the users of capital (corporate managers)." With corporate governance bodies (boards of directors) exerting much less influence over the day-to-day actions of the activities of corporate managers than occurs in other countries, there is less accountability and control than is needed for a successful system. Yet after such concern was raised regarding the threat of Japan and even Germany from the early nineties, the United States went forward with the longest period of peacetime economic growth in our history, 8.5 years. With such economic growth directly following the doom-and-gloom views of economists and academics suggesting the need for economic reform, does this mean that such views were wrong in the early nineties? I will discuss economic policy in a later chapter, but, from an accounting perspective, the views of these activists remain correct whether the volatility of the economy was positive or negative. From an accounting perspective, the problem with the growth from the nineties is that our accounting rules were woefully unable to properly reflect the financial positions of what this growth meant to our economy and to the individual corporation. Even today, our accounting rules are manufacturing focused even though the service sector was two-thirds of our output during this period of the nineties, and we've been through the dot-com era. In fact, the rules are even outdated from the perspective of today's manufacturing companies! So if ACCTGP was woefully inadequate to measure the true value of what growth meant to our economy, and companies during the dot-com era, why did the financial markets increase so dramatically in a reflection of the growth results? Instead of relying on financial statements that had rules that were viewed as too manufacturing focused, the financial markets did more of an ad hoc valuation for these companies. And in doing so, financial valuations and equity during this dot-com period went through the roof. Part of the perceived value in these companies was the elimination of the heavy capital investments, and the reliance on technology and knowledge versus labor and capital. Very few of these companies were showing profits, and their balance sheets were a mess. Scient, an Internet consulting company, had a stock price of \$133.75, a 1238% increase in price from its IPO price. A year later, the price of the stock had fallen to \$2.94. What happened? Essentially, in my view, all of the investment banks and analysts disregarded the existing accounting rules because they felt them to be too "old economy," and that was probably true. But as a severe overreaction, they arrived at formulas for valuation in the "new economy" that allowed them to make more money on commissions for companies that weren't that close to earning a profit. The analysts also overstated the impact of IT investments on productivity, and of course, IT investments were such a big part of growth boom. Therefore, it is clear that in the nineties, we learned that our accounting rules in the United States were unable to act as a controlling factor over zealous and opportunistic investment houses and other financial institutions. These rules were perceived as so distant from reality that it became okay to largely disregard them.

Financial reports for both private and the public sector are intended to provide valuable information to the financial community, but this reporting is a nebulous art form. Every national financial reporting system has its issues and must be understood as best as possible by the financial community. For one, financial statements invariably have difficulties in the valuation process of capital assets. Second, productivity and the quality of goods and services produced are difficult to quantify as well. The value of knowledge, which is so critical to corporations to-day, cannot be accurately estimated. Next, to what extent and how do corporations attempt to minimize taxes and regulatory oversight? Again, this is very difficult to measure and understand. Other gimmicks that a good corporate manager under-stands play a role in making these reports less than useful. Measuring the costs of inputs versus outputs, the distinctions between capital and operational budgets, off-budget costs, and others really make the practice of accounting very difficult. As well, with market valuations today being largely focused on human capital, intellectual property, and branding, accounting becomes even more complicated than an earlier era when market value more closely resembled book value. Ac-counting can never be 100% accurate, so it should be an objective and nonpolitical one versus something biased for the use of subjective interests.

To better understand how America's accounting rules are affecting our econ-omy, let's take a quick look at what's happening in China regarding accounting rules. Prior to the open-door reforms, China's accounting system was adapted from the Soviet-Era planning system. In 1992, China made a great deal of progress to-ward reform by enacting Accounting Standards for Business Enterprises (ASBE). The ASBE was based on International Accounting Standards (IAS) and adapted to local conditions. Despite such reforms, the Chinese system has challenged the push for publicly disclosed financial statements for the following reasons[3]:

- The prevalence of *guanxi* (connections)
- Strong government, institutional company ownership

- Government-centric accounting rules (instead of driven through enterprise)
- Draconian stock exchange rules (such as company must be profitable, pressuring bad accounting practices)
- Interlocking relationships between government and institutions
- Immature accounting and legal systems

Interesting that China's accounting reform was put in place primarily for the use of external parties in reporting, yet the greatest need for this institution is for internal reforms. There is little desire within China to use public accounting for any corporate governance or performance management that will be important for its enterprises for development in the global economy. Clearly, China's Achilles' heel will be its financial systems, or lack of one. While the U.S. accounting system is probably too complicated and draconian, China's is too infantile, and the first nation to understand and reform will have an advantage over the other.

There is a great concern from other nations regarding the number of accounting regulations that are going in place in the United States since the Enron-era scams. One of my counterparts in India told me, "We in India have grown up with so many controls over our economy, we feel that we have been sprung from them in the early nineties, and don't want to be controlled ever again. We feel like you Americans are moving in a different direction with some of your rules." Indian companies have a choice to become SARBOX compliant that helps their standing in the U.S. financial community, but it's costly and puts their executives in fear of litigation even if they haven't committed any fraud. Europe as well is complaining to the SEC commissioner regarding the high cost of American compliance rules. These heavy-handed regulations will adversely affect America's ability to compete in a global market by making it more difficult for American and foreign companies to conduct trade for the benefit of America.

At a time when America needs more innovation and competitiveness in comparison to developing competitors such as China and India, we're heading in the wrong direction. What does this mean relative to outsourcing? It means that our increasingly burdensome accounting rules will not promote a healthy environment for our corporations, and will distract foreign companies from valuable trade. According to the Hackett Group, finance costs at typical companies have increased by 18% over the last two years, largely driven by SARBOX.[4] With these increased finance costs related to compliance, finance costs are now at 1.26% of revenue.

SARBOX did not just change America's accounting rules; it overhauled how America will do business in the future. With fines of up to $5 million and twenty years of jail time, CEOs and CFOs are very focused on SARBOX. Yet for smaller companies, the costs of SARBOX can be too high. The *USA Today* reported in 2003 that hardware wholesaler Moore-Handley, with sales of $151 million, was spending so much time and money trying to comply with SARBOX that it eventually delisted from the NASDAQ to stay solvent. The estimate for cost of compliance for this company was $250,000 annually, yet its net profit was only $300,000 a year! Therefore, it is becoming increasingly likely that only companies with revenues of over $100–$200 million will be able to afford this sort of compliance, and therefore remain a public entity.[5] This will lead to a decrease in publicly traded smaller firms, the ones with innovation needed to drive our economy. Prohibiting these companies in going public will affect our economy, as smaller firms typically bring forth more creativity and innovation. Of course, this is what is needed for us to compete against lower cost providers in India and China.

A Foley and Lardner survey of thirty-two midsized companies predicted an average increase of 105% for accounting costs, 90% for legal costs, 102% increase in costs due to lost productivity, and a whopping 266% increase due to personnel compliance costs![6]

Therefore, it will be increasingly likely with accounting red tape that our corporations will make poor decisions, including the outsourcing of operations that shouldn't be outsourced. Remember, though, that outsourcing itself isn't the problem, but rather bad or over-outsourcing. How can our public corporations make strategic decisions when they are wrapped up with so much accounting red tape? They may simply outsource some of their problems instead of figuring out what the problems are, as they don't have time to do much with so many compliance headaches.

Accounting factors other than SARBOX too have complicated America's business picture. When I was in the financial services industry, we had separate sets of books for statutory reporting, one for tax reporting and one for financial (public accounting) reporting. As a growing trend, on top of this, many corporations are now keeping an additional set of books reflecting what they believe to be their accurate business reality. As well, including the interference of the various government regulatory bodies, and the interests of the Internal Revenue Service, it again becomes a question as to whether these bodies are in place for themselves, or to serve the public and the corporation.

Economic statistics of today may not be comparable to those of prior decades owing to changes in accounting policies. One example is the change of use of LIFO instead of FIFO, which may completely distort earnings reports versus those from an earlier era. Overstated profits were a problem in the 1970s because inflation pushed up risks and replacement costs. Understated profits can exist when the nation's finances are stable and risks and replacement costs are declining. Most of these shortcomings in accounting treatments are not well understood when economic statistics are produced; instead, these statistics are considered ceteris paribus in comparison to other periods, or other nations. There is a lot of subjectivity in these accounting treatments that are not well understood by the public, or even by many of the pundits who make policy decisions. Certainly, they are not well understood by the corporate managers who may make decisions based on these statistics, such as whether or not to outsource.

Not only have American accounting rules become increasingly difficult and confusing, they seem to have been lost in time and are unable to support the innovation needed for our country. Want proof? I believe that our GAAP accounting system contributed to an earlier-than-desirable decline in the positive impact of the dot-com industry on American business, and likely too fast of an ascent. With the financial intermediaries, investment analysts, and bankers making a killing in the late 1990s and early 2000s with the lack of accounting rules to control how to account for innovation, I believe that the dot-com impact on our national economy could have been more sustainable through a greater emphasis on productivity versus casino capitalism.[7] And what about the next big thrust, whether it's energy innovation or biotechnology? Will the markets, the financial intermediaries, and the government promote this or squash it with greater controls? Will our control systems support or inhibit competitiveness and productivity in the future?

Unfortunately, there is evidence to even suggest that slower investment spending for manufacturing in the U.S. economy may be attributed to variables other than higher investments in developing nations. Investment is driven by obvious factors such as interest rates, demand, and capacity utilization, but what about taxes, depreciation schedules, and other accounting considerations? Higher marginal corporate tax rates and higher compliance costs must be considered as well.

Beyond the accounting treatments of financial statements within our companies, what about the impact on the financial market itself? Today, companies are perceived as more of commodities than they are as business entities. The whole gang of institutional investors, speculators, and day traders involved in the market today are largely focused on short-term stock price and valuation as opposed to the true value of the corporation. We all certainly know this to be true, and some corporations are trying to do something about it. Companies like Alcoa, AT&T, Mattel, PepsiCo, and Sun Microsystems are no longer giving corporate earnings guidance, as they have come to realize that this action does nothing but promote the short-term mentality that promotes its executives to make short-term, myopic decisions. In fact, corporate guidance to Wall Street on earnings declined to 55% in 2005, down from 72% in 2003. Many think that such actions should have happened a long time ago, and will promote a view toward fundamentals instead of the quarter-to-quarter earnings management game. Certainly, each corporation will make a trade-off between investor relations, and the fight against corporate myopia, but the trends at least seem to be away from the damaging, short-term scope that Wall Street so desperately craves in its casino-like approach to the stock market. Once again, when Wall Street encourages corporations to look quarter to quarter for its efficiencies and growth, it rewards bad decision making instead of decisions based on fundamentals, and rewards quick fixes. There is no question that pressures from Wall Street have forced me and my colleagues to make decisions to boost my company's short-term stock price versus the financial long-term viability of the company. No corporate executive should dispute this statement.

Lastly, corporate myopia not only stems from a short-term-focused investor community, it also stems within the organization itself. There are two reasons for this myopia, in my opinion. The first is the powerful influence of stock options as a motivating financial tool within the public corporation. If you look at the list of the highest-paid CEOs in 2006, you'll see a disproportionate difference between their salary compensation and their stock option compensation. The highest paid CEO in 2006, Terry Semel, CEO of Yahoo!, had a 2006 salary of $250,001, and $71.4 million in stock options.[8]

My intention here is not to make a passionate plea against stock options (I have them myself, so that would be hypocritical), but rather to show the influence that stock options have on this short-term stock price focus. There is no question that current earnings are a poor indicator for the long-term prospects of a company. Longer-term prospects, such as research-and-development costs, employee training, and other intangibles, are difficult to quantify on a financial statement, so it stands to reason that such investments in the future may not help an executive achieve the quarterly projections as easily as could implementing a short-term, shortsighted outsourcing venture with no corresponding improvement in productivity. When corporate executives believe that hitting short-term numbers and longer-term valuation are mutually exclusive, most executives will choose the former over the latter. Given that these corporate executives make money by not owning the actual stock security, but rather through boosting the price to exercise an option truly shows the bias of short-term versus long-term. Driving up the price of the stock in the short term will help the corporate executive make more money, but digging deeper for investments that may not pay off for multiple years will not. Competition gives way to corporate myopia in many cases.

And yet, if the only and largest factor for corporate myopia were that of greed, its negative impact would be much smaller than it is today. Beyond the foolish impact that the financial market has on the typical corporation through a short-term mentality, the lack of vision and insight of corporate leaders, on the average, is probably the biggest negative factor preventing corporate productivity to emerge within its new definition. For every Jack Welch and Lou Gertsner, there are Chainsaw Al Dunlap, Jeffrey Skilling, Bernie Ebbers, and others. Charles Wang of Computer Associates was the highest-paid CEO in 2000, largely owing to accounting gimmicks involving deferred revenue. Joe Nacchio of Qwest was indicted for financial fraud, but not before he earned $102 million in 2001. I don't think that many would categorize any of these gentlemen as incompetent; most of the press regarding bad CEOs focuses on their being greedy. But what about the incompetent CEO who can't make a decision or develop a strategic vision to lead his or her company? Such stories aren't as sexy as World-Com, but many people occupying positions of leadership work in these companies, and the companies suffer poor performance as a result. As well, many of these poorly performing companies are likely to make honest poor decisions, as opposed to unethical ones. These are the companies that play by the rules, but aren't prepared to compete using the new rules of productivity.

A nation's public accounting system should be its safeguard for not only ethical factors but efficient ones as well. China's rudimentary accounting system must be eventually able to stand up to the tight reign that the government has over its private enterprise, as well as the need for an honest financial reporting system for external and internal constituents/investors. India has issues in its public accounting system, but appears to be interested in reform, while China is being more standoff-ish. On the other end of the spectrum, the United States is all too ready to legislate, and go overboard with "reform," but at the expense of creativity and innovation. While America has been a bastion for fair and honest financial reporting ever since the Great Depression, one must wonder if some of its recent efforts aren't over the top and counterproductive. It is fascinating, although troubling, to see historically bureaucratic societies like India and China trying to be more progressive and innovative while America, the historically innovative nation, is becoming increasingly bureaucratic.

Perhaps our public accounting system has to overkill its approach given the casino mentality that exists in our financial markets. What's troubling to me is that the financial markets look at the business enterprises as the means to their money-making ends, versus the financial markets in place to support our business enterprises. In China, despite the lack of a strong financial system, its mechanisms are in place to move massive amounts of capital, up to 50% of the GDP, through the system to add value to the economy. While this level of domestic investment from the financial system is extraordinary, and likely not very efficiently managed, it serves a purpose for the greater good of Chinese competitiveness. India doesn't have the level of domestic and foreign investment that China does, but it's becoming a very efficient private investment model of allocating capital to needed areas. Suffice it to say that my view is that the underdeveloped financial rules of India and China appear to be at least as efficient as our complicated and bloated financial ones that are affecting our ability to compete in a global market.

My experience as a corporate executive leads me to conclude that most leaders focus on the short-term maximization versus the longer-term, more difficult optimization. In mid-November of most years, I am trying to find a way to make my budget for the year, which will either lead me to a bigger bonus or no bonus at all. In some cases, I will be forced to make silly short-term (but legal) decisions to make my targets. Smart, savvy salespeople use the corporate myopia to their advantage by offering products and services with a deferral of payment until the following year.

The top executives at most companies are highly intelligent men and women, and infrequently make obvious, poor decisions. However, many of them will play games with the numbers in less than a fraudulent manner. If truth be told, there are few corporate executives who would deny having even done this; practically all have done so. Outsourcing, in too many cases, becomes a poor decision to make numbers. Without better options, many executives have made shortsighted decisions, such as signing a long-term outsourcing deal that delivers good first-year benefits at the expense of later years. It is almost impossible to avoid making these shortsighted decisions in the U.S. corporate model. Yet very few business people, researchers, regulatory bodies, economists, and the like are identifying this as a major business concern. Too many regulators focus on the Bernie Ebbers of the world instead of the thousands of no-name CEOs who make shortsighted decisions every day. The biggest problem isn't fraud, but rather neglect.

Our public accounting system and financial markets are in the need of reform for America to remain competitive in the world economy. As I will discuss in the next chapter, numerous statistics seem to suggest that competitiveness and productivity are not a problem within the U.S. economy. But I'm fearful that this is due to a lack of measurement of our problems. Our economists, politicians, CEOs and the like support to statistics in identifying efficient financial markets and public accounting systems. But there are other stories deeper beneath the statistics.

So what does outsourcing have to do with my concepts of ECONP and AC-CTGP? Outsourcing is a by-product of the serious incongruence between these two variables; ACCTP is what's on the investor's mind, and ECONP, the company's intrinsic value. When outsourcing becomes an *easy out*, it becomes a short-term fix more focused on making the quarterly financial statements look better than being focused on the intrinsic value of the company. ACCTP thinking is very important within our financial markets given that the business entity is more of a means for the investor to make money than it is a means for the public good. When this happens, a growing economy allows the investors and corporate managers to profit to a much larger degree than the general benefit that is provided to the workers and society in general. I'm a businessman, so I'm not the least bit averse to financial incentive and the principles of the free market. But when short-term ACCTP-focused thinking leads the CEO to poor decisions, it's time for reform.

I think that the most damning statements in this chapter are the fact that China's and India's public accounting and reporting models are increasingly free-enterprise, while America's is increasingly the opposite. We must be ever vigilant regarding whether our public frameworks are bringing value or not. Clearly, our financial markets and public accounting systems are in dire need of efficient reform, not knee-jerk populism. Outsourcing is an *easy out* practice as it is an addictive solution for the CEO to find an easier approach to cost savings. But many times, this is a clear suckers bet, through and through.

However, there is great hope for our more mature financial/accounting system in the battle of global competition. Today, the American financial/accounting system rewards managers in making shortsighted, and even disturbing, business decisions, such as bad outsourcing decisions. If our politicians and policy makers begin to understand the problems that our system causes in relation to competition and productivity, perhaps some real reforms can be undertaken, reforms that are more rational than political. However, one of the greatest limiting factors here is the difference between how our government measures economic results and the results that appear on corporate financial statements and workers' paychecks. Now, it's time to debunk some of the economic myths that exist today that support poor outsourcing decisions.

Every corporation is affected by a public accounting and financial reporting system that is used to understand its economic position within its industry. My view is that the great constraints of our system relative to others could put us at a disadvantage, and inappropriately push corporations to bad *easy out* practices, like outsourcing. Our accounting system is such that corporations are less likely to take risks, and make the difficult decisions that it must take in an emerging global economy. We must reform our accounting practices to be competitive in this global setting in order to make the right corporate decisions.

## CHAPTER FIVE

# The Economics of Who's Right and Who's Wrong

> Not a "gay science," I should say, like some we have heard of; no, a dreary, desolate and, indeed, quite abject and distressing one; what we might call, by way of eminence, the dismal science.
>
> —Thomas Carlyle (1849)

In 1849, Thomas Carlyle labeled economics the "dismal science" in his argument for the reintroduction of slavery as a means of regulating the labor market! Should economics be debated as either dismal or gay, or subjective objective? Today, we face a similar question when reviewing the economic statistics of the American economy. The *Economic Report of the President*, dated February 2007, began, "Policymakers face a challenge: productivity growth is important for economic growth and many of the underlying issues that they are trying to solve, but there is no single cause of productivity and no single policy to spur its growth." The report continued with a bright and cheery perspective occupied by the place of the United States in the major industrialized economy. This critical report regarding the state of our economy brings front and center that productivity is important to growth, but stumbles upon what to do about it, and how to measure it. Perhaps this report is referring to the new paradigm of productivity?

In this economic report prepared by the Council of Economic Advisors (2006 and 2007), the following points are noted[1]:

- Real GDP posted above average growth in 2006.
- Labor markets continued to strengthen, with unemployment falling and real wages growing.
- Productivity growth remained well above the historic average, although it wasn't explained clearly how this was so.
- Inflation remained moderate, excluding the impact of energy prices.
- Economic expansion will continue in the foreseeable future.

Regarding international trade, it was noted that U.S. exports grew at a faster rate than in 2006 (9.2% versus 6.7 percent, respectively, due to the developing markets of Asia and Africa becoming more viable as trading partners. Furthermore, the 2006 report notes, "The United States has been able to buy more goods and services than it sells because foreigners have been investing in the United States." Some would question as to whether foreigners are investing in the United States or just dumping their dollars as a function of growing imports. These reports always tend to be politically biased, regardless of the party in power in the White House. There wasn't much discussion surrounding the massively growing trade balance happening with growing developing nations.

Employment and unemployment is always an interesting topic of discussion in any government report. Per the Economic Report, unemployment declined by 0.5 to 4.9% during 2005, and fell again to 4.5% in 2006. The average unemployment rate for the year was lower than the averages of the 1970s, 1980s, and 1990s. In my opinion, this should not be a great surprise for us when we have the highest population growth rate of all developed nations. Most of this population growth is the result of immigration, not the birth rate, and this higher denominator raises some questions regarding what this truly means to our employment picture. The question is whether employment has grown sufficiently to cover the influx of new workers arriving. Per the Economic Report, labor costs (which equal 62% of nonfarm business) "have been stable, or possibly trending lower." Depending on whether you look at hourly labor cost or fully loaded compensation, you'll see a different picture on wages. For instance, if an employer pays a worker a slightly higher hourly wage but no benefits, the worker is much worse off, despite having a higher hourly wage. With a growing number of our workforce not having benefits and/or being of temporary status, this is a growing concern. We must be careful how we interpret government statistics.

The Economic Report was almost giddy regarding the labor-productivity growth for the period, noting that this factor is the primary reason for the United States having a faster GDP growth rate than any other major industrialized economy. However, the report noted, "The post-2001 acceleration in productivity, therefore, appears to be accounted for by factors that are more difficult to measure than the quantity of capital, such as continuing improvements in technology and in business practices." It's interesting that the authors weren't sure on what to base the strong productivity in comparison to other eras, where it was much easier to understand. During the 1995 era that is discussed in the report, a lot of the productivity improvements were said to be due to the proliferation of IT investments, such as giving white-collar workers PCs and adding IT investments on the shop floors. While the impact of these types of productivity improvements in the nineties were difficult to measure, given the nature of these types of investments (and the soft nature of its benefits), it is more than likely that such investments provided a real productivity improvement at the onset, although it was probably not so sustainable. Without a way to justify record productivity improvements in the economy, the economists note that post-2001 productivity numbers may be due to IT and business practices. But despite strong statements about productivity gains, the analysts weren't certain as to the underlying reasons for the gains.

It would be interesting to compare the healthy nature of U.S. productivity indicated in the economist report to that of other developed nations. However, no statistics were provided for two very important economies: India and China. In all fairness to our statistical bureaus, one can question the accuracy and reliability of data sources from these developing nations, but I don't understand how their productivity levels can be ignored from a comparative standpoint. At least from my perspective, it is clear that if China and India aren't included in the comparison, then it's not the appropriate comparison. It's simply a measurement of the old definition of productivity versus that of the new.

In a productivity equation, there are essentially three factors: labor, capital, and technology. Technology is increasingly ubiquitous in today's global market, and there's certainly an edge for America when it comes to capital, given the size of our economy and financial institutions, but a disadvantage when it comes to our record-setting balance-of-trade deficits that we are creating owing to our consumer demand. With such a high appetite for consumer products in the world's largest economy, we are truly a consumer-focused economy, unlike some of our main competitors in Asia that are so focused on saving and investment. Unfortunately, America seems to have sought recently to achieve productivity more so through labor-cost reductions than ever before, perhaps due to less success with technological change impacts, which can be seen as an innovation. This book talks about two major strategies in allowing for flexible labor: the outsourcing and temporary scenario in the United States and the offshoring of work to places like China and India. The answer is very clear as to how this productivity explosion has occurred in the United States for such a long period of time, and that's due primarily to the ability to have a flexible labor market, both domestically and internationally. Outsourcing is obviously one of the key strategies in achieving such a flexible labor market through either layoffs or the threat of losing jobs if wages are increased. Unfortunately, I don't think that a lot of this success can be attributed to the sound use of IT technology, although the capacity exists for this to happen, as will be discussed later in this book.

One part of the economic report that was indeed sober was the "Skills for the U.S. Workforce" section. With our national educational achievement falling, our productivity and competitiveness will be definitely affected if something doesn't change soon. A study of U.S. growth between 1950 and 1993 revealed that one-third of productivity growth in the period was due to increased levels of education. Now younger U.S. residents have lower a quality of education than their counterparts in other countries, we're heading in the wrong direction and becoming less competitive. At age 9 to 13, U.S. students rank in the middle of the pack (no prize) on math and science, but by age 15 are outperformed by most of their international peers. The good news is that America's college and university system is so good that we attract foreign students who learn, stay, and assist us in innovation. However, the large part of the population that makes up the working and some white-collar classes could end up being less educated than the competitors of our present and future. Unfortunately, this leads a corporate manager to seek productivity through labor plays (lower wages to lower-skilled candidates, including immigrants) as opposed to an investment in the future for productivity through better-educated and better-trained workforces. I know that it's not a popular statement to make, but we're moving in many ways closer to possessing characteristics of a developing country than an economic superpower. Our trends point to a lower educational ranking, and fewer workers with full-time employment, without benefits. This, in my mind, is not a recipe toward better effective productivity results, despite what the economics statistics state. We cannot state that our competitive intelligence as a nation is leading to improved productivity in the global economy.

In 2005, U.S. net capital inflows exceeded 6% of the GDP, which is an amazing statistic. One might reflect back on the Japan scare of the eighties and nineties and view this as just a market correction, and shouldn't necessarily lead us to believe doom and gloom. After all, the trade deficits of the nineties proceeded the largest period of economic growth in our nation's history. Given that we have the world's largest economy, we must expect capital inflows from these developing markets to grow, as they save and invest more in their economies rather than consuming more. Keeping the 1-billion-plus consumers in each of the Indian and Chinese markets partially constrained won't help our economy, but we must remember that both nations are developing. If there is to be a global economy, America must fuel the growth of developing nations, by definition. This fueling of the world economy means giving developing nations a chance to stabilize before they take on more global consumption.

What's interesting about the statistics of net capital importer and exporter nations is that in 2004, all nations either had a small surplus or deficit of net capital except Japan ($172 billion in deficit, meaning less capital infusion) and the United States ($668 billion in surplus, meaning that a lot of investment came to our country). In 1995, the United States received 33% of global net capital inflow, 61% in 2000, and a whopping 70% in 2004. This makes sense, as Japan has a savings-based economy and the United States a consuming one. But Japan's situation is an unhealthy one as well; an aging workforce and slowing growth has led Japan to need less capital rather than more. China's economy and demographics have also led to a savings-centric economy, at 52% of the GDP, giving it the highest savings rate in the world. However, the need for savings in China is a bit different than Japan's; without a sufficient safety net, or consumer lending, individuals must save more than those in the United States to fulfill certain needs. Also, by having its government tightly manage exchange rates and foreign exchanges, savings will remain high. We must also question the validity of these statistics, as the measurement of international trade and payments flow becomes more difficult and unreliable every year. The "national content" of these products and services in international commerce is impossible to measure accurately, yet the statistics suggest inevitable truths.

Some economists look at the massive influx of capital to the United States as a sign of a growing economy, and they certainly have an argument. Countries with a lower economic growth rate will need less capital and, therefore, will be less of an attractive option for investors. Japan is obviously the best example of this, with its mature economy and slower growth. However, China is a different story: with a growth rate of over 7%, it is still a capital exporter, owing to the high demand from the world for its exports slightly outstripping what is being invested in the country. As well, the Chinese government has restricted some investment in its tightly controlled economy, perhaps as a reaction to the Asian financial crisis of the late nineties. Despite such controls, China attracts more than $60 billion of foreign investment annually, in comparison to $4 billion for India. Some contend that with direct foreign investment flows into the United States being greater than that into China by substantial margins, this is a vote of confidence in the U.S. economy, but that may be a questionable theory.

Are these huge inflows of capital into the U.S. economy being used to make our business climate more competitive? Looking at the foreign holders of our debt reveals an interesting story line. In 2007, major foreign holdings of U.S. Treasury securities equaled $2.24 trillion dollars, up from $1.37 trillion in 2003! Of this debt, Japan purchased the most, with China second; China's purchases are increasing at an alarming rate. It has been alleged that China may be using the investment in U.S. securities to keep its currency, the Yuan, artificially low on the market. By keeping its currency artificially low, despite its high economic growth, the Chinese are able to keep product and service costs very low and competitive relative to other countries such as the United States. Therefore, our budget deficits now at record levels are being funded by foreign governments, most notably Japan and China, and China's purchase of U.S. securities is keeping its currency relatively lower than it should be, making its business artificially more competitive. Therefore, China is increasingly funding our budget deficits, which has hurt our competitiveness by keeping the Chinese currency artificially high, and the United States' artificially low. Furthermore, not much of this investment is going toward much needed infrastructure projects necessary to make our economy more ready to compete in the emerging global market. Why aren't the politicians and pundits talking about these issues relative to the U.S.-China commerce relationship?

One former official at the People's Bank of China exclaimed, "The U.S. Dollar is now at the mercy of Asian governments."[2] Certainly, in this example, the U.S. government has a strong direct impact on our competitiveness against other nations, and whether corporations will find it economically viable or not to off-shore. Yet, it can't be denied that in spite of these massive budget deficits being principally funded by our friends in China and Japan, our productivity growth is stable in comparison to other mature economies. As well, America is always ranked high relative to ease of doing business, and has a financial market that is massive, well designed, and easy to use as well. The dollar itself is practically the world's currency, and this bodes well for the United States. But will these facts continue in the foreseeable future for America?

Doing comparisons of economic data from one country to another is always an interesting prospect, given the concern whether the data sources are consistent from one country to another. Some interesting information came from a comparison by the U.S. Department of Labor in June of 2006.[3] India and China weren't included in the study, probably because of concerns about the validity of their data. In comparison to other "advanced and emerging economies," as noted by Elaine Chao, the Secretary of Labor, America looked very competitive. In comparing GDP per capita, the United States had the second highest GDP rate, second only to Ireland. I don't question the United States' strong ranking relative to its advanced competitors (using old definitions of productivity), such as the EU countries, Canada, Japan, and Australia, and some Asian developing countries and Mexico. One very interesting statistic from this chartbook was the employment and labor rates of these countries. The unemployment rate of Western Europe was shocking, with France (9.8%), Germany (9.9%), Italy (8.1%), and Spain (10.9%) at levels nearly twice those of Asia, the United States, and other countries in Europe. Yet despite France's high unemployment rate, its hourly compensation cost is only 72 cents higher than the United States, and over $10 an hour lower than Norway and Denmark. It is clear from some of these statistics that government policy toward commerce and tax policy has a big impact on the competitiveness of each economy. In looking at social insurance expenditures and other labor taxes, France has the highest percentage of hourly compensation costs (31.2%), almost 10 points higher than the United States (22.9%) and 8 points higher than the EU-15.

Speaking of competitiveness, the United States had one of the highest annual growth rates in manufacturing productivity at 5.6%, behind only Korea (9.1%), Sweden (6.5%), and Taiwan (5.7%). I believe that much of this gained productivity in Taiwan and Korea had to do with process, Asian competition, and lower labor rates; Sweden's growth was probably due to government policies: deregulation, tougher competitive legislation, and EU membership. Could higher U.S. productivity be due to outsourcing (same output and outsources labor not counted as an input)?

But how valuable is this research when China and India aren't included? Perhaps there are questions about China's and India's data sources, given their primitive institutions of governmental control. How would America's results look if compared to India's and China's? Very poor, I think. Simply comparing the United States to these advanced, and some developing, nations is a poor comparison indeed. America's future competitive battleground won't be Europe, it will be Asia. It is valuable for Americans to understand that our economic policy must move more closely to that of China and India than that of France and Germany; this doesn't mean that we need to have our factory workers making less than $1 an hour or software developers making $25,000 a year, but we must find innovative and efficient ways to offset these labor cost disadvantages.

Now that I've taken the reader through a fairly detailed review of governmental economics, the question must be asked: can we consider these data credible or not? Our economic statistics come from four sources. There are census statistics from polling individuals and entities (I've never been polled, have you?), data from the financial community (from securities, commodities, money markets), financial reports from businesses and governments, and studies from professional and academic sources. I would be hard pressed to call any of these definitive sources of data and, therefore, will caution the reader to use these at face value—they are more guides than gospel. One source may be valid, but is it accurate, and vice versa? However, if you read a government report, you will sense from the narratives that these data sources are incredibly accurate.

Ten years ago, in 1997, the Heritage Foundation published an article suggesting the need for reform of the Federal Statistical System. Consider the following excerpt from the article[4]:

In an economy that increasingly depends on and is driven by information, flawed data can impose enormous costs, leading businesses and agencies to miscalculate and make the wrong decisions and policymakers to advance ill-advised legislation with disastrous long-term consequences. Moreover, the impact on the federal budget could vastly exceed the budgetary costs of all the current federal statistical agencies combined. Agencies like the U.S. General Accounting Office (GAO) over the past few years have issued reports that detail the system's problems and outline recommended reforms, but little has been done. Consequently, many Americans have begun to question the quality of the data being collected and how those data are being used to prepare the statistics produced by the U.S. government.

Certainly, this is a damning statement with regard to the economic statistics that are being so relied on by our government and businesses. Having both the Bureau of Labor Statistics (BLS) and the Bureau of Economic Analysis (BEA) is confusing, redundant, and allows for data discrepancies. It has been ten years since some of these proposals have come out, and still there is little reform or discussion to reform. Consider the following issues in economic data:

- The government is wrong 25% of the time regarding whether the economy is growing or shrinking!
- Inflation and productivity are over/understated by 1 point, without much concern.
- Alan Greenspan did not use these sources as gospel, given inaccuracy concerns.
- If the consumer price index is off by 1 percentage point, it could affect the inflation number by 33%!

There are countless testimonials as to why our government statistics are so fallible and misleading. Even from the inside of these statistical bureaus are horror stories that the average American must understand. Shawn Ritenour, an ex-economist at the BLS and now a professor at Grove City College, says that "government statistics are practically useless at best, and downright destructive at worst."[5] He pointed out that BLS surveys are voluntary and obsolete in many cases before the data are distributed. He also noted that the bureau's "bureaucracy really is terribly wasteful, corrupting, and a killer of souls." Another economist, John Williams, publishes a monthly electronic newsletter that tracks government statistics and measures them using their earlier definitions before political amendments are made to the measurements. For example, he questions the central bankers stating "inflation is contained." Per Williams, if consumer price index (CPI) were measured as it was during the Carter administration, it would be at 8% versus the 2% current annual reporting. Through using *hedonic* adjustments, the bureau negates the monetary inflation through assuming the additional value of business efforts. Given that many business decisions are being made from the CPI, it is concerning that there is such a chorus of discontent surrounding the accuracy of its measurement.

Another area of concern in measurement is that of the GDP. John Williams stated, "Overstated GDP growth has meant the 1990 and 2001 recessions were much more severe than recognized, and that lesser downturns in 1986 and 1995 were more or less missed entirely."[6] If Williams is correct in his assessment, and we translate it in terms of our 2007 economy, could the impact of offshoring be having a greater negative effect due to job loss? Could the domestic outsourcing that is occurring be having a greater negative impact on wages than is being reported? These are fair questions, given the concern of the measurement of these important government variables. It was also believed that Alan Greenspan later in his career as Fed Research Chairman made some flawed assumptions on productivity numbers in the U.S. economy, likely due to bad GDP reporting. Today, a lot of people in the economic community feel that GDP reporting is now most valuable as a politicking tool, and a cheerleading prop for analysts on Wall Street.

Do you believe that government economic statistics are accurate? Much like a nation's accounting system, a nation's statistical system certainly begets a lot of scrutiny, as well that it should, given its importance to critical decisions like outsourcing. In some economies, the most difficult aspect of the economic statistics is the collection component of the measurement. Nations like China and India do not gather economic statistics to the extent that we do in America. However, the political slant to the calculation of statistics in America is most concerning, as we appear to have enough data, if calculated properly. Also, accurate data could become a competitive advantage for us in this new definition of productivity!

Famous economist Ludwig Von Mises noted in 1963 that "a judicious housewife knows much more about pricing changes that affect her household than the statistical averages can tell." The econometric equations being used, the sources of data and the subjective nature of the researcher or economist in play should make us wonder how anyone should place any confidence in the information used to produce government reports.[7] So what does this mean relative to outsourcing, and to what extent, if any, should we use those data? First, we all, at least now, know that both government entities and businesses have a lot of incentive to boost their economic results, as much as is legally possible. The rosy Economic Report of the President supports and justifies the policies of our current president, and I don't think that there is anything legally wrong, but is it objective? Using the Von Mises logic to our economy, would the average Joe read this report in agreement or suspicion? I would suspect the latter, as the numbers provided take a lot of interpretation to understand. In my mind, I believe that our economy is declining from a true productivity standpoint, as is evident in our balance-of-trade numbers. Massive trade deficits are occurring. Yet there is an interesting story occurring here, as the Chinese and others are using their excess dollars to fund our massive federal budget deficit being incurred through tax cuts on top of increased government spending. The Chinese get a lower currency rate for them to be more competitive, the government gets their policies funded without raising taxes, and our consumers get lower prices on goods and services owing to the China–India influence.

Clearly, our government is aware of the difficulties in measuring imports and offshoring. The principal data sources for imports are the Census Bureau tabulation of import documents for goods, and BEA quarterly or annual surveys for services. The problems with these surveys are, first, that importers may be missed, most likely new importers. Many of the problems associated with measuring imports and offshoring seem to suggest that imports and offshoring may be understated, which implies that output may be overstated. While the BEA seems to consider these biases to be small in scope, how can anyone tell this to be true or not? We must consider this issue as a serious one, as it implies that the government bodies may be underestimating the impact of offshoring on our national economy, and that this may lead to production and productivity being overstated in the economy.

Another big debate about government statistics has been the measurement of productivity and job growth. Since the BLS uses the establishment survey (pay-roll survey) to calculate productivity growth (for hours data), if the job growth is understated in the establishment survey, it will overstate productivity growth. Some believe that the Employment Report from November 2006 was understated, meaning that job growth was higher and productivity was lower.[8] With so much contention between factors that affect each other, such as productivity and job growth, it is very difficult to determine truly what the impact of outsourcing is on our economy through the use of statistics. Statistics can be used as guides, but we must really question their use as ultimate definitive sources. Unfortunately, govern-ment reports using these statistics do just that, and therefore explain outsourcing in ways that might not be altogether objective and accurate.

A similar issue arises when seeking to measure the productivity improvements associated with IT spending. In a simple economic equation, it is expected that IT expenditure would take on an attribute similar to technology/machinery in an industrial model. The question that famous researchers on this topic such as Paul Strassmann pose is whether companies are actually achieving the productivity booms reported regarding the impact of IT on our large corporations. Strassmann was one of the pioneers in this field. He focused his studies on Sales, General, and Administrative (SG&A) costs, rather than manufacturing costs, since computers are being used more within office settings than manufacturing settings. In October 2006, Strassmann wrote that only a little less than 50% of the 4,992 public companies achieved a positive score in managing their information technology spending in a productive manner, ten years after the proliferation of IT in corporate

America![9] Information technology investments in a corporate setting are difficult to measure given that the productivity improvements should happen within an office not production setting. Certainly, the dot-com boom, and the computer revolution of the PC and Windows led to a lot of companies investing in IT, and achieving benefits as a result. Certainly, everyone eliminated their steno pools, armies of administrative assistants, file clerks, and the like, but what about today? How do companies achieve productivity improvements in IT? Outsourcing is a big part of the savings. Much of the IT infrastructure and software development created in the 1990s in order to reduce primarily white-collar costs are now being offshored to India for greater savings. This sort of savings is a one-time cost-reduction boost that might be difficult to measure as productivity today. Economist Robert Gordon of Northwestern University suggests that the underlying growth in productivity for IT is a function of the manufacturing of the computers rather than the use of them in a business setting. I agree with this notion, and it's an interesting lesson learned from the use of IT, and the subsequent government grandstanding on IT as a major factor in a U.S. boom in productivity over the last ten years.[10] Also note that in the government's use of hedonics as a cure for an ailing economy, it shows that computers are providing productivity gains to our economy through our being able to pay the same price for a computer that has twice the processing power. Such use of statistics is one way that IT is showing to have productivity improvements in our economy.

What is needed to reform our economic statistical systems or process to distribute more valid and reliable data? First, having a single, robust, independent source of data would really help. Our economy relies heavily on the government statistical bodies that are deregulated, underfunded, and inconsistent in their methodologies. How can we support well-founded economic policies without good and objective sources of data? Certainly, our federal government for intelligence gathering for national security purposes is spending a lot of money. Shouldn't we consider economic intelligence as important as national security? I definitely think so. It appears that funding for statistical analysis is decentralized or poorly utilized, and not keeping up with increases needed to understand being competitive in the global market. Spending more money by the government to establish a super-department to manage and distribute objective economic data would be more than worthwhile.

Second, our approaches to measuring economic data don't appear to have kept up with the changes in our economy. Data sources and measurement techniques are likely the weakest in very critical areas, such as technological innovation and the service sector. The growing service sector has been responsible for practically all of our job growth, given the decline in manufacturing. Measuring productivity in the services sector is difficult for the best researcher, but especially difficult when using the primitive methods used by our government. Can we really expect voluntary surveys to be a valid source of data for such important measurements?

The last factor requiring reform is the blatant subjective and political nature of the measurement and management of economic statistics. One must wonder whether the answer to managing the economy is in the implementation of sound economic policies or through the sound management of economic statistics? Both political parties have used their tenure in the Office of the President to push the truth relative to economic data. In 1995, then Labor Secretary Robert Reich was accused of cooking the BLS data to show a story of corporations achieving record profits at the expense of workers. The Bush Administration is no different in this matter, providing misleading statements regarding the GDP growth in the U.S. economy in 2006 that could be attributed to the questionable use of statistics. For one, as is noted earlier, the White House is comparing the U.S. results to a smaller group of peer countries, not including high-growth emerging markets like China and India. Second, the growth rates presented by the White House did not net out the impact of economic growth due to population growth, which many economists believe has been the primary fuel for U.S. growth.

As we dissect the economic data that are being used for economic policy, and in discussions regarding important policy matters such as outsourcing, we must remember these shortcomings in determining the true impact on the economy. My view is that until we can reform and clean up the subjective and poorly constructed/funded sources of economic data, we must use more of corporate data and qualitative stories on the true impact of outsourcing. Both political parties have used government statistics for their own self-interest, so it's not a political issue, but rather a government issue. We cannot believe what the government says to us about the impact of outsourcing until there are valid and reliable data to prove the case.

I think that the impact of poor economic data has had a detrimental impact on our corporations and workers. Our corporations have gotten more pressure in a global economy where they have to compete against developing markets, where the local governments are using protectionism to manage their newly established markets. Our corporations, also facing greater government regulation due to the overreaction of Sarbanes–Oxley and the casino nature of our financial markets, have greater restrictions and short-term pressures to make a profit to appease the analysts and not upset the regulators. It is no wonder that our corporations are turning to an over or improper use of outsourcing as a reaction to the Chinese, Indians, regulators, and market analysts.

If our government can develop an objective, bipartisan approach to economic statistics, our corporations will have a better chance of being competitive in an increasingly challenging global marketplace. We need to take every possible opportunity to allow our companies to be more competitive; the solutions above are big steps for how our government can make this happen. Furthermore, better data will allow corporations to make suitable outsourcing or offshoring decisions that they aren't making today, in so many cases. These data will be the competitive intelligence, so strategically important to our economy for our future.

On the surface, productivity as a corporate concept appears to be easy to measure. In a basic, old definition, a worker creating extra value for the time that he or she expends defines productivity. This extra value is typically defined in terms of profit in the private sector. But when companies change product lines frequently and definitions around workers' time and effort are hard to measure as well, this variable is not so easy to calculate. Therefore, in a typical corporation, productivity can take shape through fewer labor hours and lower labor costs, as well as other factors. These factors result from either productivity improvements or technological innovations, such as the automation of a function. My research in productivity suggests that the process improvement piece must take shape before any technological improvements can accrue. Clearly, my research and business experience indicates from either an IT or manufacturing/logistics standpoint that when a corporation chooses to clean up its processes first, it will achieve sustainable productivity improvements. However, when the company seeks to achieve productivity improvements through a sole technology play with no process improvements, any productivity though achieved will net out unfavorably.

It is interesting to note that many economists believe that an improvement in productivity is the most effective factor in raising living standards. Today, outsourcing has a level of productivity that must be challenged, given the invalid and unreliable nature of our statistical system. This point needs to be highlighted, as I believe that focusing on true productivity will be good for both the company and the employee. Today, productivity is viewed actually opposite of the statement above; instead of allowing for better living standards through better *true productivity*, corporations are achieving false increases in productivity by reducing labor costs. How are labor costs being reduced? Through the use of domestic outsourcing, temporary workers, and offshoring. If productivity continues to be sought through such outsourcing methods, our economy will be affected in a negative way.

There are certain areas in our current economy that every effort should be made to increase productivity. In our growing services sector, the whole concept of productivity is relatively untapped, and waiting to happen. Why? One, it is harder to measure and manage productivity in the service sector than it is in the manufacturing sector. Two, as a result of a lack of clear measurement, there are few techniques or approaches to achieving those productivity gains in the service sector, as what is happening in manufacturing. The trends toward services and away from manufacturing will lead even an amateur to conclude that really focusing on and tightening data sources and measurements will pay off for our country in the long run.

Lastly, I'm not a big fan of the conventional wisdom that suggests that America doesn't really need manufacturing, and therefore doesn't need to focus on it as much as on services. In a nation with a growing population, much of it from immigration, a cognizant decision to forgo manufacturing is a big mistake as well. We need to evangelize this point that our economy will only be able to grow so much without a manufacturing base, particularly in view of the massive future opportunities given the introduction of hundreds of millions of Chinese and Indians to a consumer middle class. Not taking this American manufacturing concept head on would be a serious drain on our future growth opportunities. The Death of Manufacturing, as it has been called, tells a story in history that is very painful for me to hear. In 1950, manufacturing accounted for a third of the economy. In 2003, it was 12.5%, and it continues to decline today. In Benson's Economic and Marketing Trends, in February 2006, it is stated that

Considering the stupendous list of America's manufacturing achievements and the vulnerabilities associated with foreign dependence when a nation lacks strong domestic manufacturing, it is alarming when economists are warning the U.S. is facing the gutting, hollowing out and closing down of the American manufacturing forever.

Wow, think about the economic statistics that have been presented in this chapter: highest four-year productivity growth since 1948, expansion of the U.S. economy for four straight years, employers creating 2 million additional jobs in one year, and so on. This is the language that our economists speak, and document for official statistics that are used widely in the market and in the business environment. But what do these numbers mean to the average American? What does the average American think about the economy? Per the American Research Group in May 2007, 32% of Americans approve of how President Bush is handling the economy. For the past year, this rating was never at 40%.[11] Gallup data from October 2006 showed that 58% of Americans thought of economic conditions as "only fair" or "poor," 54% thought that it was a bad time to find a quality job, and 52% thought that the economy was getting worse versus 38% who thought that it was getting better.[12] This dismal view of the economy from the polls occurs despite the economic statistics, strong growth in productivity, and the relatively low unemployment rate. In another poll in March 2006, Americans were offered two statements, with one noting that "people face increasing uncertainty about employment," and the second noting, "people can expect to better themselves." By a 2 to 1 margin (64% to 32%), respondents chose the first statement over the second. In defining their concerns with the economy, the three problems most important in their evaluation were

1. The number of jobs moving overseas (offshoring)
2. Jobs for lower-paid workers that lack health and retirement benefits (outsourcing and temporary labor)
3. The federal budget deficit

Interestingly enough, Americans were concerned about things that the economic data told them they shouldn't be concerned about. In this same survey, Americans were given four choices to describe the economy, from very cheery to very gloomy. Only 4% of the respondents chose very cheery, while 47% chose the gloomy option. In a separate poll, 90% of respondents agreed that "25 years ago if you worked hard and played by the rules, you will be able to have a solid middle class life." This was compared to only 49% that agreed this characterization for today. Lastly, the Pew Research Center survey released Labor Day 2006, which asked respondents to compare how the average working person was faring today versus twenty or thirty years ago. On job security, 62% said that there was now less job security, 11% thought there was more, and 24% said it was the same. Survey after survey define the American as pessimistic, while the economist is defined as optimistic. So who is correct, the housewife or the economist? I choose the housewife.

So today, we must understand *the economics of who's right and who's wrong.* Today, Americans are working longer hours, with less security, but economic statistics state that we're better off, at least in comparison to other countries. On one side of the coin, we have statisticians and government officials telling us how much better off we are, while on the other side, we're feeling less secure and increasingly concerned. Outsourcing and offshoring are sometimes noted as a necessity for our economy in a global marketplace, or as a betrayal and a symbol of the insecurity and concern that we have toward our present and our future. But does either side of the statistics really tell the story? What if the statistics are so weak and inaccurate that they are irrelevant? Then, what do we use as reference data, as a source of truth? Perhaps we agree with Von Mises, and use the housewives and the laid-off workers to tell us the story.

Can these sources really tell us the story, or must we consider other sources? I believe that we should utilize statistics, but done right. However, the statistics should just be used as a guide. We must also understand the pulse of our workers and our corporations. In order to do so, we must understand the contentious relationship between the worker and the corporation in today's global economy. Once we understand this, we will better understand America's addiction to outsourcing.

CHAPTER SIX

# Screw It, I'll Outsource

> The principal object of management should be to secure the maximum prosperity for the employer, coupled with the maximum prosperity for each employee.
> —Frederick Taylor, "The Principles of Scientific Management" (1911)

Rationalism by itself is rather unconvincing because it assumes that logic is real, and that our human senses can be unreliable. Rationalism for business purposes was first used to solve problems of mass production and assembly-line procedures in the late nineteenth century. Elements of rationalism were used in a process applied to measure units to a system with a plan to achieve a desired result. Such a process seeks to dehumanize the work effort and reduces every element to a repetitive action.

In his famous 1911 work, Frederick Taylor sought to improve the lot of both the worker and the employer through the use of rational, scientific management or, as we call it today, Industrial Engineering. The four major principles of Scientific Management are as follows[1]:

1. Replace rule of thumb casual work methods with methods based on a scientific study of the work.
2. Scientifically train, select, and develop each worker versus expecting them to learn on the job.
3. Cooperate with the workers to ensure that the scientific methods are being adhered to.
4. Divide the work effort equally to ensure that the managers use scientific methods to plan the work, as the workers will to execute the work.

The marriage of workers and machinery didn't begin well at the onset of the Industrial Revolution with lockouts, strikes, sabotage, and battles between the workers and the private armies of the employers. Socialist parties and trade unions started to take center stage in this struggle, and it was looking like our nation was heading toward class warfare. Owners felt the need to control labor within the factories, and the workers were seeking more control over their workplaces. The owner's desire to discipline labor accidentally found Frederick Taylor or, perhaps more properly, Frederick Taylor found the struggle. In 1874, he became an apprentice machinist, learning about factory conditions at the floor level; this was unheard of for someone of his social standing. He came on this fate despite his upper class status owing to poor eyesight that prevented him from attending Harvard. He was able to observe what he found was the unnecessary contention and blame that existed between the workers and management of the company. Through rationalism, Taylor felt that the danger and inefficiency of politics and class struggle could be avoided. Taylor testified before Congress in 1912, stating

The great revolution that takes place in the mental attitude of the two parties (capital and labor) under scientific management is that both sides take their eyes off the division of the surplus as the all-important matter, and together turn their attention toward increasing the size of the surplus until this surplus becomes so large that it is unnecessary to quarrel over how it shall be divided.

This statement personified something important and necessary in employee relations, sometimes ignored on both sides of the bargaining table even today; that is, both sides can achieve more by working together. Taylor felt that management should stop looking for the theoretical extraordinary man, and start implementing scientific processes that prevent the inefficiency that negatively affects industrial operations. He sought to convince the managers/owners of these shops to invest in their people and operations in order to improve productivity that would lead to a win–win for both workers and owners. First, he pointed out that factory conditions needed to be improved. These workplaces were often dimly lit, too noisy, crowded, and generally poorly organized. Second, he felt that these operations needed additional management supervision over and above the foreman. A professional manager would ensure that scientific management principles would be implemented, and managed from a productivity standpoint. The foreman of these operations was typically a taskmaster, and more concerned with whipping the workers into working harder through draconian methods. Lastly, Taylor felt that management needed to provide incentives to the worker to improve.

Taylor not only asked for concessions from the owners, he also asked for concessions from the workers as well. Back in Taylor's era and still today, many workers considered themselves to be artisans, and believed that they were specially qualified to complete the task owing to their personal knowledge, skills, and experiences. Today, many workers still believe that tasks are completed through special worker skills, particularly if they have been in the job for a long period of time. This makes sense from a psychological standpoint; a worker wants to humanize his work as a function of self-worth. I have faced this scenario in many cases when I was involved in outsourcing or other restructuring exercises. The question in corporate productivity is finding the right balance between humanizing work for the workers' benefit and dehumanizing it to achieve repetitive, rational responses and results.

These revolutionary methods of rationalism, along with that of science, allowed the Allies to win the Second World War through superior industrial techniques, and have since then helped to drive us to the economic superpower status that we enjoy today. However, when industrial engineering principles are applied, the worker can feel like a cog in a machine, and that her experience is not being valued. This is the classic art-versus-science scenario. Frederick Taylor didn't see that much good could come out of the artisan approach during the early twentieth century for America. Many of the factory workers were immigrants and, in his book, Taylor mocked their butchered English as evidence of their limited capacities. The labor unions took the other side of the argument, and wondered how a scientific approach to dehumanize the worker would help our economy. But scientific management wasn't dehumanizing as it was liberating; factory conditions were improved, and compensation increased. In comparison, many labor unions weren't able to make similar improvements through their methods.

Today, Frederick Taylor is often unknown or misunderstood when the topic of the history of modern management is discussed. Productivity as a science is also misunderstood and misdiagnosed. To the day of his death, Taylor maintained that the primary benefactor of productivity should be the worker, not the owner. Back during his time, the unions were "craft monopolies," in the words of Peter Drucker, and, as such, considered an apprenticeship to be a special privilege and a rite of honor to achieve. Members were sworn to secrecy, and nothing was written down. Taylor determined that work should be documented, analyzed, and broken down into tasks, and this took all of the mystery and rites out of work. The Unions petitioned Congress to ban time studies, and Taylor was vilified as suggesting that work could be broken down into routine, repetitive functions. Labor unions hated him, and saw his efforts as contrary to their interests. While one may think that such contention with the labor unions glorified Taylor and his efforts in favor of the owners, he called the owners "hogs," and always made a point to contend that his efforts were focused primarily for that of the worker. It's hard to argue with the success story of Taylorism, with some blue-collar workers making $80,000 and up past $100,000 even today.

Taylor's rational, scientific approach to neutralizing the contention between workers and managers was a much better option to violence, or even concessions to more socialistic political solutions (that are plaguing many European nations today). There is no question that this friction still exists today between workers and management. Today's modern manager must find a way, in Taylor's words, to increase the surplus associated with running the business. This surplus can be achieved either through growing the top line or reducing the bottom line. In the early days of the American Industrial Revolution, our nation was a fast-paced growing one, much like China is today, and our focus was on top-line growth. Unlike in Europe, machines were introduced in the early twentieth century, and yet jobs continued to grow. Therefore, productivity could be defined in a way that was beneficial for both the worker and the manager, in Taylor's term. For generations after the Second World War, America was the sole superpower because of its manufacturing productivity, through the use of scientific methods. Later on, other nations like Japan started to adopt better practices around scientific management and, as a result, started to compete against America in the global marketplace. Given that America's economy was (and still is) so much larger than these emerging economies, this was not a problem, as economic growth in foreign markets created greater consumer demand for American goods and services. Outsourcing and offshoring became an effective way of importing the American Way across the globe, allowing for us to become even more prosperous as a result.

Perhaps business conditions are cyclical in nature: it appears to me that in many ways we're right back to the early days of the twentieth century. Contention between the worker and manager is unusually high today. Today's worker feels like an unvalued commodity, feels squeezed without any support from a lackadaisical workforce, and business processes are fairly irrational. Sometime between the Second World War and the start of America's manufacturing decline, we started to lose our passion and consideration for scientific management. Workers stretched beyond middle class living and started expecting wages that couldn't be justified in a more competitive, global economy. These workers started to feel as if they were this extraordinary man, even if their productivity levels couldn't justify this title. The loyal worker gave the company his career and, in return, received a cushy salary and retirement plan. Productivity was an afterthought, an outdated afterthought at best.

The professional manager lost focus on productivity as well. The classic 1987 film *Wall Street* provides a great stereotype of the professional manager in Gordon Gecco's "Greed Is Good" speech. He speaks of management not having any stake in the company, and too busy on hunting trips, flying around in first class to understand, or care what's best for the organization. While a bit too stereotypical, the professional manager has and makes a comfortable career without much at stake. Much like the worker, the professional manager has been provided a nice lifestyle for his family through understanding the politics of the company, and following the path set before him by predecessors and bosses. Typically, these professional managers became above the fray as they graduated to management level, and stayed away from the factory floor, or processing center. Now being separated from the production of work, they reverted back to the days before Taylor with the strong lines of demarcation between management and worker. Decisions were made unscientifically, and without consideration of productivity.

Once again, the term *productivity* is a battleground contention between manager and worker, as it has once again become a win–lose proposition. Today, Frederick Taylor's words ring true, almost one hundred years after he shook the worker–manager standards. After so many decades of wealth sharing between workers and managers as a function of a greater surplus being created through productivity, the money pie began to shrink, and both sides started fighting for their fair share. Collaboration and harmony in office/factory settings disappeared, and distrust took back over again. A lack of job security, the erosion of benefits, and increased global competition has led to this awful environment at our largest corporations. More workers have decided to not care at work, as she has seen too many cases where workers are laid off, their jobs shipped to China or India, or their positions turned into temporary positions (or permatemps, as they call it), thus marginalizing their security and loyalty to the company. Professional managers, because of the very nature of the work that they perform, find themselves fighting the workers in a battle to achieve that outdated definition of productivity that means "eliminate as many workers as you can in order to increase surplus." After the first steps in the early nineties of layoffs to cut the fat, computerization was used to reduce staff. Consultants then emerged and gave new ideas for restructuring. And now, today, the option of outsourcing or offshoring is the new *easy out* to management's problems. In an era of increased global competition, the workforce and management of American business cannot afford to be contentious toward one another.

As a professional manager myself, I feel that the environment between the worker and the manager might be at an all-time low since the days of Frederick Taylor. Owing to our accounting policies and short-term market pressures discussed in an earlier chapter, the professional manager now is trying to win in the emerging global economy using an outdated definition of productivity. This is because whenever productivity is defined in a win–lose proposition as it is today, productivity can never become sustainable. During my career, I have been faced with many win–lose battles I knew that I thought I could win as a member of management, and yet the productivity was never sustainable. As an ex–Big Five consultant, I felt not just the desire but the obligation to proceed with restructuring strategies that would forcefully tear through the existing social fabric of the organization. I have been a part of them myself, as a 25-year-old analyst working for an insurance company. Back then, a swashbuckler executive took over United States and Fidelity & Guaranty, a large insurance company, and largely affected my hometown of Baltimore. After "reengineering" this company to death, the once-proud organization finally lay by the roadside waiting to be acquired by another insurance company (St. Paul's), which eventually got eaten up by another company (Traveler's). The moral of this story is that ripping the heart of the social fabric of the company is not a successful strategy because of the damage that's done in the relations between the worker and the manager.

On the other hand, I have worked for companies that underwent transformational change in a different and more effective manner. When I spoke of my Big Five approach at the Coors Brewing Company, they made me understand quickly that such change would not happen without a healthy dialogue and approach with employees. Today, a lot of change is happening at Coors, and a lot of good will come out of it for its future, and I think that a lot of this is due to an approach that takes into consideration the importance of maintaining a good worker–manager relationship. I will discuss strategies for this, and it's never easy, but a chainsaw will never lead a corporation in a competitive marketplace. Understanding how outsourcing and offshoring can be appropriately used is an important matter to understand and implement.

A very basic and outdated definition of productivity is "a measure by quantity or quality of output to the inputs required to produce it." Today, the Bureau of Labor Statistics (BLS) definition is simply the total output divided by the total input. This measurement seems to focus on labor rates involved in production more so than other factors, such as quality, process efficiency, and logistics costs. With a measurement bias toward labor rate, how can workers and managers within America strike a healthy relationship? With a system that rewards labor-rate reduction over process efficiency via measurement bias, the answer is that it is increasingly difficult for a corporate manager to achieve this balance. Given these biases, managers are increasingly outsourcing, using permatemps, and sending work overseas, all in the name of productivity. I know this to be true because I have done so myself. As leaders of public corporations, we feel as if we have no other choice, and yet could, if the measurements of productivity were more valid.

Can we compare Frederick Taylor's effort for efficiency to what we need in 2007? First, our economy is the world's superpower versus a developing one. Second, working conditions have significantly improved compared to what Taylor saw in 1911. Yet despite these major differences, our need to focus on rational business process and productivity is relatively not much different from the need to do so in 1911. In fact, there may be a greater need for industrial engineering in 2007 for America than there was a need for Frederick Taylor in 1911. Just because the lighting on the floor is better it doesn't mean the processes have been fixed.

Today, our national economic policy is without imagination and outdated; our financial market system is creative and efficient, yet overbearing and self-serving; our scientific approach to work within our corporations is severely lacking, and without passion when it is; and our educational system is deplorable. It seems as if the primary passion in the workplace is the growing contention that exists between the worker and manager. All of this adds up to a corporate structure unprepared to compete in the global marketplace, and the use of lifeless, sterile one-size-fits-all approaches such as outsourcing and offshoring. This leads the corporate manager to say "Screw it, I'll outsource," taking the *easy out* instead of fighting a battle that he doesn't think can be won. Yet what happens when the "Screw it, I'll outsource" saying takes shape for an entire industry? Can America afford to throw away its manufacturing operations under the rallying cry of "Screw it, I'll outsource"?

Statistics fly around left and right on this topic. The number of jobs lost during the twenty-first century in manufacturing to offshoring seems to sit at a gross of 3 million, which seems to be a lot of jobs, when not considered along with the concept of creative destruction, which notes that jobs are destroyed in place of more suitable jobs in the economy. But have those suitable replacement industries arrived yet? Many workers would think not, yet many economists think this is the case. While the pro-offshoring pundits would note that sending profit-less manufacturing offshore and keeping the profitable is the right approach, we have to wonder if such a thought process is consistent with the new economic rules of the world. The question "Does manufacturing matter in the United States?" is a very important one for Americans, and a question that will be critical to answer properly for the sake of America's future in the global market.

The question that needs to be answered is whether America needs manufacturing, and the answer will give us a good clue if outsourcing and offshoring are a good thing or not. In 1900, 41% of the population worked in agriculture, and today that number is 2%. In 1970, there were 421,000 workers making good money as switchboard operators; today, there are about 75,000 operators, at best. Shouldn't manufacturing follow this same pattern in our country?

The first point often cited regarding our industrial decline, and the offshoring of jobs is the statistics of job loss. From 1998 to August 2003, 3 million manufacturing jobs were lost. Since 1993 and NAFTA, 700,000 textile jobs have been lost from the United States. If losing jobs in manufacturing wasn't a big deal to our government officials, why did the Economic Report to the President of 2004 ask "What is manufacturing?" and question whether the assembly of a fast-food burger could be seen as much of manufacturing as the assembly of an airplane?[2] Indeed, it is likely that this won't be the last time that this question is asked, as a lot of those ex–manufacturing workers are shifting to the lower-paying service industry. Wherever I go in the United States, I find that manufacturing matters deeply to the people of this country. In 2003, Patrick Buchanan wrote about a town called Weirton, West Virginia, and questioned, "What's next for us?" The population of this steel town is around 25,000, and at one point in time, the steel mill included 13,000 jobs. Today, there are 1,200 jobs remaining at Weirton Steel, now a subsidiary of Arcelor Mittal, a European-based company. What do you think has happened to the psyche of this town? How has the standard of living changed in this small town now that 5% of the population works at the mill, versus about 50% during its heyday?

Consider this quote from Pat Buchanan from *The Great Betrayal* (1998)[3]:

Manufacturing is the key to national power. Not only does it pay more than service industries, the rates of productivity growth are higher and the potential of new industries arising is far greater. From radio came television, VCR's, and flat panel screens. From adding machines came calculators and computers. From the electric typewriter came the word processors. Research and Development follow manufacturing.

But, I wonder, would manufacturing jobs really matter in these communities if a suitable replacement existed? For instance, would the people of Weirton, West Virginia, care as much if the steel mill left and was replaced by a new industry with equal pay and greater job security? Probably not. Job displacement is a clear rallying point for workers, and while most likely have never heard of Joseph Schumpeter, they would nonetheless be able to articulate his theory in general and clear terms as to why manufacturing matters if there is no clear employment alternative. Today, too often, manufacturing job losses are replaced with service sector jobs that are frequently lower paying, and perhaps without any benefits at all. Give the worker an equal opportunity for work, and you'll see that manufacturing doesn't matter. But it's unrealistic to replace higher paid manufacturing positions with the same level of pay in a service industry. Working as a Wal-Mart greeter or at an Ace Hardware store will not yield the worker the same wages and benefits. So, at least in the short term, the question cannot be answered by giving the worker an equal opportunity for pay in some other industry. Creative destruction hasn't taken shape in this sense, and it will likely take time, if at all, for these workers to have a comparable opportunity in another industry without significant training, education, and American competitiveness.

Another reason why manufacturing competitiveness is so important to our country gets down to simple economics. In 2004, our trade deficit with the world was $484 billion. In 2006, the deficit mushroomed past $600 billion, easily beating the record of $497 billion. It has almost reached 6% of our Gross Domestic Product! While a good portion of this increase has had to do with fuel prices, a lot of it still is a function of better productivity results in other nations than in the United States. This deficit must be also linked to our record-setting government-spending deficits, and the overstated value of the U.S. dollar. This combination of U.S. economic policy is a bad one as well for the worker in a manufacturing setting, as higher U.S. deficits and an undervalued Yuan/overvalued Dollar puts China more in the driver's seat relative to trade balance. While I don't believe that our politicians are in favor of exporting jobs overseas, I do see our government losing the battle to China in setting up a more conducive business environment. So at least the answer to this question relative to job displacement or replacement is yes, manufacturing matters, but not if a suitable replacement job exists for these individuals on the horizon (we'll see).

At least in the short term, Peter Drucker's vision of manufacturing workers turning into knowledge workers hasn't played out as expected. Perhaps we have let our manufacturing workers down by not supporting an industry without a suitable replacement for employment, or by sustaining well-paying manufacturing jobs. But what about the concept of the multiplier effect; will the United States get more of an economic boom from keeping the jobs in the States, or shipping them overseas? Our current conventional wisdom clearly points to seeing a greater multiplier by shipping work to China or India versus keeping it in the United States. This must lead us to believe that our policy makers see greater opportunity in developing middle class markets in these countries than in maintaining more middle class in the United States. In my opinion, economics is truly the battle of the middle class; for the twentieth century, it was clear that this battle was easily won by the United States. Not only was America's middle class growing tremendously after the Second World War, in many cases, the only-in-America dream came true for so many of our citizens, the middle class was even getting rich! While standards of living, in relative terms, always seemed comparable between Europe and America, there is a reason why it is called the American Dream, allowing immigrants and natural citizens to become well off if they worked hard. Certainly, there was greater opportunity for individuals within a poorer social class to move up the ranks through the American Dream in our nation. Therefore, while shipping jobs overseas can provide a multiplier effect, we have yet to see a study showing how it has benefited the working and middle classes as a result. This doesn't mean that it hasn't had benefits for them, or that it can't, but it is clear that policy makers need to do a better job at either innovating replacement industries for middle class job security, or maintaining the same paying industries.

There should be no question that an emerging China and India means a rapid expansion of their middle classes at the expense of ours. Factory workers previously in America, and now in China means a plus for China's middle class, and a negative for America's, all other variables constant. The same logic applies when software programmers move from America to India. In December 2006, the Federal Reserve Chairman Ben Bernanke visited China to ask for concessions surrounding Chinese economic reforms. Items of discussion were the Yuan being undervalued (due to government control), and the need for growth of domestic markets (to promote more consumption of U.S. products, thereby reducing the balance of trade). Despite the massive potential of its market, China has yet to liberalize its consumer market to the degree anticipated by U.S. business. America sees a lack of reforms in China as already affecting both the middle classes of both nations. China will counter with a need to invest in its own country versus a too quick move toward consumerism (when large portions of its population remain poor). And yet, China already has 300,000 millionaires!

An American trade policy mandate for China and India to open its markets to American goods and services, a la American style, is unrealistic. Both of these countries must invest in their infrastructures and peoples before go–go consumerism takes place. Given America's dependence on cheaper oil, cheaper goods, and cheaper services, we are at the mercy of the world, and must win through being better versus asking others to emulate our culture. The American corporation learning to not misuse the outsourcing option is one of the first steps to efficiency. This is not to say that America shouldn't seek to negotiate better trade agreements, for sure, but the primary focus of this strategy I propose is better real productivity within our corporate setting.

Certainly, growing consumer markets like China and India are compelling, but taking our eye off the American middle class will be a serious detriment to our corporations if we're not careful about it. What do I mean by taking our eye off the middle class? Consider the following impacts if we take our eye off manufacturing[4]:

1. Manufacturing has an output that is highly tradable.
2. There are large impediments in trading services, making it harder on the global market.
3. As is being proven today in a wired global world, services are becoming highly mobile, making it difficult to become a competitive advantage.

What will become America's competitive advantage in the future? Peter Drucker seemed to think that America would become an elite nation of knowledge workers, yet other nations will share such work, as technological advancements and simultaneous economic takeoffs of India and China has made our expected monopoly a pipe dream. Perhaps a case will be made for America to be the innovation and research-and-development capital of the world, but can we make this happen with the current trends in our educational system in comparison to the rest of the world? Given the socioeconomic and technological trends happening in the world today, we would be foolish to write off manufacturing as a core competency.

There is no question in my mind that our workforce understands the current state of affairs happening across the world better than management gives them credit of understanding. The workers do understand that management is devising ways to reduce blue-collar labor cost. I have been this person for quite a few companies, and it's a terrible spot to be in. The workers also know that they are sitting ducks, and the contention between the two sides is unbearable. While it's inevitable that companies in our economy today will address  workforce challenges to a certain degree given market and accounting conditions/rules, there are certainly right ways (like I've seen at Coors), and wrong ways (like I've seen at countless companies) of doing this. If management is able to break the chain of contention, should we expect the workers to concede as well for the greater good? Workers in the past have frequently made wage concessions, but how many times have such actions helped them? Agreements and concessions should truly become mutually beneficial, and based on applying the science of work to the situation.

In my mind, there are virtually endless opportunities of upside in the use of scientific principles at work in order to improve productivity and competitiveness in today's U.S. corporations. Today's management must take more risks in order to be competitive, but the risks should be in breaking the stodgy cultures of their companies versus perpetuating irrational business practices. In choosing a scientific approach to work, there is little risk, but the risk comes into play in challenging one's own organization to adopt these approaches. Almost one hundred years after Taylor challenged the American owner and manager to collaborate, to create a bigger pie for all to share; many of the same problems exist today. The American psyche calls out for people to be unique and independent, but work should be organized and disciplined. I frequently tell my staff that "we are not splitting atoms at work," and it's not a bad reflection on us or what we do if we simplify and tame our efforts. Repetition and order may create boredom, but for most workforces today, it's what is needed for success and improvement. I think that it's deep within the fabric of American culture for us to consider ourselves creative and independent, but many work activities are typically not the places for this. We need to execute with science at work to succeed. We can't be such cowboys.

The "Screw it, I'll outsource" decision is made when the American worker chooses to celebrate his or her independence over the work, and the manager cannot tame the processes, or chooses not to. Then who wins? As Taylor noted, the only way to success is through making the worker successful. In today's outsourcing arrangements, it is clear that this is rarely the case, and management is not shy about making it a point to note such actions are about survival. We need to teach our corporations to be creative and disciplined in setting forth its futures, and stop taking the *easy outs*.

This discussion has been focused on the manufacturing sector, but what about our service sector? Consider Peter Drucker's comments in his book *Post Capitalist Society* (1993) about the service industry and outsourcing[5]:

Even more drastic, indeed revolutionary, are the requirements for obtaining productivity from service workers. Service work in many cases will be contracted out of the organization to whom the service is being rendered. This applies particularly to support work, such as maintenance, and to a good deal of clerical work. "Outsourcing," moreover, will be applied increasingly to such work as drafting for architects and to the technical or professional library. In fact, American law firms already contract out to an outside computerized "database" most of what their own law library used to do.

These are interesting thoughts from Drucker before the proliferation of the Internet and dot-com boom. Drucker goes on to note that outsourcing is needed to make service workers more productive, and that senior management within an organization outsources these functions largely out of a lack of interest in them. Today, over fourteen years after Drucker's thoughts, and what appears to be a lifetime of transformation in our thinking due to electronic networks and innovations, the same thinking applies: service work is outsourced to improve productivity (read—reduce labor cost) and senior managers really don't care about these functions. When you read this sort of diagnosis regarding the service sector, does this sound like how we want our fastest-growing industry to be? In America, our workforce shall proceed with functions that are our core competencies, ones that cannot be outsourced (for various logistical and legal reasons), and jobs that are outsourced. Is America set up to become the service sector for the rest of the world, as it was the industrial engine for the world during the twentieth century? This was never very likely, and now appears to be less likely with the proliferation of high technology across the globe to make services less labor-intensive and more ubiquitous.

So here's the scenario laid out for the professional manager: government economic statistics noting how glorious the U.S. economy is, with strong productivity, a strong labor market, and competitiveness with overseas markets. However, in many situations the manager faces cost pressures like never before, given the direct or indirect pressures from overseas markets. The manager also faces an increasingly disenchanted workforce, as she places additional pressures on the employees. You continue to hear of the silver bullet from overseas, or the specialist company in the States that can do the same work at a 30–100% cost reduction, and you're tired of hitting your head against the wall. As well, she is also tired of hearing the finance people talk of her competitors who are outsourcing. Eventually, she chooses the *easy out* and outsources. But what we'll discuss in the next

chapter is that she hasn't really solved the problem and, in fact, may have created
an even bigger problem by doing so.

Here's the scenario laid out for the worker at the large U.S. corporation: government economic statistics tell as well how great the economy is growing and how
stable labor wages are, but she doesn't see it. Earlier, it was just the blue-collar
worker struggling to remain middle class, but now the same fate applies to the
white-collar worker. Who would have thought that white-collar work would be
outsourced as well? Even Peter Drucker didn't guess that it would have happened
to the extent that it has, as great as he was. Now both the white- and blue-collar
workers are searching for job opportunities to provide to them the expected middle
class lifestyle, with the expected level of job stability. Yet the fastest-growing sector of the U.S. economy, the service sector, typically isn't providing well-paying
jobs to cover the jobs lost. No, this is not a statement suggesting that managers
shouldn't say "Screw it, I'll outsource," as some may suggest, but rather to ask
why they are saying it. Have our economic statistical bureaus provided data to
help us win in the global economy? Obviously not, because it was alleged that
even a past Fed Chairman (Greenspan) didn't believe these statistics. Have our
corporations done much to help the United States win in the competitive global
economy? Again, obviously not, as corporate profits have increased or remained
the same, but America's contribution to this through workers is dwindling and fast.
We cannot expect a corporation to ignore obvious competitive opportunities, such
as lower labor rates in foreign markets, but how come these U.S. corporations are
ignoring true productivity opportunities as well? Because they choose the *easy out*.
And what about the workers, what have they done for us to win? Our workers have
taken for granted that America would always have a robust middle class workforce
and, as a result, our work environment is not the most conducive for many corporate operations in a global competitive environment. And blaming this change
entirely on lower labor rates in other nations is really missing the point of what's
happening.

Lastly, the "Screw it, I'll outsource" phrase is also an indictment of our national
educational system. The trend of our competitiveness in the world market relative
to education keeps getting worse, and we must wonder how our nation's workers
will be seen as viable if they are falling so far behind other developed (and even
some developing) nations. Truly, this is a trend that must be reversed immediately
for our own economic security.

I was born in the first year after the baby boomers, and I've seen in my
lifetime quite a shift in the American persona; today, we're at the point of which
every American must wonder what they can do to make our national culture
and well-being stronger. We are gluttonous in our desires to eat, own material
things, and in being self-absorbed. In Frederick Taylor's day, Americans were
a rising breed, with goals of working ourselves toward becoming an economic
superpower, and we achieved our objectives. My parents and grandparents taught
me the honor of taking responsibility for myself, and in the dignity of work.

Today, our American culture has been corroded with overconsumerism, self-absorption, and victimization. These attributes can almost justify corporations in taking the *easy out* and outsourcing. We Americans must dig in and resurrect our golden days in order to achieve and reclaim what we once had on the world stage.

# CHAPTER SEVEN

# The "Difficult In" over the "Easy Out"

> I shall be telling this with a sigh
> Somewhere ages and ages hence:
> Two roads diverged in a wood, and I—
> I took the one less traveled by,
> And that has made all the difference.
>    —Robert Frost, *The Road Not Taken* (1916)

In this book, I contend that the two roads that diverged in the woods are the roads of the *easy out* and the *difficult in*. In the previous chapters, I have discussed the *easy out*, and linked it with the practice of outsourcing and offshoring. Given America's business climate, too many corporations have taken this *easy out*, and outsourced to make a problem go away. Many of these companies that either inappropriately or over-outsource have learned the hard way that their problems don't go away when they outsource; in fact, many companies actually create greater problems as a result. My experience is that while workers may not like it when a company outsources its jobs for good reasons, they typically can accept such decisions when they are logical. However, when companies outsource inefficiently or over-outsource, the remaining workers are bitter and upset because they can't make sense of the corporate decision. This mentality can run through an organization like wildfire and seriously damage the management's leadership credibility.

This is the point of the book that it is laid out clearly to America what those two roads diverged are, and that is the *Easy Out* and the *Difficult In*. Here are some attributes for each of them (Table 7.1).

I find it interesting that the term *productivity* has more meaning in a macroeconomic standpoint than it does in a microeconomic corporate one. For the economist, the term *productivity* measures the output achieved given the inputs used. This is, of course, a very general statement. A corporate manager cannot use

**Table 7.1**
**Easy Out vs. Difficult In**

|  | **Easy Out** | **Difficult In** |
|---|---|---|
| **Approach** | Strive for "Best Practices"<br>• What's best for others isn't what's best for you | Strive for What's Best for the Company<br>• Disciplined, detailed approach in making the best decisions |
| **Execution of "Strategy"** | Leadership Experience (Artisans)<br>• Leaders who implement high-level strategies without understanding the details.<br>• "Management Capitalism"<br>• Throw decision "over the wall" | Scientific Leaders<br>• Leaders who understand the detail before they even consider a strategy.<br>• "Owner-focused Capitalism"<br>• Use approaches like Six Sigma |
| **Incentives** | Short-Term Accounting Gains (ACCTP) | Short- and Long-Term Economic Gains (ECONP) |
| **Response to Adversity** | "Compliance"<br>• Compliance means being ruled by rules.<br>• Leads to mediocrity | Integrity and Courage<br>• Ruled by logic, and adheres to rules, not ruled by them.<br>• Leads to market leadership |
| **Worker– Manager Relations** | "Schizophrenic"<br>• Either afraid of or brutal to workers.<br>• After a while, contention is created through "management cowardice" | Joint Respect and Incentive<br>• Both parties get risk/reward in equal shares.<br>• Managers' #1 goal is to take care of workforce = #1 productivity goal.<br>• Workers' #1 goal is to work hard for company. |

such a simple measurement in a work setting, as there are so many other factors involved in the equation. Achieving true productivity at a corporation becomes a very detailed and complex endeavor, like unraveling a strand of DNA. Corporate managers who look at their operation in this manner are like scientists, seeking scientific methods to explore productivity.

The first attribute to consider regarding *easy out* and *difficult in* at a company is the objectives of the leader within the corporation. Each corporate leader needs to decide what approach he or she is going to take relative to achieving productivity; will the leader choose Best Practices as a course direction, or will the leader choose a specialized understanding of what's best for the specific company? In Chapter 2, I discussed Corporate America's obsessions one after another: consulting, dot-com, and then outsourcing. With each of these crazes, the business communities became flooded with the opportunists who capitalized on the crazes, the pundits who wrote articles and books, the politicians who based campaigns on them, and many others. I myself have ridden the waves of many of these fads, and these behaviors will continue as long as Corporate America remains obsessed with being obsessed. Not only this, Corporate America is obsessed with playing "follow the leader," which in some ways, is what Best Practices is about. In my view, Best Practices represents a sort of business stereotyping; expecting that the DNA of one company in a market segment is practically the same as that of its competitors. There has not been one industry that I've been involved in that avoided the drum beat of the notorious Best Practices. I like to call this the "Airline Magazine Craze," as many a top executive while in flight will read about fads from reading those airline magazines.

In 1919, Frederick Taylor noted that "among the various methods and implements used in each element of each trade there is always one method and one implement which is quicker and better than any of the rest."[1] This is the definition of the *one best way* of doing things that Frederick Taylor spoke of during the early twentieth century. Yet when we discuss Taylor's thoughts, we must remember the environment that Taylor was relating to, and why he suggested that there existed one best way of doing things. Today, standardization is very important from a process standpoint to reduce defects, but largely as a function within the company, process by process. Why should competing companies within an industry seek to be standard in strategic activities? Today's interpretation of Best Practices has encouraged just that. In my view, it has become the great equalizer, the "anti-innovation." In the 1990s, the Big Five Consulting firms became all the rage with the Fortune 500. A couple of management gurus, Michael Hammer and James Champy, stirred the business community by reinventing the term of *reengineering* and having corporations take notice of how to improve their operations. As a result of this, and thoughts from other management thinkers, the nineties became a golden age for consulting, and benchmarking/best practices became a big part of it. I remember when I was in Big Five that so many of our clients wanted to know so much about their competitors, and I always wondered why? Such is the world of the *easy out*; learning to improve based on what everyone else is doing, and stifling innovation in the process.

The outsourcing craze is very much in the same category. Much like the term *reengineering* drove the consulting craze, the term *core competency* has driven outsourcing, allowing corporations to take the *easy out*, and move their problems off to other companies in the United States and in distant lands. But for what? What did these companies move? Without an understanding of those processes, being core or not, I don't understand how leaders can rationalize outsourcing decisions. Terms like *reengineering*, *benchmarking*, *Best Practices*, and *core competency* often stir up the follow-the-leader progression. The opportunists of course welcome such actions, as the drumbeat means revenue to the consulting firms, the outsourcing companies, and the gurus and pundits. But what does a company get for doing a benchmarking exercise that all of the rest of its competitors are doing as well? Companies that have achieved innovation in their business models have not followed the leader. Wal-Mart, Dell (particularly during the earlier years), and General Electric stand out as companies that have dared to be different, that have taken the road less traveled.

I'm not saying that benchmarking and Best Practice reviews aren't important as points of data for companies, because they are. However, too many companies in Corporate America today are obsessed with such data, without understanding that it is only a guide, not a revelation. Nobody ever won in competition by trying to be like the winner. A leader for a company that I worked for once told me of an old sales saying of "the first to market always wins." The *easy out* companies hang on by imitating, and are failing in the process. The *difficult in* companies learn from their competitors, but are more focused on achieving efficiency and innovation by understanding their own DNA. This most certainly cannot be done without a complete understanding and knowledge of the company's unique characteristics. Wal-Mart redefined retailing by doing this. Companies that too quickly outsource its operations without fully understanding its own operations sells short on a potential opportunity. Who knows how many companies avoided potential market winning ideas by outsourcing a problem instead of figuring it out? As is mentioned frequently in this book, outsourcing per se is neither a bad nor a good activity, but rather an overused one. The overuse of outsourcing is almost without fail a loss of innovation for American companies in their need to be more competitive in the global economy.

I can't tell you how many times I sought innovation through creatively trying to understand process, and was shut down before I was able to do so. Yet when I was responsible for e-business for a large insurance company in 1998, I was allowed to take a different path than others in my use of offshore software development. Having spent a good amount of time in India, I knew that the software development process that my company needed was a more interactive process than simply shipping everything direct to India. I couldn't afford to ship everything offshore from a quality perspective, and hope for the best, like the company had done earlier with a Y2K project. I needed the software developers to understand the nature of our business, and I needed our business analysts to understand how the code was going to work. I took a different approach to offshore software development to be consistent with our business model, and outsourcing worked; this was possibly through an understanding of process. By bringing Indian developers into our U.S. operation, I bridged much of the cultural gaps of development being done twelve hours away. To the contrary, I have worked for a large company that chose an IT outsourcing firm based on the CIO's past relationship with a top IT company. Having had success with this large IT firm in the CIO's past, the decision was made to use this company for the CIO's new company, and the decision was a major mistake. In this case, a decision was forced through the organization as a result of best practice principles. The *easy out* not only allows for "follow the leader" decision making, it also perpetuates poor execution. Sometimes even when good leaders take the right approach and make the right decision, poor execution principles often prevent such decisions from being successfully implemented. In

Frederick Taylor's day, the manager/owner of the operation was far removed from the actual process of the work. Back then, workers were workers and managers were managers, and never the twain shall meet. No considerations were made toward one right way of conducting work until Taylor came along and, as a result, he originated the idea of the Scientific Manager. Ironically, many casual readers discuss Taylor's scientific management as a tool for the workforce, but rather it was a tool for managers. Today, almost one hundred years after Taylor's efforts, the same question is raised in corporate settings all over again. I have walked through so many factories, warehouses, processing centers, and even corporate centers, and found managers incapable of running their facilities in a scientific or rational manner. An artisan approach considers the manager's subjective nature to define his or her facility. This operation is run as a function of the manager's experiences, personality, biases, or even whims. Back in Taylor's day, this was very understandable because of the large educational canyon between that of the worker and that of the manager; it was very hierarchial. Today, with our workforce being relatively educated, and not illiterate newly arrived immigrants, how is it viable for the hands-off artisan to remain?

An artisan manager is one who seeks the *easy out* in the operation of his department. Artisan managers operate from feel or experience, from having learned from a mentor *how things work*. Therefore, principles of productivity remain the same as they were fifty years ago when America was the sole leader in the global economy. Times have changed, and so has our definition of productivity. These artisan managers cannot operate the same, using feel and experience. They must use science and innovation in an ever changing, maliciously competitive global economy. Yet how many organizations are training their managers to become these new productivity warriors?

Psychology also comes into play for the artisan manager. This individual wants respect and attention as a function of his title. In too many cases at corporations today, the person's individual psyche needs overrides what's important for the corporation. Without a strong corporate governance program to hold what's important to the corporation over that of the individual, the manager's personal desires come in first. For those reading this book who has worked in any type of organization, you know what I'm talking about. Obviously, leaders are going to bring personal baggage with them to work, but the problem arises when there is no governance to prevent this from affecting business results. As I mentioned earlier, the human psyche is irrational by nature, and we want work to be repeatable and rational; we expect some irrational behavior to exist, but the corporation must come first, not the person.

Artisan managers often follow popular culture within their industry by reading journals, speaking with colleagues from other companies, and going to trade shows and conferences. Artisan managers are often followers, and learn of pop trends later than others. Frequently, by the time they hear of an idea, it's already a buzz in the industry, and winning cannot happen by being second, third, or fourth. Seeking to show their bosses that they are progressive, they are very willing to jump on the bandwagon of an idea without sufficient detail to support its viability within the operation. And as the cult of personality for the operation, they are likely to make this decision a stamp of their own personality, or in many cases, to prevent this new idea to come about because it doesn't fit the culture. This is the scenario that leads to poor outsourcing decisions that has happened countless times in business today. One financial services company that I worked for was a storied, two-hundred-year-old operation in a very traditional market. During the nineties when e-business was the hot pop culture item, the CEO of the company decided that he needed an e-business guru to reinvent our business model for the eventual progression of this storied company into a dot-com entity. His guru decided to tear apart our business model, and venture into everything and anything; online pet supplies, a Web site for seniors, and other ideas were "hatched," as it was called, and yet these ideas had nothing to do with our core business of financial services. Not only were these ideas not core to our operation, the online ventures of pet supplies (pets.com), and senior citizen Web sites (various) were already implemented by first adopters. Our company spent millions of dollars on these ventures without any end product before the venture finally ended. Yet nobody was paying attention to the company's core operations that were bleeding money. As a result, the CEO and his staff were eventually fired when it became almost too late to save the company. This is an example of the artisan manager; someone who makes whimsical, high-level decisions, typically on the wave of some hot fad.

This artisan manager is also the perpetuator of managers' capitalism, which in the words of John Bogle, the founder of the Vanguard Group, is "the corporation came to be run to profit its managers, in complicity if not conspiracy with accountants and the managers of other corporations."[2] In this distortion of capitalism, in Bogle's words, corporate ownership is so diffused that no responsible owner exists. The ownership of our Fortune 500 companies is faceless, but one with a very clear slant. The largest managers of pension funds and mutual funds own half of all U.S. equities. These institutional investors are focused on short-term gains from these companies, as the long-term doesn't matter given their belief that stock ownership is a liquid financial instrument, and not a going operational concern. With a strong bias toward short-term profits versus long-term investing, the overuse and misuse of outsourcing is more prominent than if long-term investing were the strategy. There is no question that as the perpetuation of managers' capitalism grows, the artisan manager is protected from greater corporate governance oversight, and is more likely to be protected in making high-level, whimsical, short-term, bottom-line decisions regarding outsourcing.

There is no question in my mind that the artisan manager is protected in Corporate America as a function of managers' capitalism. The artisan manager in America is protected to make decisions in favor of poorly protected fads in whims of outsourcing versus true productivity. If a whimsical decision becomes a failure, what does the corporate manager lose? Sometimes she loses her bonus, but sometimes she doesn't, and rarely does the leader get terminated. But if that corporate manager was the owner of the company, the person would lose a lot of money, and maybe even ownership of the company. The professional manager is more apt to throw a poorly constructed idea over the wall to see if it works, and is not as concerned if it doesn't, as it's not his money at stake.

Unfortunately, I believe that the artisan manager is becoming more prominent in American business today rather than less so. As company ownership becomes more of an investment than a business activity, it is an obvious conclusion. Even though we have known for almost one hundred years that the discipline of management can be applied as a rational science, the lack of corporate governance and participatory ownership leads to worse, not better management behaviors. Today, scientific management needs to come back into fashion out of necessity. The words of Frederick Taylor do ring true in more conventional implementations, such as Six Sigma. But will these companies know what to do, or will principles of scientific management simply be the next fad? It's a question worth asking, as many companies are desperate for success, and may once again move toward another solution that they don't understand. Because of managers' capitalism, the artisan manager is stronger than ever in terms of importance in the U.S. corporation.

Much like the practice of outsourcing, there are likely more poor Six Sigma implementations than there are good ones. Today, some feel even that Six Sigma is a fad that has past its prime. Consider this quote from Tom Davenport of Boston College: "I think it has (Six Sigma's moment passed). Process management is a good thing. But I think it always has to be leavened a bit with a focus on innovation and (customer relationships)."

Six Sigma consultants are busier than ever, living and being rented at some of America's largest companies. But is this a choice between creativity and efficiency, or can Six Sigma be flexible to consider both? Besides the transactions that occur, does the manager and consultant understand the human dynamics of the group, the interaction between workers and customers, business processes and machines, and so on? To a certain extent, but scientific tools must be more than measuring and fixing defects. The whole point of scientific management is to measure and study processes to perfect them, and in Taylor's words to find the one best way of doing things. Business today is obviously more complex than it was in Taylor's day, and the manager who uses science seeks to uncover as much as is possible about an operation will find efficiency and creativity. In my past, I ran an operation with two different outsourced providers. One sought efficiency in a canned, almost Six Sigma way, while the other sought efficiency and creativity concurrently. As a result of moving to the second provider, our productivity more than doubled and cost cut in half! It's ironic that Frederick Taylor's lessons from one hundred years ago are as critical today as they were back then.

The concepts of Six Sigma, Kaizen, and other strong approaches to scientific management are only as good as those who implement these programs; they cannot be seen as "out of the box, all things to all people." Unfortunately, these ideas have become as much of cottage industries in themselves as have concepts of the past, such as dot-com, and other fads. I'm skeptical about any program that becomes rule-based versus logic-based. Those who become Six Sigma blackbelts and look at it as a cure all have lost focus on what Jack Welch and his GE team accomplished with the concept. In the end, each situation needs to be based on sound data and logic, and Six Sigma is a good approach, if not taken too literally. Any sound scientific management approach will do to cure the irrationality of the modern corporation; focus on the fundamentals, not the clichés!

Please don't necessarily confuse a Six Sigma or Kaizen approach with an approach of a scientific manager. While Six Sigma is obviously a great tool for companies seeking to be more disciplined, and thorough in making wise decisions, just because the company uses a formal approach it doesn't mean that in execution it will succeed. In many cases, scientific management can be a lot simpler than complex computer modeling and rule sets associated with formal approaches. Sometimes, even an artisan will use a fad approach like Six Sigma to demonstrate his or her aptitude in doing the right thing. But the right thing should be viewed as the most understandable, logical approach of understanding the process of work; like outsourcing, sometimes the Six Sigma–type approaches just confuse matters. Just look at the number of Six Sigma consultants popping up today, similar to what happened with Big Five consultants in the 1990s! Six Sigma can become the *easy out* fad of the decade, while detailed process understanding, without the buzzwords, can be the *difficult in*.

For the manager wanting to consider an outsourcing initiative, he should start by mapping every aspect of his operation before even considering the initiative. This is tedious, detailed work that most corporate managers don't want to undertake. Process maps, time studies, engineered standards, and others are the keys here, but frequently are avoided like the plague. In many cases, the manager enlists a third party to do the mapping and detailed analysis instead of his employees. This is one of the biggest mistakes of outsourcing, as the customer company will never understand the nuts and bolts (and culture) of exactly what the outsourcing company can or can't do. Let's consider an example in manufacturing: in some industries, American corporations are outsourcing manufacturing operations to China and elsewhere without understanding the manufacturing process itself. Particularly when it comes to more complex manufacturing processes or rapid product lifecycles, the Chinese may not be a sound decision when going to market. On the IT side, I have seen companies outsource application development to India sight unseen, and without any appropriate documentation of the processes. Some of these customer companies even outsource application development to IT firms that score high on the Capability Maturity Model Integration (CMMI) as justification, yet these highly ranked companies accept assignments without the customer understanding its own detail (which is a no-no for CMMI!). It's truly amazing how many times this happens in outsourcing arrangements. Only processes or functions that have been appropriately mapped, studied, and managed should be sent to a third party, with no exceptions!

So why are so many managers unwilling to adopt the scientific management side, or *difficult in* of their jobs? Is it because they don't understand, or is it because they simply don't want to? The answer appears to be a little bit of both. Most managers haven't been trained as industrial engineers, and don't understand the importance of process focus. For most corporations, there is nothing complicated about the details of the operation, particularly for managers who are typically more highly trained and educated than the average worker. Having been in the trenches in financial services, consumer products manufacturing, and other industries, I must say that never have I been overwhelmed intellectually in the details of any of the processes. While some Six Sigma blackbelts may seek to amaze the average worker with her methodologies and models, it really takes a stomach for detail and common sense to understand process plus innovation. There are no shortcuts for digging deeply into the nuts and bolts of the operation, and owning these details. Yet managers need to be trained to have a process approach to their work; to think through all issues/solutions with an emphasis on understanding detailed processes. Process-focused managers, taking the scientific management approach, are curious about the ins and the outs before they consider outsourcing. Understanding process is not hard, but can be tedious work. Innovation and market leadership cannot occur without the details, the *difficult in's*.

I'm amazed about how lacking the study of industrial engineering is in most business schools. So much effort is placed in the M.B.A. being versed enough in accounting, finance, marketing, economics, and even information technology, but not much at all regarding how to run and manage a company/operations in a scientific manner or how to make proper decisions through the use of scientific management. I have experience in M.B.A. programs as a student and a professor. In both, there was little discussion of time studies, engineered standards, or true process mapping. There are discussions about reengineering as a theory, and even Six Sigma, but not the nuts and bolts. Corporate managers are more likely to need knowledge and training in creating rational business processes than they are creating a marketing plan; are our business schools focused on the right areas?

In a recent implementation, I had my team map detailed processes, metrics, and objectives across the entire enterprise before a decision was made regarding outsourcing a specific operation. By doing so, the decision process regarding outsourcing made it very clear that it was a worthwhile endeavor. Interestingly enough, the organization learned of a different rationale for outsourcing; instead of the commonly held view that outsourcing was solely for labor-rate savings only (that aren't sustainable), the organization learned that considering outsourcing along with an improved understanding and implementation of process added to productivity improvements across the enterprise. This implementation would also support an increase production capability and innovation that would increase revenues. One more point, by taking a process-focused implementation before the consideration of outsourcing, the selection process for the third party changed dramatically, and really gave a large advantage to well-functioning 3PLs that wouldn't try to trick us.

As discussed in earlier chapters, the *easy out* manager focuses on ACCTP, or short-term accounting profits. I find it fascinating that no less than the founder of one of the most successful mutual funds, Vanguard founder John Bogle is a proponent for calling out this managers' capitalism, as he calls it. Per Bogle, the casino economy, which is in place today that handsomely rewards the CEO is a result of "ineffective gatekeepers," such as legislators, regulators, rating services, attorneys, public accountants, and corporate directors. In 1980, the pay of the average CEO versus the average worker was a multiple of forty-two, versus a multiple of 280 in 1994; today, it is still higher at 179 to 1. This is definitely due to stock options, and the rewards built into a short-term accounting system. The mutual fund mentality adds to this, as the power of these largest financial institutions almost forces the corporate manager to focus on the short term versus economic value. The quarterly earnings obsession is a puppet string affixed to the artisan manager. Without a good understanding of the operation, or even a desire to understand, the artisan manager will kowtow to the power of the quarterly earnings statement, and even use financial engineering to manage earnings, and make them look good for the institutional investors. Since the institutional investors really don't care whether you sell cigarettes or aspirin, they are more concerned with the accounting statements than they are about the viability of the business operation. The artisan manager is well suited to play this game within his or her company, and with the financial community. A 2004 Thomson Financial study found that since 1998, companies missed only 16% of the time.[3] If you dig into the details of this study, you'll find that the level of accuracy over the company results is impossible to believe. Of course, the stories regarding Bernie Ebbers and Dennis Kozlowski are obscene and extreme, but the financial renumerating that occurs on a daily basis in many companies is much more pervasive and still very dangerous.

The artisan manager is more willing to craft a detailed strategy around ACCTP management than he or she is in scientific management and understanding the process of the operation. So if an IT firm as an outsourcer presents an opportunity to a corporate executive that transmits a favorable view on the accounting statement, but wreaks havoc on operations in a year or so, there is too great a likelihood that the corporate executive will take the outsourcer's offer. An ACCTP favorable position is that of an offshore outsourcer who has lower labor rates than the company's internal operation. An artisan will be able to sell the outsourcing deal without understanding that an offshore operation will save on labor rates, but consume additional costs (as an example) owing to a lack of understanding, inefficiency, and even logistics. Through taking a scientific approach, it is unlikely to happen, as the outsourcer who potentially could offer lower rates and higher costs is sniffed out. And how many times have leaders introduced innovative market positions through accounting ploys? Not many.

An ECONP approach is truly a *difficult in* approach, but one that pays off for the manager who takes the time to do so. Regardless of accounting rules, the outsourcer must add economic value through an understanding of detailed processes. There is very little correlation between accounting rules and detailed business processes, but a lot of correlation between these detailed processes and an economic view. In most of the outsourcing deals that I have conducted, I have rarely chosen the lowest-cost provider in the bidding process. Does the outsourcer understand our business processes? Will the outsourcer take financial responsibility for their results, and seek competitive advantages for us? Sometimes, outsourcers who bid the lowest price don't have margins that can support taking financial responsibility for events that may occur, or the innovation needed to improve the business. In too many cases, I have seen unethical outsourcing firms offer lower costs, but indicate an unwillingness to sign the deal when the customer demands that it take financial responsibility for the results. An artisan will gloss over this, and show his or her manager the paper savings. A corporate manager who favors ACCTP over ECONP is more of a corporate accountant than he or she is a business owner. Nothing against corporate accountants, but the battle isn't won or lost in corporate accounting, but rather in the trenches in the operations. Enron, World-Com, and Qwest were all ACCTP plays. Outsourcers who take advantage of their customers typically do so on the ACCTP route. This is obviously not the way to proceed with a partner, in my mind.

This very clearly leads to the next point of distinction: how does the corporate manager respond to adversity? The artisan, in an explanation that ties to his bias toward the rules of ACCTP, has a compliance-based view of the world. This manager is ruled by rules, and cannot extract herself from this setting. A rules-based setting means that the manager understands her marching orders from others in supporting the *easy out*. If the manager's boss believes that she should no longer have a staff to complete a certain function, the manager will comply and outsource. If you think about this in football terms, most quarterbacks in the NFL will listen to the instructions being given by the coach regarding the play and execute that play. Peyton Manning, the best quarterback in football, often calls his own plays at the line of scrimmage based on what he sees developing on the field. There is often a big gap, in my mind, between the rules of the corporation and the surrounding logic that exists. Through a rational understanding of work processes, the scientific manager is not threatened by rules, for the most part. In fact, one key role of a successful manager is to use experience to manage rules, not to blindly follow them. Yet in today's corporation, leaders who push back on rules can often be seen to not be team players in many organizations. They may be viewed as unwilling to follow rules, or being insubordinate. However, that is not always the case. Frederick Taylor proposed essentially one set of rules, and that rule set was the one right way to conduct the process. Despite all of the different flavors of scientific management today, the corporate manager should not tie himself so tightly around either company rules, or even the rules of a certain methodology, such as Six Sigma. I have seen some very large companies being as blinded by their own narrow focus on Six Sigma as they have been on their own cultural rules. While it sounds somewhat contrary, an artisan manager will follow a rule set to avoid really understanding the process, and as an *easy out*. The scientific manager will follow process thinking through being ruled by logic and detail, and not worry about perceptions of adherence. Today, it is almost a given in the IT community that you offshore application development. In logistics, it's almost a rule that your freight management must be outsourced. The *difficult in* manager will not be afraid to stay high on integrity and, while following rules, will make decisions based on detail and logic (and of course, legal).

In my mind, when companies are facing adversity, they are more likely to make rule-based versus fact-based decisions. Rules are vehicles to use when covering your butt, and are easy to understand, for the most part. In a lot of company cultures, the term *compliance* is seen as one that draws support through being loyal. Managers who are confident and unshaken by difficult cultures and situations dig into and stay with the facts as their saving grace. I have always said in my career that if I'm going to face being fired for not following rules or for making bad decisions, I will choose the former (as long as the rules aren't legal ones). As a scientist manager, you can fight the adversity, and lead your company down a new path of success. I have taken this approach in some of my most successful outsourcing arrangements. After all, leaders aren't paid more money to follow company rules, they are paid well to develop and execute proper strategies.

The last question to consider when discussing the *easy out* versus the *difficult in* involves manager–worker relationships. Ever since the beginning of the Industrial Revolution, there has been a lot of discussion concerning how management should treat its workforce. During the early twentieth century, workers were considered commodities necessary in the production process. Today, there are areas of the world where this philosophy still exists. During my last visit to India, I was watching the host company's sparkling new office building go up in the last phase of the project. The shimmering steel and glass building was as modern as any new skyscraper that I had ever seen in the United States, but the difference was that there was work being done high above the ground by workers supported on bamboo supports. While during these trips I was as mindful as possible about the differences between Indian and American culture, I couldn't help but ask my Indian hosts about the safety of the supports. I was told that the migrant workers working on the building were day laborers with few rights beyond getting paid for a day of work. If the worker fell as a result of the poor support structure, there were few, if any, rights that would protect this worker as a result. This reminds me of documentation that I've read from the American Industrial Revolution when workers were subject to cruel working conditions. Back then, workers weren't seen as any more valuable as the machinery that they operated and, in some circumstances, even less so. Outside of the craft unions, labor union support for unskilled workers really didn't appear until 1905 with the Industrial Workers of the World (the Wobbies). This union was only in place for 15 years before being routed by the Palmer raids after the First World War. Industrial unionism was later revived by John L. Lewis in 1933, and then twenty-two years later, the AFL merged with the CIO to form real union power in the country.

During Taylor's day, labor unions hadn't as yet achieved any real power for the protection of unskilled workers, but were beginning to exert their position within the American lexicon. This whole concept of worker–manager relations was just starting to come into prominence, and yet much differently than the way we think about it today. Back then, employee relations almost had a class struggle notion to it, as the owners and managers were largely rich Anglicans, while many of the workers were poor immigrants. This underlying tension created between management and the workers was not only a social problem but was a productivity one as well. Taylor's development of scientific management was a savior to business because it prevented a growing social problem from causing a large business productivity problem as well. In Europe, there still is a large correlation between the social aspect of workers' rights and the productivity of the private enterprise. In earlier chapters, I discussed how much Europe has struggled with becoming more productive as a result. If it weren't for Taylor's scientific management, the same would have happened in the United States, and even affected us today. Furthermore, the use of the scientific management approach allowed the United States to become an industrial power. However, labor unions still disagree with Frederick Taylor's methods of *Principles of Scientific Management*. Why is this true? Because most labor unions think of workers' rights in the sociopolitical sense, and Taylor viewed them from a productivity standpoint. Even today, labor unions make the point that corporate actions are harmful to society when they do things such as outsourcing. Outsourcing to them is a betrayal against Americans, and this becomes a sociopolitical argument, one based more on emotion than fact. In today's global economy, the sociopolitical argument loses its teeth when the corporation is multinational. The labor union needs a different approach, as will be discussed later.

Taylor's argument is so timeless because his promotion of worker–manager relations ties what's best for the corporation to what's best for the worker. When labor unions collectively bargain with management, a win–lose situation is created. When *Principles of Scientific Management* are promoted, the situation is win–win. The *easy out* manager of today has been taught that workers' rights are important, and that "our worker is our no. 1 asset." Many managers not only say such things but they truly believe them as well. Most *easy out* managers have been promoted to the level of manager as a result of having good people skills. How this has happened is not accidental. These managers treat their workers like they are family, and frequently have their families commingle with the families of the workers. When I was growing up, I frequently went to picnics with the families of my father's workers and his boss's sons. Such intermingling was very commonplace in the past, and still exists today with the *easy out* manager. In the companies that I have worked for during the last fifteen years, this environment of *family* has been very prevalent at some companies. Of course, it becomes difficult to terminate the employment of a poor performer under those kinds of circumstances. Within American industry, loyalty became a much more important virtue than competence given the lack of any true outward competition in so many industries. In the auto industry, there was enough business for GM Ford and Chrysler until Japan Inc. came around, so quality was for many years definitely not "job one." For so long in American business, scientific management was disposed in place of humanism, and the belief existed that the worker had as much right to employment as the customer did to a quality product or service, or even more so.

In the 1980s for the blue-collar worker, and the early twenty-first century for the white-collar worker, all of this began to change. This is when schizophrenia began to surface for the *easy out* manager, particularly around decisions of outsourcing. Turning a blind eye to the growing competitive environment, particularly from overseas, American managers had an employee relations nightmare to face; should they focus on humanism or productivity? To many of them, this became a one-or-the-other type of question. After all, in their mind, you'll have to either treat the worker like family, as has been done for decades, or throw them out, and outsource to meet the new demands of global economy. Amid these questions, the labor unions and politicians began exerting their influence and making this out to be a sociopolitical question. This makes the corporate manager a bit of a schizophrenic; being saddled with guilt or concern over his or her own career with taking necessary action. This is an *easy out* in worker–manager relations through either remaining loyal to a workforce that isn't productive or slashing and burning this same workforce to save the manager's own soul. I've heard many a manager articulate an outsourcing decision as "You know that I'm one of you, but the company is making me do this." I've also heard the very same manager earlier state that "We care about our employees, so we won't outsource," perhaps only six months earlier. The *easy out* is simply avoiding what is inevitable after a *difficult in* opportunity was missed.

*What else can I do* is typically the cry from the *easy out* manager when being forced to outsource, or perceives that he's being forced. For the *easy out* manager, I will repost the beginning words of Frederick Taylor in his *Principles of Scientific Management:* "The principal object of management should be to secure the maximum prosperity for the employer, coupled with the maximum prosperity for each employee."

The answer of what to do is rather obvious for the corporate manager: to not take the *easy out*! What Frederick Taylor speaks of is not impossible, but admittedly is difficult. It is easier for the artisan manager to believe that effective employee relations is to treat the employees like family, but if in the end you have to lay off family members, is this really effective employee relations? Of course not. In today's new global marketplace, the worker doesn't need a friend, and some place where he or she feels like a member of the family. What the worker needs is an environment of joint respect and incentive, the same one that Taylor proposed one hundred years ago. However, this environment is cultural and one that doesn't happen overnight. The effective corporate culture must be one that considers the welfare of both the employee and the manager in time to avoid any rash decision at the last minute, such as outsourcing.

How does a corporation create an environment that is jointly respectful to both management and the worker? Today, it is not so easy, given the obscene level of executive compensation, and the soft, unwillingness of the many workers to make a difference. It is important to note that the contention in today's environment is not altogether the fault of management. What has the average worker done for the enhancement of American productivity during the last few decades? Perhaps compared to Europeans, the American worker is respectful and diligent, but possibly not to a sufficient degree to compete against the emerging economies. Note that a key message of the *easy out* versus *difficult in* is the importance today of workers and managers in stopping this seemingly unending outsourcing of American jobs overseas, or within the United States to very-low-paid employees. As Taylor noted, management and labor must come together to create an environment of success for both sides. Today's casino economy promotes the benefit of the investor and manager over the worker, for the most part. During earlier decades, the worker was highly compensated given a lack of a competitive global marketplace, but those days are gone. Outsourcing is simply a reaction of management within the casino economy, given the lack of joint respect and incentive that doesn't exist today between the two sides.

This is where the *difficult in* needs to begin between the workforce and the management of the corporation. In the very competitive global market where U.S. wages are fifteen to twenty times higher than its Asian competitors, why wouldn't the management and labor of a company want to cooperate, and seek to win together? Does management really believe that its best solution to the problems is this sort of schizophrenia where they are nice to the workforce, as family, until the functions of the workers are outsourced to overseas, and they are underemployed? Does labor believe that its best option is to blindly fight for higher and higher wages as it did twenty years ago, before the emergence of China and India, among others? Today, corporate management must make decisions, not whether to outsource but, rather, whether to be competitive. Outsourcing is often a deflection rather than a strategy. Corporate leaders who choose the road of the *difficult in* have an opportunity during this very difficult period in our economic history to inspire our workers to compete within a new world as opposed to living in the old one. Later in this book, I will lay out a prescription for how management and workers must come together to maintain our productivity and competitiveness. Perhaps it's not possible to turn around how our corporation's managers and workers unite in today's fast-changing world economy, but if we stop the bleeding now, we will understand this new definition of productivity, and win in the global economy.

Many business books of today address the behavior of company management, but rarely, if ever, do authors take on the problems of our workforce. While it is true that the state of America's workforce is nowhere as bad as the situation that exists in France or other European nations, our situation is no longer as healthy today as it once was. And before the politicians and labor unions seek to rally the forces around retro strategies of the seventies and eighties, the workforce needs to understand clearly some of the impact that it has had on why corporate managers are taking the *easy out* so often. Executive compensation can be obscene relative to average workers' wages, and contention with management is higher than it has been since the Second World War. But the worker must take responsibility for part of the blame as well. What the worker in America needs to be today is neither the pampered, enabled euro worker of much of the more socialist EU, nor the severely unpaid and abused workforces in Asia. The American worker must become the partner with management to take on this new definition of productivity, to be able to compete against workers in China or India, who make a fraction of a wage. The worker who is willing to fight to maintain his higher wages versus expecting them via some devine right. Note that the *easy out* existed before outsourcing, before management consulting and the dot-com era. It had permeated into American business as a result of stagnant competition from other nations. Now that this competition exists, American workers must get out of their funk, and contribute to the greater good.

One last point to make about the relationship between the manager and worker in the U.S. system: statistics would lead us to conclude that it's working great, and the combination of jobs going overseas, stagnant wages, and high productivity (measured in a less than jointly respectful, win–win environment) has made our economy, and the workforce a better place. For those who believe this to be true, ask the average worker if he or she believes that there is more or less security and opportunity in the economy today than previously? I believe that the workforce is more concerned over their futures than ever before, and this belief is validated when workers are surveyed. That is the reason why outsourcing has become this big bogeyman, so to speak. Outsourcing represents a major indication of how America is losing its competitiveness, no matter what the statistics may present. Americans are smart enough to understand this, yet are being persuaded to fight the message instead of changing it. Workers and even managers cannot fight economic environments, regulations, conditions, and policies that lead us toward the *easy out*, but they can commit themselves to core fundamentals of good business that will turn things around. That is the course that everyone should take—the hard road of the *difficult in*.

There is no question in my mind that some readers will examine this part of the book, and conclude either that the message is prounion, antiunion, proworker, antiworker, socialist, globalist, or whatever; those who do so will be missing my points. The pure genius of Frederick Taylor's ideas was that they weren't sociopolitical ideas at all. They were truly ideas searching for the core and the one right way of conducting business that still exists today. One hundred years ago, the labor unions invoked a nasty campaign of character assassination against Frederick Taylor as a result of his theory of the study of work. Ironically, everyone has heard of Karl Marx, but very few have heard of F. W. Taylor; each saw and responded to the same socioeconomic conditions, but both dealt with them differently. Marx felt that struggle was needed to free the worker from these chains, and Taylor felt that struggle wasn't necessary. Taylor's approach is definitely more American than Marx's, and yet Marx is better known than Taylor.

This thought of a *difficult in* is rather ironic as well. Many political pundits or labor-union proponents have solutions to our current economic issues that are less than ideal, and yet they receive a lot of public support. In 2004, John Kerry received a lot of support from various groups when he called CEOs "Benedict Arnolds" for offshoring jobs. That's the voice of the *easy out*. So where's a similar voice of the *difficult in*, asking American workers and managers to search for real productivity and competitiveness in an environment that is pleasant to both parties as well as the investors? Much like America faced during Taylor's day, we face a true two roads diverged, as Frost wrote for us in 1916. And like Frost's poem The Road Not Taken, it may be tricky to determine which path is best for us. What is important to understand is that we need to choose, and we need to do so quickly. The choice must happen one company at a time, one worker and manager at a time. While it would be helpful for government economic policy to support the correct path, today's corporation cannot wait for it, and must forge ahead itself. And with behavior that will definitely feel like being contrary to how corporate managers must decide in our short-term casino economy, the manager must choose against his or her experiences that lead them to the easy out, time and time again. The future will be decided now with the choices that we make.

# CHAPTER EIGHT

# Fear of a Global Planet

The world stage is perfectly set for China and India to blossom as economic powers while America focuses on world political struggles. Focusing on the Middle East is important, but should that sole focus be at the risk of our economic competitiveness? Shouldn't we have a domestic policy that makes the *difficult in* more viable than the *easy out*?

China is emerging as the most efficient manufacturing platform ever, surpassing the efficiency of the United States. What's amazing (and scary) is not that a relatively poor nation like China is able to compete with high tech and low wages as well as it does, but rather in the speed in which they accomplished it. Everyone is aware that China is competitive in high-labor industries like textiles (provides 50% of textile products to America), but when it becomes efficient in the sophisticated electronics industry so quickly, we all must understand that a new paradigm has been developed relative to manufacturing prowess. China is no longer just a low-cost-labor assembly operation; it can now efficiently handle design, components, white-collar work, freight/logistics, etc.

The myth that China and India will be the sweatshop while America will be the brains behind manufacturing is becoming increasingly farther from the truth. Instead of using American engineers to design products, Chinese engineers are emerging to design products that are assembled in China. In the high-tech semiconductor industry, the U.S. Semiconductor Industry Association warns that a "gravitational pull" could continue to take talent, capital, and R&D from the United States. Never before in the history of modern economics had such a transformation occurred so quickly in manufacturing. These nations will not be satisfied with being low cost providers only, and we need to take notice of this fact quickly!

What's happening with business process outsourcing (BPO) in India may be even scarier to U.S. industry. Indians aren't just answering your phone calls about your laptop, they are also processing insurance claims, researching legal matters, testing pharmaceutical products, and preparing tax returns, you name it. India's sweet spot is services—which now constitutes 60% of the U.S. economy. The possibilities for American job elimination via the Internet from India, a largely educated, English-speaking population, are mind boggling, and just scratching the surface. India is already the world's largest manufacturer of motorcycles, tractors, fertilizers, soaps and detergents, cutter and polisher of diamonds, and one of the largest bulk drug manufacturers: what will be next?

If the America public is paying attention to what's happening in the world economy, it sure has a funny way of showing it. More importantly, if our politicians are serious about solving the causes instead of the effects, it's difficult to see the results. In mid-December 2006, the United States sent a high-profile entourage to China to discuss reducing the swollen U.S.–China trade imbalance, and the need to reduce controls over the Yuan. After two days, the Americans left China with nothing more than empty promises, as is evident by this quote:

"We agree on the need for balanced, sustainable growth in China without large trade imbalances," U.S. Treasury Secretary Henry Paulson said.[1]

Really? If China invests 50% of its GDP in infrastructure investments, and its economy is one-sixth the size of the U.S. economy, how can there be enough money left over for it to eliminate the trade imbalance? This isn't possible, and furthermore, not even desirable to the average American. It's in China's best interests to keep conditions exactly how they exist today in order to support their economic expansion, and a case can be made to state that it's equally desirable for the United States. It is certainly admirable for Henry Paulson and Ben Bernanke to push the issue with China, but are the end results what we want? Even so, politicians and government officials can only do so much from a trade relationship standpoint. Instead, a greater focus must be placed on making us more competitive against the growing Chinese economy under the new definitions of productivity. Outsourcing and offshoring will continue as long as the prevailing environment makes it so fertile to do so. America must fix the problem, not simply address the symptoms. America needs to negotiate from a point of strength, not weakness, and that cannot happen under presiding conditions.

Let's hope America won't wonder five years too late why we didn't take the time to better understand China and India when we had an opportunity to do so. After all, neither of these nations are mysterious kingdoms that have recently emerged in front of us; the history of these proud nations goes back to long before the days of Christ. Americans must understand the Chinese and Indian cultures in order to decide how our nation can best remain economically competitive, and be in a position to face our *difficult in's*. China and India have made a point to understand and embrace American culture. They have studied our ideals, our systems, our language and, most important, our culture. For decades now, the globalization of American culture has had a much greater impact on the rest of the world than it has had on us. It is impossible to miss the familiar lights of McDonalds, Starbucks, and Kentucky Fried Chicken, to name just a few, in virtually every country in the world. The rest of the world has more reason for concern over American brands in their culture than we do today for foreign brands/manufacturers in ours. And the Chinese and Indian populations are more fearful of what's happening in the global economy, in some ways, than are you and me.

So who is this China that we face as a global competitor? For thousands of years, China has become what it is today as a result of a unification, disunity, conquering, and being conquered. And in each consecutive period, the nation added to its culture and that is so important for us to understand today. To understand China, one must begin with the Qin Dynasty in 221 B.C., the beginning point of Imperial China. During this period, the Great Wall was built, a legalist government existed, and a clear and absolute legal code was written, including the absolute power of the emperor. The emperor during this period, Qin Shi Huang, evoked a brutal silencing of opposition, including the killing of scholars. Some contend that this sort of government laid the groundwork for modern China's desire for collective rights over indivdual rights, and the need for a fortress to protect its people from outside forces. The next dynasty, the Han Dynasty, became the first to embrace Confucianism in 202 B.C. In Imperialist China, it was considered the state religion, and inserted a much different religious phlosophy to the Middle Kingdom than did Christianity to the West that was about to flourish just a few centuries later. Consider the Confucious view of ritual in society[2]:

Lead the people with administrative injunctions and put them in their place with penal law, and they will avoid punishments but will be without a sense of shame. Lead them with excellence and put them in their place through roles and ritual practices, and in addition to developing a sense of shame, they will order themselves harmoniously. (Analects II, 3)

The use of ritual places emphasis on politeness and one's place in society. It places a greater importance on the collective whole versus the individual, and sets clear guidelines regarding how individuals should conduct themselves to avoid wrongdoing. The ritual also divided people into categories, which established hierarchies believed to be essential in managing the population. Later on, Maoism sought to undo some of this, but the Confucian rituals still exist today in how Chinese citizens are expected to conduct themselves within societal settings. Discipline, respect, hierarchy, and collective good are all attributes that remain from the Imperialist Chinese, and they are important in that they play out on the world stage today in offshoring and the Chinese economy.

The Han Dynasty through defending the homeland from Huns and others, established the first formal trading connections with the West in Silk Road. China's love–hate relationship with the world is epitomized by this interconnection of these routes that cross the middle of Asia into Europe, and sea lanes to Japan and Korea. Actually, it was Alexander the Great a couple of hundred years earlier who had sought to harvest this route, but not until the Han Dynasty did it become important for the Chinese to do so. With the Roman conquest of Egypt in A.D. 30, trade with the Roman Empire began to prosper, and Rome and China had somewhat of an equal relationship. Silk became a popular dress item within Rome, although the

Roman Senate sought to ban such attire as too seductive (the attempt to ban was never successful—the power of the consumer market at work!).

During the seventh century, the Tang Dynasty established Buddhism as the state religion even though it had been founded in India a good six centuries earlier. This period is thought by some scholars to be the most prosperous time in Chinese history, and trade routes were extensive and far reaching. Many foreign merchants set up shop in China. A few years after the advent of the prosperity, one of the warlords, Huang Chao, captured Guangzhou and proceeded to kill most of the citizens, including a large contingent of foreign merchants. As a result, China fell into disunity for fifty years, and became a multistate system consisting of many regimes covering the country. Eventually, the Mongols consolidated the nation through the first use of firearms around A.D. 900. Later, Kublai Khan, the grandson of Genghis Khan, was the first to rule the Dynasty with Beijing as the capital. Also during this period, Marco Polo arrived at Khan's court, and established a venture that lasted seventeen years, with permission to travel freely across China. From these travels, Marco Polo wrote of the wonders of China that has not dulled in the eyes of the Europeans ever since.

Finally, in 1368, the Ming Dynasty was established by pushing the Mongolians back to the steppes, and occurred largely through peasant revolts. During this period, the population doubled after having fallen during the Mongol rule. Large urban centers started to sprout up and despite the widespread xenophobia, foreign trade began to flourish. A strong and central government became increasingly autocratic and bureaucratic. This was certainly a golden era in China, albeit a protected and guarded one. During this period, the remainder of the Great Wall was constructed. There is some history to suggest that this era exemplified what is important to China; open trade, but with a guarded nature toward foreigners, and great innovations in technology and innovation, yet a growing government bureaucracy. Perhaps China learned that the massive bureaucracy of the Ming Dynasty contributed substantially to its failure, and as a result, the modern Chinese government has sought to enable business through less bureaucracy. There is a lot to learn from this era about current-day China.

After this period of prosperity, the Qing Dynasty was founded when the Manchus defeated the Han Chinese, and quickly adopted Confucian traditional Chinese government. They invoked a political and legal system (Eight Banners) in an attempt to assimilate this into Chinese society. During the late period of this Dynasty, entering into the twentieth century, the Qing control weakened, and Western penetration increased. With the Opium Wars, the Taiping Rebellion (whose impact was on the Christians), and the Boxer Rebellion, China was in a struggle between old and new, of national versus foreign influences. Finally, a group of young officials and students overthrew the Qing government. As a result, the Republic of China was founded.

In 1919, an important, yet hardly newsworthy, movement started to take shape in China called the May Fourth Movement as a response to China's treatment in the Treaty of Versailles agreement ending the First World War. The Chinese government had entered the war on the Allies' side, on the condition that all German spheres of influence would be returned to China after the war. However, then Japan also entered the war on the Allies' side, and proceeded to attack these areas of German interest within China. When negotiating the Treaty of Versailles, the Allies were more focused on punishing Germany than keeping the promises made to China and, as a result, China was left with an unfair settlement. The May Fourth movement was largely antifeudal, and led to the development and success later of the Communist Party in China. The Versailles Treaty was seen as a betrayal, and Wilson's Fourteen Points were viewed as Western slanted and biased. Students took part in this movement, and formed the future of the country with the foundation of the Communist Party.

The nationalists took over in the early stages of the twentieth century, but did little to relieve the suffering of the poor. The Japanese invasion in the late thirties, including atrocities on this nation as horrific (but not as well documented) as that of the German Holocaust, made matters worse and demoralized the people even more. At end of the Second World War in 1945, the Chinese people were tired of fighting, had quite a few fractional divisions within the population, with high inflation rates, and a government unable to establish authority over the lands formerly held by the Japanese. Without sufficient resource funding to bring this country back together again, the Nationalists continued to lose their grip on power. While the Communists didn't have a lot of resources either, they did build on a large grassroots support effort, and played on the imcompetence and corruption of the Nationalists. Finally, in 1949 when Mao and the Communists took over, they were faced with an enormous land mass, including half a billion rural poor seeking greater hope and prosperity. Seeking to transform a country with thousands of years of tradition, Mao inaugurated erratic and poorly developed economic policies, and was an ideologue to a fault, seeking to rule through political concepts and ruthless purges. In his three decades of rule, millions of Chinese were killed, justified as for the "greater good."

Mao was certainly not an economist, as was evident in many of his policies. He believed that the masses were the answer to any economic question; that by enabling them, he could energize the entire nation. In 1958, farmers started organizing into immense communes, working as a team for the collective good. Instead, Mao's Great Leap Forward is seen as one of the greatest economic disasters in modern history. From 1958 to 1962, an estimated 25 million died in the most severe famine in Chinese history. A few years later, in 1966, Mao sought reconciliation through the Cultural Revolution. Mao sought to change all aspects of Chinese life, and the Communist Party bureaucracy was challenged as never before. Over the next ten years, millions of intellectuals and capitalist wanna-be's (per their definition) were forced into manual labor, and thousands more were killed by the Red Guards. Scholars debate whether Mao undertook these actions in furtherance of the revolution or to eliminate his enemies and consolidate his power. Yet, for whatever reason, the Cultural Revolution decimated the Chinese economy, and only after Mao's death did reformers have a chance to make changes. Deng Xiaoping, who came to power in 1978, is frequently given credit for putting China back on the path of economic recovery.

The history of Mao and the Communist Revolution in China tell us a lot about China, and how even a market economy in China is much different than that of the United States. For centuries, China was a military and bureaucratic hierarchy imposed on a large population of peasants. The imperial system in place was largely inefficient owing to the extent and remoteness of the peasant systems all across the nation. Peasants were the heart of the nation, but were an exploited group, done so through a great deal of tradition. The farmers in Mao's China changed the identity of the nation. Peasant farmers became benefactors of their labor, rather than the serfs that they were before. However, as the population started to swell, the nation had to become more efficient with its use of farming to feed its billion-plus population, and also use its land for other purposes such as housing and manufacturing. Just as in America, China was facing an industrial revolution that it needed to win and as a result, its nation could no longer thrive as a commune farming kingdom. For the Chinese people, it was viewed as good that Chairman Mao's revolutions prevented foreign intervention, but it was bad in that decades of social strife through the Great Leap Forward and Cultural Revolution led to a new caste system within the country without needed foreign innovation and investment. Post-Mao leaders recognized this, and started the next experiment toward industrialization.

As dreadful as the Mao Communist era of China was in its economic growth, the growth stage thereafter was a historical success story. Since 1990, the country has had a 500% increase in Gross Domestic Product (GDP), has lifted over 400 million people from poverty, and a half of a trillion dollars of foreign investment has spilled into China, creating a lot of employment and additive growth. It's hard to believe that foreign investment has been legal only since 1979, and the stock market reopened only in 1990! This is a story that cannot be lost on the American public; how a largely poor and battered communist nation with historic levels of starvation in 1958 in a closed economy has achieved amazing heights as an economic superpower less than fifty years later!

There is no mistaking China's emergence as an economic superpower today. A country that accounted for 1% of the world's economy in 1978 that now accounts for 4%! In 1981, the trade between the two countries totaled $5.5 billion dollars, $3.6 billion being U.S. exports of agricultural products. In 2005, this number multiplied to over 50 times at $285 billion, including $42 billion of U.S. exports and a whopping $240 billion of Chinese exports to the United States! Only one eighth of the $42 billion of U.S. exports is in agriculture, while the majority of it is in categories such as machinery, aircraft, optical equipment, medical equipment, and such, a much more sophisticated list.[3] China's list includes the old staples of toys, clothes, and footwear, but is getting increasingly complex in the types of goods that it offers to the United States and the world. Surely, China has burst onto the U.S. economic stage, and while our politicians have focused some energy on discussions from a protectionist standpoint, there have been faint discussions as how to not halt, but rather compete against this juggernaut.

China's star has just begun to shine on the world market. In China, there are pockets of economic prosperity, but areas that are relatively untouched. The most prosperous area in China is the Yangtze River delta region, anchored by Shanghai. In this region, there are over 80 million people, and it serves as China's main commercial center. It is very accessible to international locations via the East China Sea, and the Pacific Ocean. Shanghai's port has capacity for over 21 million units (TEUs), a staggering volume![4] The next largest commercial location is in the Pearl River delta area, anchored by Guangzhou (formerly Canton). This is the area near Hong Kong (two hours) with a population of around 50 million. This commercial center is right on the Pacific Ocean as well, in the southeast part of the coastal region. For these two regions, the infrastructure in place is either as good as or better than most U.S. cities. Besides these two major commercial areas, China has others as well. The Northeast area that used to be called Manchuria, adjacent to Korea, is well known for heavy industrial production. The fourth major commercial region is the Fujian province, which has had the benefit of gaining investment from Taiwan, which is adjacent to it across the China Sea. It should be noted that all four major commercial areas are all centers on China's southeast coast, where infrastructure is conducive to economic barter and trade. A huge investment is being made in infrastructure, but it is still being strained, and investment must continue. Since the 1980s, 5,323 kilometers of rail, 20 airports, and 15 berths at ports have been financed by the central government, an amazing level of investment![5] Between 1989 and 2001, the Chinese government poured $761 billion into 1,553 infrastructure projects, with investment since then growing even faster.[6] This investment has paid off, with eight of the fifty largest ports being in China, and 25% of the world's workload of rail carried on a Chinese track.[7]

Certainly, China's star will burn even brighter when its noncoastal, western provinces are fully linked into the public infrastructure. Today, 75% of the nation's population lies within the four eastern districts, which account for 44% of the nation's landmass. Only 25% of the population lies in the Yunnan province and northwestern districts that occupy 56% of the landmass. The Yunnan province is the one that is adjacent to Tibet, and has quite a diverse mix of ethnic groups. Worse, this province has more poverty-stricken counties than any other province. However, help is on the way for this province, as it has added, and is adding, more roads than any other province. The official plan is to connect all towns and capitals with expressways by 2010, and a high-speed road network by 2020.[8] It also has projects seeking to link it to Tibet, Myanmar, Laos, Vietnam, and Thailand, opening up more trade opportunities. In the coming years, China will double the size of its 34,000-km highway network, already the world's second largest, to the United States. The pace and scale of their infrastructure projects are almost unbelievable.

Another big development project, the "Development of the West," is in Urumqi, a city in northwest China which, incidentally, is in the Guinness World Book of Records as the most remote city in the world, being 1,400 miles from the nearest coastline![9] However, being on the frontier of the Central Asian Republics (CAR) that are oil rich, the Chinese government has big plans for the growth of this area of the country.[10] One initiative is to lay 7,000 miles of rail track in Western China by 2010! In view of the fact that large areas of this vast country are untouched from an economic standpoint, the future growth of China should continue well beyond the next couple of generations. As China spends much of its economic gains on the infrastructure of these underdeveloped areas, its muscles will flex even greater as an economic powerhouse. Furthermore, when inner areas are linked to the seaports, the cost of Chinese goods should remain stable as a result of inflation being tamed by lower-cost economic markets off the coast. This will allow the Chinese economy to grow at a high rate without having to face enormous inflationary pressures.

China and India provide unique threats to the United States, given their culture and potential. While China is a disciplined, centrally planned, overcontrolled, and growing but wasteful market economy, India is much different. China's growth is largely due and controlled by its government influence; India's is in spite of it. China's growth is disciplined and calculated, while India's is marvelous and wild. China's growth has been based on simple manufacturing processes, while India's growth started with white-collar work, and is now expanding out. China is a communist/socialist political system with more capitalist features than most people would believe. On the other hand, India is the world's largest democracy, but with more socialist features than one would think.

India also has ancient roots, economically speaking. Trade existed between the Indus Valley and Mesopatmia as far back as 2600 BC! At the start of the eighth century AD, trade existed off and on between India and Arab regions, and invasions occurred frequently as well. In the 1500s, Europe came to the party, with Portugal starting trade and colonization in India, and Holland and Britain followed closely behind. During the 1600s, Britain had a monopoly with the East Indian Trading Company, which lasted for centuries. In the middle of the nineteenth century, the years of colonization paid off, as Britain invested in infrastructure and education in the subcontinent, and these British actions were the beginning of India's language, medical, and engineering improvements. After India's independence a century later, the public sector dominated industry, which eventually led to economic ruin in just a few decades. Finally, in the early 1990s, with an impending threat of a significant financial crisis, India opened and reformed its economy, thus fostering the growth that it enjoys today.

Since these economic reforms, India grew at an average growth rate of 6% per annum until 2002, and a rate of over 7% for the ensuing years. India's hardened world financial position has changed, and now it has foreign exchange reserves of over $100 billion, although this has been achieved in non–debt-creating flows, leaving the nation still with debt to pay from its socialist days. Yet given its strong economic growth, India is paying back its debt at an accelerated pace, and becoming an interesting place for foreign companies to invest. Its corporations are being run by some of the best managers and engineers in the world, largely due to the strong educational system (Indian Institutes of Technology and the Indian Institutes of Management). With growing dominance in software, design, services, and innovation, India may have even more control over its economic future than the emerging star of China!

The secret to India's success has been its unparalleled scientific and management talent. At the onset, the British tried to encourage native forms of education, but these schools failed from a lack of patronage by fellow Indians. In 1835, the British implemented English-language education with the hope that science, technology, and law could be introduced without disrupting religious or social life. Instead of this education seeping downward into lower social classes, those who gained the knowledge of English used it as a passport to advancement, rather than as a missionary to the lower classes of society. Although this educational system allowed for advances in engineering, medical, and legal progress, unintentionally, it also led to the modernization of the higher classes at the expense of the lower ones.

Today, some of the best engineering and management schools in the world are located in India, and its secondary educational system is very strong in math and science, which is always a key factor to economic growth. In India, a software programmer may have a Ph.D. in electrical engineering, while an American programmer may just have an associate's degree. The vast canyon of difference between the trend line of Indian education for white-collar work in comparison to that of the United States is mind boggling. This model of excellence toward math and sciences is reminiscent of a few generations ago in America in the Space Age, during the time our school system focused on these disciplines. The Indian young are very diligent toward their studies, given the competitive nature of the educational system. This level of intellectual competition really drives excellence in the Indian school system, something that America could benefit from replicating. As India continues developing its highly skilled, educated, young workforce, companies, both foreign and domestic, will tap into this potential for outsourcing/offshoring benefits. The Indian gains from the information technology area will pale in comparison to what will be possible if these trends continue into other disciplines, such as medicine, biopharmaceutical, BPO. In the eighties and nineties when Peter Drucker wrote his famous management books explaining the *Knowledge Based Society*, he could have been referring to India. The Indian educational system and workforce is much more pertinent, sadly enough, to what Drucker was talking about than is our current American educational system and workforce. Perhaps even more so than China, India has great economic potential. America's addiction to outsourcing/offshoring will continue to grow unless we understand the potential of these economies.

There is no question that India will be an economic powerhouse for decades to come. With GDP growth that has been over 5% or greater for ten straight years, strong forex reserves, and declining inflation levels on top of a strong service and growing manufacturing economy, India is poised to be a giant. However, outside of the Mumbai (Bombay) area, there isn't a great port presence or sufficient infrastructure to support Chinese-type manufacturing growth. Its poor physical infrastructure, bureaucracy, high/unreliable cost/use of utilities, high cost of business entry/exit, underdeveloped consumer markets, and high level of regulations and restrictions will impact its future potential as a manufacturer. For container traffic to rise dramatically from its current state of 1% of world traffic, many of these issues must be addressed immediately and dramatically.

While China is focusing on building physical highways to link itself to the world, India may be more focused in building virtual highways of bandwidth to work with the world. At the Indian Economic Summit in November 2006, Shakeel Ahmad, the Minister of State of Communications and Information Technology noted that expanding broadband in India will be a key factor in the achievement of both economic and social reforms.[11] Having been to India many times, and driven through some of these rural areas, I find this to be an interesting, perplexing thought concerning the issues of the rural poor in India. While India is investing some in infrastructure, its own government freely admits that its physical infrastructure will be its bottleneck for continued development. Recently, the Finance Ministry admitted that "weak infrastructure continues to be the Achilles' Heel of the Indian economy." While China has set revenue aside for massive public projects, the Indian government has admitted to unproductive expenditures that divert funds from much-needed infrastructure projects. Even when it does invest in public projects, implementation is often hindered by the social responsibility of maintaining employment rather than efficiency.

Besides infrastructure challenges, India faces an unacceptable number of its citizens living well below the poverty level. In Bombay alone, there is one ghetto that houses 1 million poor, the largest ghetto in Asia. Towns outside of the major cities are poor and underdeveloped, without any apparent plans to change the quality of life in these locations to any significant degree. Government data indicate that 200 million people earn less than $1 a day, when they can find work.[12] While the percentage of those earning less than $1 a day fell from 26% in 1999 to 20% in 2005, this is an obscene social issue to address. No economic superpower can be burdened, either economically or ethically, with this degree of problem. I have discussed this matter with Indians; they understand the major issue of poverty, but the sheer size of the problem means it will take time to address.

With such rapid economic growth in the private sector, coupled with the government's responsibilities with the burdening masses of poor, India is having greater difficulties managing inflation and its financial system. Its tax system is woefully inadequate, with a very small percentage of the population officially paying an income tax. In addition, India must reduce the barriers in its economy that are lasting remnants of pre-1990 reforms. The government still conducts itself somewhat like a socialist system, and private enterprise succeeds sometimes in spite of the government. If the government has policies that enabled better growth (better tax system, appropriate infrastructure, fiscal responsibility, empowering the population through better social services, more foreign investment), India has amazing future possibilities.

Despite the promise of the Chinese and Indian economies, both have Achilles' heels that could prevent them from being major economic competitors with the United States. For China, its private industry is exposed by having poor managers, who typically have climbed the ranks through communist party connections, and who lack formal training/innovation in growing their organizations. As was mentioned earlier, China's financial system is a mess. Its industries are wasteful and polluting, and its marketing approach to new products lacks innovation. There are problems with counterfeiting. There is an aging population (due to the one-child rule). There aren't adequate labor laws to develop an environment of worker–management relations that will be efficient for its future. Energy and oil demand is exceeding supply. If you look far enough under the covers, you'll find that China Inc. is a competitor that can be beaten, if we choose to compete.

India may have more potential than China in the long run, and possibly more risk. An unbelievable level of poverty (without population controls of China) that will likely take generations to overcome, if ever. Its financial system is also underdeveloped, with bank loans going to government projects and connections rather than the most efficient uses. Its physical infrastructure is horrendous, and it's inconceivable that interstate commerce can take place without major improvements across the country. New Delhi (the seat of government) is chaotic, with a lot of corruption and cronyism. A nation with such a large percentage of its population below the poverty line operates under a much different brand of democracy than in Western societies. And lastly, even though progress is being made for an individual to be able to move from one social class to another, barriers still exist.

Russia is yet another nation to keep our eyes on economically. While Russia isn't viewed today as a direct threat from an offshoring perspective like China and India are to the United States economy, this nation has some attributes to it that will be deceptively powerful relative to competing against us in the future. First, while the Russian economy is roughly half the size of the old Soviet economy before *glasnost*, it continues to possess an amazing volume of the world's natural resources, has a highly educated and Western-knowledgeable workforce, and has sufficient expertise in manufacturing as a legacy of its Soviet days. Today, Russia, not India or China, is the fastest-growing food consumer market in the world. However, immediately following the dissolution of the Soviet Union, Russia spiraled into a severe financial crisis, and in 1992, the first year of economic reform, retail prices in Russia increased by 2,520%! This was due to a decontrol of prices; inflation eventually came down to 240% in 1993, and 224% in 1994.[13] In 1994, the ruble plunged by 27% in one day due to monetary policy. However, Russia started turning it around in the late nineties, at or above 5% growth every year since 1999. For a five-year period of 1999–2004, Russia had a 6.8% average annual economic growth, higher than every country but China. With crude oil and oil products accounting for 45% of its merchandise export revenues, Russia has a solid foundation for trade that is the envy of a lot of nations in this oil-obsessed world. If Russia can parlay these natural resources into a well-founded program for other exports (getting into offshoring programs), Russia will become another viable competitor for the United States.

By the end of 2006, the Russian economy continued to show very strong performance, with Russian stocks hitting record levels. Russia's benchmark stock index, the RTS, hit record levels in 2006, and climbed by 70% during the year. Since Vladimir Putin assumed power in 2000, Russian stocks have increased eighteen-fold, and the economy is now in its eighth year of growth. The world financial market's confidence is high regarding Russia, and we shouldn't be surprised if we start to see Russia evolve more as a player in the game of outsourcing/offshoring.

There are certain attributes that China, India, and Russia all possess that the American public must be aware of in order to respond to the global threat of competitiveness. First, all three of these nations are the largest, most populated nations in the world (China, no. 1; India, no. 2; Russia, no. 3), and the largest landmasses (Russia, no. 1; China, no. 3). Second, all three of these nations were communist/socialist planned economies during the Cold War, and started a liberal-ization/modernization of their economies through the eighties and nineties. Third, all three have been periodically invaded by foreign powers through their history and, therefore, are conflicted in their dealings with foreigners, particularly with the West. Lastly, and perhaps most important to this discussion, is that all three of these behemoths must grow their economies by large-digit growth percentages in order to restore national pride and to remove various nagging social problems, including a large amount of underdevelopment in pockets of the country. Economic power is a source of national pride, particularly where competition with the United States is concerned. These nations will be our largest and most pressing competitors in the future decades. Furthermore, all three of these nations understand America better than we understand them, and they are positioning themselves for success against us in a global competitive setting.

Should America fear a global planet? It has always been a global marketplace, but in the past, it was one where we were always the winners. Today, the playing field is getting flat, and other countries are making a case for their share of the pie. Look at what's happening in China to understand the power of a nation to thrive as an economic superpower. No matter what trade representatives we send to China to ask for concessions, the drum beat of hypercompetition will prevail, and not in the favor of the beggar. In his book *The World Is Flat*, Thomas Friedman recalled when his parents would tell him to finish his dinner because people in China and India are starving. Today, he notes that his advice to his daughters is for them to finish their homework, as people in China and India are starving for our jobs. Having myself looked into the eyes of thousands of Indians with the American-Dream–style hopes and ambitions, I can definitely understand what Friedman means by this statement. This generation of Indians is much like the generations of Americans over the past one hundred or so years that desired and focused on having a better lot in life than their parents had. These individuals are willing to work hard in school, and sacrifice at work to get from their career what they desire. As a purchaser of Indian offshore software development services, I saw this intensity and desire whenever I was in the position to compare Indian firms with American firms. The comparison of the American programmer versus the Indian programmer, or the American manufacturing employee versus the Chinese counterpart, is what America must focus on. Our educational system has become a holding pen for children to be passed through until they graduate. Our workforce is woefully inadequate to be a factor of success in a global economy. These are the areas that we must concentrate on.

Despite all of the good news coming from China and India, I dare to suggest that their populations may *fear the global planet* as least as much as Americans do, and probably justifiably so. China's transformation in becoming a manufacturing power is equaled in significance to its alarming environmental problems. Today, pollution problems cost China 8–10% of its GDP, and 400,000 people die every year on pollution-related problems.[14] Furthermore, only 38% of all cities have acceptable air quality, and 70% of the country's lakes and rivers are seriously polluted.[15] Given the state of the problem, the Chinese government is finally starting to address these issues, but is it "too little, too late," and at what cost to their industries? Pollution might be a bigger threat to China's industry than any foreign competitor.

China needs to only look to India to understand what impact environmental problems can have on a manufacturing economy. India has not only had polluted bodies of water for some time, it is also up against water shortages. Using coal for 50% of its energy needs has left the air in India brutal to breathe, as if there's something always on fire. It's almost inconceivable to understand what the profile of its environment would be if it became a more serious global manufacturer, and perhaps this is one of the main reasons as to why it hasn't. Since 2003, Indian activists and Pepsi have been embroiled in a battle of whether Pepsi has poisoned this nation's groundwater and overconsumed precious water resources. Such battles draw a fine line between the truth of corporate responsibility, and the *fear of a global planet.*

America must understand that the emergence of China and India won't be solved at the negotiation table, but rather the tables of our classrooms, dinner tables, and boardrooms. America must understand that offshoring is a symptom of a larger problem that must be addressed at home and not at trade negotiation tables. By the time it reaches the negotiation table, it is too late. We need to understand the history and the cultures of these great nations in order to understand where they have been; where they have been will in turn give us indications of where they want to go. China has had a love–hate relationship with the world for centuries, and yet it understands today how critical the world market has become to its collective prosperity. Given the dismal failures of Mao, it is moving away from collectivization and protectionism. India too is responding to decades of socialism and colonialism. Despite its social and environmental ills, it is a surprisingly resilient culture, and its younger generations are focused on becoming a global power through intelligence and innovation. Russia wants to regain its glory through utilizing an educated workforce, and significant natural resources. None of these nations are looking back when it comes to outsourcing/offshoring. If anything, each of them wants a much larger piece of the world economy, and is willing to work hard to make it happen.

I have asked the question "Is anyone listening?" In my opinion, America's greatest global threat is that of losing its status, not as the world's military superpower, but rather losing its status as the world's economic superpower. Never before in the history of man have two major nations shown such remarkable growth trends after having such poverty and underdevelopment. Never before has not only one but two economies been able to resist conventional economic thinking by means of having low wages and high-tech capabilities. It is a new world that is emerging, with significantly changed economic realities that our nation must understand in order to succeed. Now are you listening?

# CHAPTER NINE

# The Last of the Spirits

> "Ghost of the Future!" he exclaimed. "I fear you more than any spectre I have seen. But as I know your purpose is to do me good, and as I hope to live to be another man from what I was, I am prepared to bear you company, and do it with a thankful heart. Will you not speak to me?"
> —Charles Dickens, *A Christmas Carol* (1843)

The theme of the classic novel *A Christmas Carol* is an appropriate segue to a discussion of how outsourcing has, and will continue to have, an impact on the workers and businesses of America. Today, in 2007, we need to become Ebenezer Scrooge, and see the past, present, and future of the American economy in the new global marketplace. First, we have seen our Ghost of Christmas Past—not long past, but our past. Our past of being a British Colony, and essentially being born from outsourcing. In the nineteenth century, we became an industrial power, fueled largely by immigration, and set out on a manifest destiny to establish what would represent a new definition of an economic power. Then came the twentieth century when America focused on industrial production, while Europe was preoccupied with wars. By the middle of the twentieth century, our nation was firmly entrenched as the leader of the free world, and the world's greatest economic superpower of all time.

Next, we consider the warnings of the second of the three spirits, the Ghost of Christmas Present. In a twist of fate, America is the nation preoccupied with war, and China and India are the twin success stories to the likes of which has never seen before in the history of capitalism. Until very recently, America has been the uncontested superpower of the global economy, with no serious competitor overall. Our politicians are currently focused on war more so than corporate productivity. Our corporate leaders are realizing unabated levels of personal stock options and bonuses by taking advantage of our short-term–focused accounting system, using methods like outsourcing. Our workers make twenty times more than comparable workers in India or China, unless they are a part of the growing permatemp population who do the same job for 50% less. Our government sector analyzes productivity using old definitions and compares to developed nations instead of new definitions of developing superpowers (India and China). India and China are evolving from low-cost, low-tech providers to low-cost, high-tech providers, breaking the mold for economic development in a global economy. Each of these factors could be viewed as our Ghost of Christmas Present.

Right in the middle of this storyline of the Christmas Present is the whole saga of outsourcing. Is outsourcing good or bad for the U.S. economy? The Ghost of Christmas Past provides healthy evidence to support America's emergence as an economic superpower as a direct result of outsourcing/globalization. Its important for this ghost to appear to the American people so that they can understand how they have benefited greatly in prosperity due to outsourcing, and they can once again. The great American Dream has been at least in part to a net result of the importing of immigrants from all over the world to our country, and the exporting of our ideas and products as a function of our economy. John Kerry, Ross Perot, Pat Buchanan, and other protectionists are fighting our historical precedent. Why not listen to our past?

America is still by far the world's largest economy, albeit slipping ever so slightly (now it's larger than the no. 2 through no. 5, versus no. 2 through no. 6 in 2003). We ask the ghost how is it possible for us to have such serious economic might, and yet feel so increasingly poorer? How can our middle managers be losing their jobs to India when we are so overwhelmingly stronger than other nations? How could our factories be shutting down, with once prosperous and vibrant cities having become war zones today? The ghost points his finger to what we Americans don't typically take the time to look at, either because of our lack of understanding or lack of concern for the rest of the world. The ghost flies us over the challenging landscape of India, and of the children determined to become a part of their growing middle class through education and sheer will. It shows us the determination and hard work present in the country, that same grit that our nation once possessed. Next, the ghost flies us over China, once a nation of peasants, due to Chairman Mao and his dastardly Cultural Revolution, but now brimming with national self-confidence. The ghost shows us a nation working for the common good, with the government vying to support the emerging capitalist enterprise. We see students who were very serious about earning a better living than their parents could earn, an almost exact replication of what the working class went through in America during our Industrial Revolution. Our future as an economic power must start in our classrooms. We see a lot of China and India's present that is eerily similar to our past.

The ghost takes us around the world, to Vietnam, Cambodia, Korea, Poland, Russia, and Brazil—all areas seeking to fight and work harder for greater shares of the world economy. A world with many economies smaller than some of America's largest corporations. When these countries were asked which nation in the world has the largest economy, they all knew the answer to the question.

We were shocked when the ghost presented this picture to us: "You mean, these nations are still in awe of us and our economy? They are working this hard, and they want to take more away from us?" We are shocked to see such competition, such energy to take from us what is ours.

Next, the ghost flies us over some parts of Western Europe. In some of these areas, we see an even greater level of discontent between the workforce and management than we have in the United States, and this surprises us. The ghost points to some brave European politicians who are trying to take on the entrenched establishment of trade unions, farmers, workers, and politicians that are crippling some of these economies, and were banished as a result. As Asia grows, these historic European economies continue to slide farther away from world competitiveness.

The ghost flies us back to America; instead of flying us over our corporations, the ghost takes us over many of our educational school districts. We see that fifteen of our largest cities have graduation rates of 50% or less.[1] As we fly over the inner cities, we see empty spaces in some old schools as a result of high absenteeism and we see outdated methods of learning. As we fly over schools in the inner cities, rural areas, and suburban settings, we see our children being taught in the same manner as they were taught thirty years ago, with little or no recognition that our world has drastically changed. Back when I was a child, there were no personal computers, and not as much of a need to speak foreign languages. Today, the ghost shows us the lack of focus for such programs. Not only are our schools deficient in teaching new skills, we are losing competency in long-term critical ones like science and math relative to the rest of the world. Our standard scores are woefully inadequate and reflect the failure of the system needed that we must maintain the world's largest and most innovative economy. Forget about the low-cost manufacturing jobs in China, our children must be properly educated to maintain higher-paying blue- and white-collar jobs desired by children in other nations. The battle today is in the corporations, but the battle of the future is in today's classrooms. As the ghost shows us, we are not well positioned to win this battle of the future. This is a horrible vision presented to us by this ghost. There is no passion for us to build our educational farm system for competitiveness.

The last scene that this Ghost of Christmas Present presents to us is that of our current state corporations. Awash in a financial system that resembles a casino more so than an economic growth generator, the ghost takes us to New York City during the end of 2006, and shows us record bonuses for Wall Street traders. According to New York Comptroller Alan Hevesi, these bonuses are rose by 17% to a record $23.9 billion in 2006.[2] While there is certainly nothing wrong with the financial community making a lot of money in a free market system, one must wonder whether such a method of profit is an efficient multiplier to future growth or not. Did these individuals contribute to our economy at these levels, or is it truly the casino mentality at work? Whether or not you as a citizen believe that such levels of dividend should be allowed (personally, I think that it's okay if within reason), were these bonuses earned for the right reasons? This is where I would disagree, and say that they haven't been. Today's financial community is rewarded for achieving quarterly earnings that may be contradictory to a use of financial capital that adds value to our economy. If the focus is on short-term quarterly earnings and consumption over longer-term corporate value, and more public investment, would our present state view within the world economy look differently? In America today, it is a boon for our economy to encourage the wide-open, casino approach to the financial community, but how will this affect us in the future? We must tie outsourcing as the *easy out* to this question. We cannot silo outsourcing/offshoring through sterile, isolated conditions, but rather to include dynamic, economic factors that come into play, many of them being quite destructive.

Before we can even begin to consider what the *ghost of our future* will bring, we need to open our eyes to what is really happening today. We are in the midst of declining quality of our educational system, little emphasis in our private sector on true competitiveness and worker-manager relations, a casino mentality for the financial community that doesn't focus sufficiently on investment for longer-term wealth creation, and a lack of a competitive spirit! Ironically, while there is a general understanding of how concerning our present situation is, we really don't understand the ramifications of the problems. We let the politicians play games with us on the problems of outsourcing, and we may have some inkling of how bad manager–worker relations are becoming. If you are a parent like I am, you certainly can't feel very good about our public educational system, no matter where you live. We feel the dangers of the present, yet refuse to act; are we afraid, or unable to take action? Perhaps we are so consumed with everything happening in the world around us to take notice. So many other headlines steal our attention, yet the truth of the matter is that none of these other stories hit home as closely as the economy. Most of us feel like something is wrong, but we choose not to act. That is why we need a visit from the Ghost of Christmas Future.

As you can see from Figure 9.1, the early years of the twenty-first century have provided a continuation of remarkable world economic growth, but this pace cannot continue. China and India have been the key drivers to this growth, and both economies still need growth to sustain their large populations, but both have serious environmental growing pains, among others. China's growth may drop slightly from the 9.5% range, into the high 8%s, while India is likely will see higher growth, more in the mid-7%s for the next five years. In a world economy enjoying record growth, with two juggernauts needing to sustain high levels of growth, the pressure will build tremendously upon the developed economies of Europe and the United States to compete in this environment. The near-term future world economy will only get more competitive as growth slows.

With a tightening global economy, and China and India needing massive growth to fuel their capitalist hungry societies, look for some attention to be paid to the global economy in the 2008 Presidential election. Will any presidential candidate challenge our nation to return to our proud past, and sacrifice in order to become more competitive on the world stage? It is unlikely to be the case. Instead, the Republicans may point to job growth (through their own statistical bodies)

**Figure 9.1**
**Gross World Product**

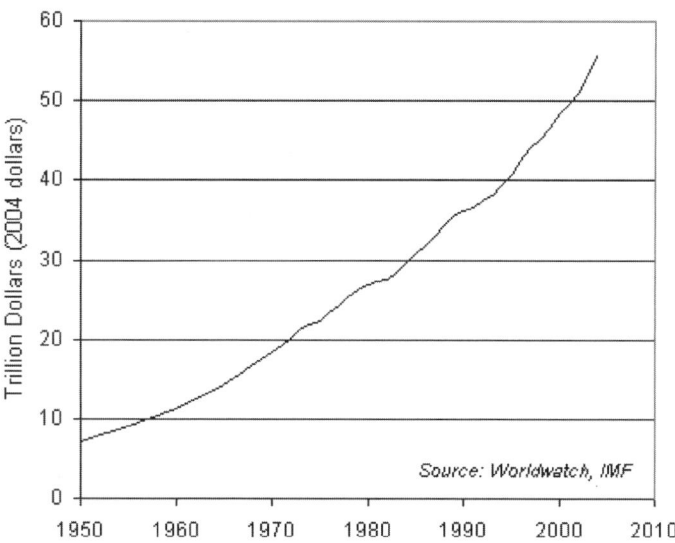

Gross World Product, 1950–2004

*Source: Worldwatch, IMF*

and wealth creation (as noted earlier with the Wall Street traders), suggesting that the approach has been beneficial to all classes of Americans. The Democrats will counter with documentation of inadequate wages for the working poor and high underemployment and will rhetorically focus on the loss of jobs to India and China. They will also cite the record Wall Street profits as another opportunity to play nasty class warfare, as they know that such storylines play well in Middle America. Essentially, both sides will play politics over policy. The *Ghost of Christmas Future* lambasts both groups for not providing the straight story to the American public, or even bothering to understand beyond the rhetorical. Will our politicians take the *easy out* or *difficult in* when it comes to laying out a strategy for outsourcing and globalization for the next four years?

As China, India, and Russia's middle and upper classes grow, it will be increasingly difficult for their governments to contain the enormous pent-up demand of their growing consumer markets; those nations that win the *battle of the middle class* will ultimately win the battle. Today, China already has more mobile phone users than America has citizens, and India's markets are swelling as well. India is even creating market demand among its poorer populations through innovative manufacturing approaches that will make consumer products affordable. Russia is the fastest-growing consumer food products market of all. While a lot of demand will occur for consumer electronics and other products not traditionally produced in the United States, there will be some product opportunities in these countries for manufacturers that take time to learn about local culture and tastes. An increase in the consumer markets for these developing nations will likely be good for business for America's top companies. However, with a consumer market not having as much potential as China or India, America's economy will become less of a consumer of world production, leaving the United States less of an important partner from a trade standpoint. In the new economic realities of the global economy, America's production and consumption becomes less critical, and this starts to become understood right after the 2008 elections.

Although I believe that manufacturing should be an important part of our national economy, when creative destruction does not produce sufficient replacement jobs (36% of those outsourced can find suitable-paying replacement jobs), the real pain occurs on the outsourcing of America's service sector, wherein 60% of our jobs exist today. We haven't even seen the tip of the iceberg when it comes to white-collar outsourcing, or business process outsourcing; in 2005, it was a $22-billion industry in the United States, and in 2014, by some estimates, it will equal $148 billion![3] Personally, I think that this estimate is rather low, because India's managers haven't begun to focus on all of the white-collar opportunities that exist in business today. Knowledge work, which was built up to become the future of work in America, will be possible to be done in every corner of the world in the near future, with an amazingly educated and managed workforce in India leading the charge, supported by a continuous improvement of technology advancement.

In the next five years, India will trend toward a greater role of the *brains of the world*. High-tech innovation labs have been established in India by Microsoft and General Electric to take advantage of an excellent, yet low-cost, educational system, with some of the most intelligent young minds in the world. Eventually, in the late first decade of this twenty-first century, these labs will become Indian, not American, entities. Therefore, the multiplier of job growth that the pundits discuss with respect to outsourcing will diminish greatly. India itself already believes that this will happen.

India will also become prominent by the end of the first decade of the twenty-first century in business process outsourcing as companies begin to understand and connect to how these functions can work in an overseas model. The customer service and IT sector will remain prominent, but other white-collar functions will grow as it begins to dawn on India's managers that much more is possible. All of the white-collar jobs today are on a whiteboard in India, and someone is trying to imagine how to turn these dreams into reality. It will happen later during this decade, and will rattle America's middle class to the core. And yes, it will happen at your and my expense.

Today, 25% of India's GDP is from farming, yet tied to a whopping 70% of the population! Later in the first decade of the twenty-first century, India will develop policies of government that more closely shape China's planned approach to government in a democratic model. Today, 60% of India's growth is due to private sector spending.[4] While this is very healthy for India today, the clog of capital resources within the farming sector, and within the government bureaucracy must be cleaned up. India's leadership will find a national focus to do so in a few years and when it does, it may become more powerful on the global stage than China. Today, India's limitations and constraints are as massive as its creativities and potential. The Ghost of Christmas Future predicts that this will be a focus for India and start to take shape during the late part of our present decade. And when this happens, watch out! India has the most healthy, collaborative environment of brainstorming within the private sector, including foreign enterprises. In 2006, it held its twenty-second annual Economic Summit in partnership with the Confederation of Indian Industry (CII) to address such issues.[5] In my opinion, such thinking will soon rattle the cages of the public sector enough to make a difference, and move more toward a private–public sector collaboration to solve its social problems without stunting growth.

Across the world, other economies will emerge in the next few years as swing economies, which are those providing benefits via lower labor costs and stable sociopolitical conditions in a global economy. Using the China model of manufacturing, these countries will rely on multinational corporations to use their workforces as temporary manufacturing assembly centers that offer more prosperity to their citizens than would exist without such work. Given the flexibility needed today in a global economy, multinationals will leverage such nonstrategic outsourcing opportunities whenever possible, but in a different manner than relationships with China and India. For instance, such arrangements may be used as leverage with these developing powers, or in situations where it just makes logistical sense to manufacture in the Philippines or Indonesia, for example. As these nations emulate the China Model, greater competitive pressures will be placed on all players involved, including the United States. Wal-Mart and other corporate behemoths might well start to form new alliances, and such programs may be leading indicators for where the next big manufacturing opportunity may exist. Many of these swing economies could be enterprise zones of strategic or political importance, such as a region of the world deemed important to stabilize with economic opportunity. America itself has these zones, being its inner cities; why not do the same here?

The Ghost of Christmas Future shows us this picture of the next five years that is unbelievably dynamic, primarily across Asia, and into Eurasia as well. The state of the global economy in the next five years will make the first five years of the twenty-first century look like we were standing still. All we can do when seeing this picture of the near future is open our mouths in awe. This ghost is not trying to shock us, but rather to show us how the trends of today will play out in the future. Again, it is a dynamic picture of the future, and one that should lead to very positive global ramifications from an economic and political standpoint.

The picture shows three prominent regions of the world not as prominent as they should be. The first region on the sideline is that of Western Europe. In the words of one of its most famous philosophers, Jean-Jacques Rousseau, "Man is born free, but everywhere is in chains"; this exemplifies the state of Europe's position in the global economy. As long as much of Europe steadfastly rejects the reforms needed for its industry to be more competitive, it will not realize a growing portion of the world economy. Efforts within the EU to lower protectionism and fix an unhealthy manager–worker balance could make a difference, but it may not happen in the next few years. If Europe doesn't get serious about such necessary reforms, the total EU economy, slightly larger than the U.S. economy, will be significantly smaller than that of the United States, and fall from world relevance.

The second region is the Middle East. This region of the world has distracted itself, and has become a distraction for some countries in the world, notably the United States, and the countries of the EU. Given the importance of oil in the world economy, many of the oil-producing nations of this region could use the revenues of this limited natural resource today to build its industries of the future, and to invest in public infrastructure to support future growth. For instance, it is reported in a journal from the National Academy of Scientists that Iran's oil revenue is dwindling, and if such trends continue, their oil revenue could "virtually disappear" by 2015.[6] The near-term prospects of Middle Eastern nations using their oil revenues to form investments in future GDP is not very promising. With the wars embroiling much of this region, the prospects are unfortunately bleak. It is a wasted opportunity for this region to use its revenues on war instead of future industries.

Unfortunately, the economy of the United States is the third economy that has the potential to lose prominence in the world. From a public policy standpoint, it doesn't help that our nation is distracted by war, weakened by a poor education system, and saddled with a mismanaged commerce infrastructure. From a private standpoint, we have corporate leaders without imagination, trending poor worker–manager relations, and are focused on short-term gains as a function of our financial system. Furthermore, with the growth of the wealth and consumer markets in Asia, America will become less important to world production. Despite government economic statistics (regardless of how accurate they may be), this is a picture of an economy on the wrong side of growth, if changes are not made.

Yet, despite the warnings, and the sensationalists who will prompt the citizens to focus on the economy but use the wrong message, we will not focus our national attention toward this newly emerging global economy. This hypercompetitive global economy began in recent years as countries like India, China, and other developing nations learned rules, played by them, and developed the necessary technological tools to be successful. This amazing hypercompetitive global economy is very new and misunderstood within our American culture. An example of this is in Iraq, where we have 1,000 diplomats, yet only thirty who speak Arabic. This is a cultural, rather than a political, shortcoming. It is the result of our arrogance and cultural ignorance of the rest of the world. It would be hardly surprising for anyone to believe that we are choosing not to focus on the future stars in this hypercompetitive global economy. Yet as the Ghost of Christmas Future warns us, this will be a dastardly mistake, one that we may not recover from in an attempt to maintain our economic dominance in the world.

During the next phase of the future, the next ten years after the first decade of the twenty-first century (the teens), we will perhaps begin to understand what globalization and the emerging economies of China, India, and Russia really mean. *Outsourcing* as a term will have changed in meaning; today, when a corporation moves a part of its operations to another organization with better competencies, it identifies it as a strategic decision. During the teens, *outsourcing* will be an obsolete term, and *globalization* will simply be a catch-all term. Instead of the MNCs (multinational corporations) competing against each other by using low-labor-cost markets, such as those of China and India, MNCs will compete against home-grown nationalistic corporations in India and China, some of them private enterprises and some quasi-public entities. Outsourcing and offshoring, as we understand them today, will be obsolete, and the new definition will be much more fluid and dynamic.

The fulfillment of true globalization (what I am calling the hypercompetitive global economy) will in effect be the only model of production, with the exception of a nationalistic protectionism by nations such as China and India seeking to flex their newfound muscles against remaining an assembly factory or call center for foreign MNCs. What will the obsolescence of outsourcing mean to the U.S. economy? This is the next vision provided to us by the Ghost of Christmas Future. This vision is one of America becoming a shrinking exporter and importer of goods: fewer exports as a result of an undisciplined worker–manager relationship, due to a casino financial marketplace that places more emphasis on short-term profits over long-term investment, and due to an educational system that is trending away from a first-world category. As a result of these factors, America will continue to lose ground in a dramatic fashion for ten consecutive years following 2007 in economic growth, and soon will be competitive in much fewer categories of goods and services. As a result of so many years of lost productivity and a tumbling share of the world's economy, the standard of living in America will decline as well, hampering our ability to be the consumer market of the world. Sometime around 2020, we will be no longer the world's largest economy; we will lose that title to China. Perhaps three to five years later, we will become no. 3, with India overtaking us. Of course, we will still be very relevant owing to brand-name recognition of large consumer products and other commercial goods and services tied to MNCs, but more along the lines of how the United Kingdom or France are relevant in the world economy today.

The Ghost of Christmas Future shows us a glimpse of the political pundits and economists in the year 2020 that will wonder how we let this happen in the years 2003–2007? Some historians from 2020 even will wonder how far this problem existed, perhaps as early as the seventies? And in analyzing our discussions during the early part of the twenty-first century regarding outsourcing, they laughed at our collective ignorance. How could America ever fear a global planet? How could we let the protectionists prevent us from seeing that we have seen the enemy, and the enemy is us? In the year 2020, we may finally seek to learn from these other cultures, but it will be too late; why couldn't we have learned in 2006, or 2007? We could have compared the energy and talents of our workforce and management to what existed in these other societies. We could have learned of the ultracompetitive environment that exists in their school systems, having children very much compete to get into college, and the social structure built around the importance of education. We could have looked at our sagging physical infrastructure in the nation, including that of many of our inner cities. We could have looked at the creation of the marginal workforces through domestic outsourcing, which was far more dangerous in the early twenty-first century to our workforce relations than was offshoring. All of these factors were items that we could have controlled but chose not to do so.

The Ghost of Christmas Future allows us to look even further into the future, to the thirties. During this era, the complete transformation will occur to the world, being Asian-focused. America has transcended into a nostalgic consumer market, still holding onto major world brands, and leading innovation as a result of its strong emphasis on R&D. However, the standard of living of the average American was no longer ten to twenty times higher than these Asian countries, but rather barely higher than some, on par with others, and perhaps lower than a few. In this sort of economic setting, where such a dramatic transferral of wealth happened over such a short period of time, the end result was a world economy truly based on an equal playing field for the most part. Much of Asia and Eastern Europe is on the same relative scale as is America and Western Europe, and a few South American countries joined in as well. As a result of such massive technological inventions and transformations, the world is equal to compete among itself, even peer to peer. This became a model that America cannot succeed within, as was the case within much of Western Europe. Being too bloated for too many decades, and even centuries, these first-world countries couldn't keep up once the world truly became a global economy. It was a sad vision indeed, and a painful one for us to see, only fifteen to twenty years into the future. From a demographical standpoint, evidence supports a growing Asia and a declining America; we must not wait for it to happen.

One other vision that we saw from the Ghosts of Christmas Present and Future was the current threat to our environment and the future consequences as a result. In the past, America has always been the leader in solving the world's problems, such as better food and medicine development/production/distribution that helped much of the world population prosper. Today, both India and China have significant social problems in the environment and their societies that could be solved by American innovation and know-how. Hopefully, America will win this *brain game* and be able to outsource to these countries, instead of vice-versa. In earlier chapters, I asked the question, what will American workers do if we outsource more manufacturing and white-collar work? Here is an opportunity for us to fill in the gap with a lucrative and important future industry. In a global economy, this is creative destruction at its best; why aren't we thinking this way?

But then, in the beginning of 2007, we awoke from the visions that we saw from these three ghosts, the Ghosts of Christmas, Past, Present, and Future. We as a nation collectively leaped to our feet and realized how much of our wealth and potential was squandered over the past two decades or so. Now it was a time to change, but only after viewing how scary our future will be unless we repent, and reform.

For those who may think that my tale of the ghosts of Christmas is a sensational one, or an unrealistic one, think again, and think about how the practice of outsourcing fits in to the story of our past, present, and future. Our past, in some ways, was similar to China or India. We began a colony, and eventually, we grew tired of being economically used, as colonies are, and chose to seek our independence. Having been born out of commerce, and having an abundance of natural resources at our disposal, we grew from a foe of outsourcing, to becoming amazingly wealthy as a result of it. Steaming into the twentieth century, and truly becoming the world's economic superpower after the Second World War, not many Americans were complaining about outsourcing during this period. Incidentally, we became the economic superpower when the prior (Europe) was engulfed in war! The *baby boomers* born after the Second World War have lived in an incredible level of prosperity unparalleled in history. As a result of the greatest creation of a middle class ever seen in modern history, we should obviously praise the practice of outsourcing as enabling this.

But the future awaits us, and it may not be positive today, unless we change our course. Contributing factors to our decline have been a spoiled workforce, spoiled management, the cottage industries always finding a way to make a buck, and a casino economy without enough discipline to sustain economic growth. We are the enemy, not China or India; these nations are simply lapping up what we are dropping. With outsourcing, it has begun to happen, and Americans are starting to feel the pain. Those who profess that the pain is too small need to take a ride with the Ghost of Christmas Past. As a corporate executive watching it unfold, I fear terribly for the state of American business, given the road that we have inadvertently chosen.

As you can see from these dreams, the *easy out* is less about what outsourcing is as an effect, and more about what we need to do to fix the cause, which is somewhat cultural. Many of us born in this country have been handed wealth since the moment that we were born, but today we're competing against Chinese and Indians who have been born into poverty, social strife, and sometimes both. For them, the *difficult in* of business may be seen as nothing compared with the trauma experienced in their lives. For many of our citizens, the *difficult in* of business is the most terrible thing that we will ever face. For example, I was raised middle-class, and never had a major worry in my life, right up to the present day. I have Indian and Chinese counterparts who are much hungrier than I, both literally and figuratively. As Thomas Friedman has noted, there are Indians and Chinese dreaming of ways to take my job from me. These dreams of the future are to warn us that more of this will happen in the future unless we begin to change our course right now.

So you may be asking yourself how you purchased a book about outsourcing and ended up reading about America's lack of guile in corporate productivity, and its weakening social structure with a weak educational system. True, you aren't reading a typical outsourcing book that focuses on blaming every CEO for what's happening, or providing the corporate executive the justification in any case for making it happen in his organization. Furthermore, you may even classify me as a hypocrite, as I have outsourced multiple types of work, and you may perceive this (even after reading this much of the book!) as anti-American. None of the books written thus far have done much to change our national perspective regarding what the real problem is, or even whether or not our nation has a problem relative to outsourcing. Simply making a case on either side of the argument leaves the reader with nothing more than what she started with before she started reading the book. What America needs are some game-changing ideas that we must try as an alternative to doing nothing, or the continuation of destructive patterns. The balance of this book therefore will do just what I have described to be lacking in other discussions on outsourcing: to give the American people an alternative to watching the future unfold as the Ghost of Christmas Future describes it. What this debate needs more than anything are ideas that will make a difference, rather than more cute theories from management consultants seeking to create the latest buzz on the topic.

The next chapter will lay out the major solutions that need to take shape in America to address the problems that face us in our declining ability to compete in a hypercompetitive global economy. These recommendations will address the root causes of the problems, as opposed to the effects. For instance, outsourcing is an effect of a much greater cause. Once American corporations start focusing on strategies that address causes, their competitive skills will improve. The next chapter will lay out a gameplan for all of the parties (private and public), with a particular emphasis on the private, corporate sector.

# CHAPTER TEN

# Solutions, What If...

What if Sitting Bull had a machine gun at Little Big Horn? What if Columbus landed in India after all? Random and potentially insignificant events occur everyday, which have lasting impacts on major themes within a nation, or even the world.[1] Today, events are no different than in the past, no more or less random than how they have played out for thousands of years in recorded time. For us to succeed in the future, we must study the past, not just for facts, but also for patterns. What we must learn is that random isn't so random at all!

What if we learned from the past and the present, and redesigned our future? What if we looked at what the future might be, and tried to determine the impact that our present actions might have? This chapter presents my view of what we need to do today to reshape how the future will play out. I believe that we have an opportunity to make things different, to start a new path. We've all seen recitations of what is wrong; in this chapter I offer solutions. Whether you agree or disagree with my points, what is important is that you take a stance to wake up our corporations, our politicians, our educational administrators, our labor unions, and our workers, to start taking steps forward in this hypercompetitive global economy, to do something. Outsourcing and offshoring aren't *causes*, but rather *effects* of a much larger problem in our economy. For any book to focus on solving an effect without directing attention to the causes would be irresponsible. Beating the drumbeat of protectionism, or high executive compensation, no matter how striking, will not solve the ills of outsourcing, as such approaches have never worked in the history of capitalism. The answers to the problems of outsourcing will not be found by simply labeling outsourcing a problem. We must become practical and focused on solving the problems, or we will not succeed.

Now, I will present the outline of my solutions to the Easy Out (see Figure 10.1).

**Figure 10.1**
**Solutions to the Easy Out**

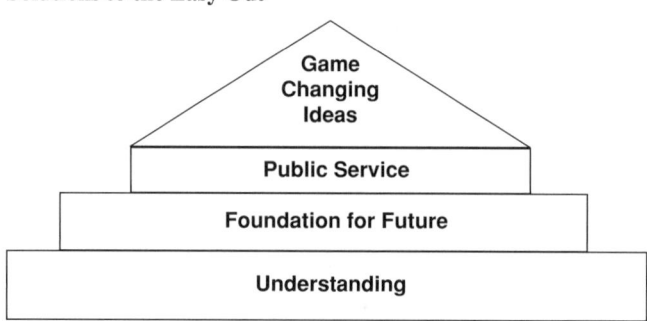

## UNDERSTANDING

The foundation to my solution starts with *understanding*. To solve a problem, you must first understand it. Perhaps many of our leaders (private and public) don't truly understand the problems that exist in private industry in general, and with outsourcing in particular. Without an understanding, corporate leaders often move to ineffective solutions, such as over or inappropriate outsourcing, and offshoring. I am not saying that our leaders aren't smart enough to understand what needs to be done, but rather that they perhaps haven't taken the time to understand the problems and possible solutions. These solutions aren't complicated because, as I mentioned earlier, history continues to repeat itself, over and over again. We've always been a nation that is moving forward, and that mindset has been beneficial for us, but it has sometimes led to us ignoring lessons from the past.

## SOLUTION 1: UNDERSTAND HISTORY

In *understanding* outsourcing, three factors need to be understood by America. First, protectionism doesn't work. Second, outsourcing/offshoring has been our friend since the beginning of our history. And third, competition has made America what it is today.

History tells us that the alternative to open markets—the protection of goods and services with taxes and subsidies—is ineffective. America's history has been relatively clear of protectionist activity, but whenever it has occurred, it has been a disaster. It only leads to inefficient companies, supplying to consumers what they don't want, at artificially high prices. Protectionism won't keep corporations from outsourcing within the new rules of today's global economy.

It is a relatively safe bet that one or more candidates for President in 2008 will proceed on a protectionist platform. Yet, there is no evidence to support that tariffs and subsidies to various sectors of the economy will help the sector improve employment. Furthermore, as is evident through history, the protecting of one sector may cause ramifications in a trade war toward another sector that's not protected. What would happen if we sought to impose any tariffs on Chinese goods? In 2006, Senators Schumer (D, NY) and Graham (R, SC) proposed legislation that would impose a 27.5% tariff on all Chinese imports if they didn't raise the value of its currency.[2] In 2007, other politicians are moving toward similar legislative paths. Per an AFL-CIO report, China artificially lowers the price of its goods by 40% through a fixed currency rate.[3] However, in looking at the documentation provided by the AFL-CIO on the topic, there is no substantiated evidence to show that Chinese currency policy artificially lowers the costs of its goods by 40%. In fact, there is more evidence from academic writings and private enterprise agreements that the market conditions within each private deal will make adjustments for any currency fluctuations, even if the Chinese currency is fixed. In any deal between companies of two different countries, currency cost needs to be considered as a function of the deal. For quite a long time, the Chinese yuan was fixed to the U.S. dollar at about 12 cents/yuan. Today, in June 2007, one yuan is worth 13.1 cents, and this minor currency reform hasn't had an impact on trade balances between the two nations. What can't be denied is the differential between labor costs, and even China's growing competitiveness in low-labor industries, like consumer electronics. Another factor that wasn't addressed is whether activities and worker–manager relations in the United States is helping our manufacturing economy or not; despite government statistics, I haven't seen much evidence suggesting that worker–manager relations in the United States is having a positive impact. An education of the history of what tariffs have brought to our nation appears to be in order. Tariffs will not solve this problem that we have with our addiction to outsourcing, or even our love for lower priced Chinese consumer items. Therefore, the first solution of this chapter is for our politicians, labor unions, and business leaders to read the history of protectionist policies, and its impact on the U.S. economy.

Second, outsourcing and offshoring is our friend, but only when executed properly. Unfortunately, pundits haven't presented clear rationales in detail of outsourcing initiatives in large corporations that have worked, ones that have not, and why they worked or didn't. They didn't bother to articulate or understand the differences between domestic outsourcing, offshoring, and temporary labor and articulate or understand why these help or hurt the economy. And our leaders and pundits don't have a strategy for each that will assist our nation in winning the battle of global outsourcing and competitiveness. History supports the healthy use of outsourcing within a global economy.

With respect to the history of economic competitiveness, Karl Marx and Frederick Taylor have spoken to us regarding what to expect in the new world. Marx felt that the economic value of goods was a function of the labor put into it and that this labor was being exploited because the "instruments of production" fell into the hands of the bourgeoisie. Therefore, a struggle between labor and management was  necessary to create a new distribution of wealth. In this view, a class struggle is necessary. Frederick Taylor's view was the direct opposite of the Marxian view of the need for struggle; Taylor felt that competition could occur in a mutually beneficial manner, even if not totally equitable. Competition occurs when an incentive exists for improvement; if the CEO is rewarded greatly for his or her work and the laborer profits as well (but not as handsomely), that is a mutually beneficial model that promotes productivity.

Taylor believed that competitiveness should mean that parties prosper together, not separately. History shows us that mutually beneficial competition and productivity has been good for America, and that the gains achieved have in the past encouraged strong worker-manager relations. Today's model of competition is not good for all parties involved; surveys note the worker's growing insecurity among high bonuses of executives and financial traders. Our leaders who are looking for answers to questions such as the outsourcing/offshoring question must consider the lessons from history regarding competition; do we want our strategy to be win-win, or win-lose? The answer is clear. Our politicians and other leaders should rally around win-win policies that don't promote class struggle, on either side. We should not prevent corporate managers from earning large bonuses, or outsourcing as strategy dictates. However, corporate governance policies should be put into place to ensure that its leaders only receive bonuses commensurate with their contributions, and that workers get a piece of the pie. Taylor was correct, and Marx was wrong.

History tells us that when outsourcing is properly executed, it is the pinnacle of competition, and creative destruction occurs as a result. History also tells us that strong worker-manager relations are key to productivity and competitiveness, and America can have an edge over China and India by encouraging win–win corporate solutions. Even though there appear to be shades of collaboration between China's corporations and its government, the same cannot be said about its management and the workers. Can productivity continue without workers' rights in a growing economy? In 2004, about 3 million workers joined a total of 57,000 protests in China according to Labour Bulletin, a labor rights group, and over one hundred thousand workers are killed every year on the job.[4] Can an economy that violates workers' rights to this extent continue high growth? America should use this as an opportunity to become more competitive with a joint worker–management focus to compete against China and India Incs.

History repeats itself in the world economy as well. It is estimated that in the early nineteenth century, India and China made up half of the world GDP, but they missed the opportunity of the Industrial Revolution; today, they are a combined 6%. What are India and China learning about what they missed, and what can we Americans learn of history to make sure that it doesn't happen to us? Some are predicting that China's economy will surpass the United States in our lifetime (estimates between 2015 and 2040); we must be prepared.[5]

## SOLUTION 2: UNDERSTAND OTHER CULTURES/LANGUAGES OF THE WORLD

We must gain a better understanding of other cultures and languages in the world to be more competitive. Our schools, corporations, and government must place a greater focus on this for us to continue as an economic as well as a military superpower. Around the world, there is a race among the young to learn English unlike any other period in history. Nonnative speakers of English now outnumber native speakers by a whopping three to one![6] Per language expert David Crystal, "there's never been a language that's been spoken by more people as a second than as a first."[7] In Asia alone, there are 350 million speakers of English, more people than the entire population of the United States! Besides our language, our culture is everywhere you go in the world, on every corner. The world knows us, they *understand* us, and now, many places are trying to master us. They are looking at taking what's best about us, and putting it into their cultures and their business environments. They are looking at competing by learning about their competitor, and everyone's competitor in business is the United States. Everyone wants to be like us, and everyone wants our jobs, our prosperity. But Americans don't understand the rest of the world at a level even close to what will be necessary for us to win this hypercompetitive global economic battle, or even care to. What can be done to change this disturbing trend? There have been some plans in place to change the trend from the Senate, but the execution of these plans is lacking. Senators Lieberman and Alexander proposed the U.S.–China Cultural Engagement Act of 2005, which became the U.S.–China Engagement Act of 2006 that was introduced in April 2006, now referred to as the Subcommittee on Educational Reform.[8] Nothing has happened on this bill, but Senator Alexander sponsored another bill in 2006 that actually made it quickly through the Senate that "statements of national unity, including the National Anthem, should be recited or sung in English." We need to revisit our priorities.

By the time this bill ever winds its way through Congress, if it ever makes it through, hundreds of thousands of Chinese will have mastered the English language, and are ready to compete against the United States. And pitifully, we Americans continue to keep our heads buried in the sand. In February 2006, The Committee for Economic Development (CED) published a statement entitled "Education for Global Leadership: The Importance of International Studies and Foreign Language Education for U.S. Education for U.S. Economic and National Security," asserting that[9]

In order to confront the twenty-first century challenges to our economy and national security, our educational system must be strengthened to enhance the foreign language skills and cultural awareness of our students. America's continued global leadership will depend on our students' abilities to interact with the world community both inside and outside our borders.

Today, only one third of seventh to twelfth graders study a foreign language in America, versus practically every nation in the EU requiring it upon graduation. Of this small amount of students studying foreign languages in the United States, the large portion of the students study Spanish (70% in High School, 50% in College), with a large percentage studying other Romantic languages, like French. As a point of comparison, there are 70 million French speakers in the world, and 1 million Americans studying it, versus 400,000 studying Mandarin Chinese and 1.3 billion speakers in the world! Obviously, in today's world, the Romantic languages aren't as strategic/critical to our future as are Mandarin, Arabic, Persian, and Russian. Even after 9-11, which should have been a wake-up call for us, only 0.8% of foreign-language enrollments are for Arabic! Certainly, we cannot be expected to win the War on Terror or the hypercompetitive global economy with such low numbers of enrollment in Chinese, Arabic, and Russian. During the Second World War, thousands of Americans were trained in Japanese, German, and other critical languages. As is noted by the CED, the critical languages of today are those of Chinese, Russian, Arabic, and Persian, but little effort is being made to encourage the development of these language skills.

How can our nation expect to win outsourcing contracts from China and Russia when we don't speak their language? How can we expect that India, China, and Russia won't win contracts in the United States when they speak ours? The average number of languages spoken by an American business executive is 1.5, while that by a Dutch is 3.9, with most countries somewhere in between. I can dabble in three or four languages (including Mandarin and Russian), and some business colleagues find it to be humorous, but not useful. However, if I were to compare my language skills to those of an average European or Asian, and I would be considered a cultural disappointment. What I've learned by teaching myself multiple languages is a deep appreciation of other cultures, and most importantly and surprisingly, is my improved ability to communicate in my native tongue. There is something about struggling to converse with someone in a nonnative tongue that makes you more clear when communicating in your native tongue.

Perhaps even worse than the lack of foreign-language skills in most high schools is the minimum, if any, coursework in world history, geography, and studies of different areas. As a result, young Americans were second to last (only Mexico was worse) relative to their knowledge of basic world geography. As someone who has spent time volunteering in the secondary school system, and as an adjunct professor at a well-known university, I am shocked and embarrassed regarding America's lack of knowledge of the rest of the world. Comparing my international students to Americans in my MBA classes was embarrassing as well. In the CED report, one corporate respondent noted, "If I wanted to recruit people who are both technically skilled and culturally aware, I wouldn't even waste my time looking for them on U.S. College campuses." This is a sad commentary on our understanding of the world. And given my own personal experiences with American versus international students, I wholeheartedly agree with his notion, unfortunately.

Look at the growing global marketplace; 70% of Coca-Cola's profits are from outside of the United States. With only 5% of the world's population in the world's largest economy, the growth opportunities for our nation economically lie in these other markets, and in defending our markets from increasingly competitive foreign companies. Without a sufficient knowledge of these cultures and languages, what chances do we have at success? What is true at the boardroom is the same on the battlefield; while translators and translating tools can be used, there is no substitution to speaking face to face with the local officials in China, or the citizens in Iraq. General Petreus, when he was the Commander of the 101st Airborne in Iraq is reported to have noted that "we had terrific situational awareness; what we lacked was cultural awareness."

This problem, in my mind, might be one of the most critical issues facing America today; how to become/remain important in a dynamic, interconnected world. Too many of my counterparts from around the world look at us as a bunch of boorish, unworldly, and worst of all, uncaring people. To quote President Bush,

Learning a language... is a kind gesture. It's a gesture of interest. It really is a fundamental way to reach out to somebody and say, I care about you. I want you to know that I'm interested in not only how you talk but how you live.

There is no question that beyond the need to perfect functional skills in the mathematics and sciences, our students must come to understand that the business of America is the world. America must be dedicated and focused on foreign languages and cultures as a matter of priority. I agree with the CED and its recommendations regarding making Foreign Languages and Cultures a top priority[10]:

1. That international content be taught across the curriculum and at all levels of learning.
2. Expanding the training pipeline at every level of education especially critical, less-commonly taught languages such as Arabic, Chinese, Hindi, Japanese, Korean, Persian/Farsi, Russian, and Turkish.
3. National leaders, political leaders, business/philanthropic, and the media inform the public about the importance of improving education in foreign languages and international studies.

Certainly, these recommendations are lofty goals, and they won't be easy to accomplish. Budget dollars are tight, but gaining in foreign languages/cultures will most likely be at the expense of other critical areas of reform. Even if funding were available, where would we get the language teachers needed at all levels of our public educational system? Today, our military branches cannot attract enough of these linguists, so how will our educational systems be able to do so on such a widespread scale? Who will train the trainers? Certainly, the questions of who will train and pay for our future teachers to teach our future business people and military personnel is not a simple one. Given current foreign language educational trends, we should expect China, India, and other nations to continue to gain outsourcing opportunities as a function of their growing abilities and interest, and for America to not, given the lack of such achievements. Shouldn't we consider this to be a critical factor relative to outsourcing?

Today, we cannot solve our outsourcing *easy outs* without understanding the root causes. There is no way that a root cause undiagnosed will ever be solved. A national focus needs to occur to open the eyes of all of our citizens regarding what's happening today. Without this foundation of understanding for our politicians, our business leaders, the media, and professional and trade groups, we have no chance in this hypercompetitive global economy or, for that matter, in a world inspired by terror as a means to an end.

## FOUNDATION FOR THE FUTURE

For America to be economically competitive, our politicians and business leaders must build the foundation for the future. Our leaders must be able to articulate a vision for America that involves sacrifice, because an investment in building this foundation for the future can only occur if we sacrifice to make it happen. Let's face it; Americans aren't great at making sacrifices of any sort. We are a nation of self-interest, and we have succeeded in the global economy through an individual entrepreneurial spirit of can-do-ism. Our history is filled with individual spirits: Henry Ford, Thomas Edison, Orville and Wilbur Wright, and Alexander Graham Bell, to name a few. However, now is the time in our history when we must learn the powerful virtue of sacrifice, such as that which occurs in other countries, such as India and China, both cultures of teamwork and the collective good. In the past, we have succeeded as a result of learning from America's shining light of individualism and innovation to compliment their society over individual culture. Perhaps with the new rules of the global economy, we need a little more focus on our collective infrastructure to allow us to be competitive as a nation.

Not only is our private enterprise system a short-term gratification system, so is our form of government. Public elected officials have two, four, or six years to present a compelling story to their constituents, often from a special-interest standpoint. House of Representative officials who serve two-year terms are more likely to curry favor to their constituents by the addition of a government contract to their home state than they would a long-term investment strategy. When our elected officials are up every two years, and our CEOs are under scrutiny every three months, it is easy to see why our mentalities will remain firmly entrenched within the short-term camp. If our business leaders and elected officials really understand, perhaps they can begin to sell their shareholders and constituents on a longer-term foundation for the future. Such an approach by an elected official will take guts and conviction, but isn't the American public ready for these values? Is the American public really interested in more two-year promises that cycle over and over again for decades? I think not. Instead, I believe that the public is informed well enough to understand and accept a well-articulated foundation for the future. Likewise, I believe that the stakeholders of large corporations are ready for this message as well.

During the Great Depression, F.D.R. sold the American public on public works programs that solidified much of our foundation that contributed to economic success over the next six to seven decades. Our schools, our cities, and our infrastructure became the finest in the world, and all collectively were conducive to a remarkable period of economic growth. Today, China is investing 50% of its GDP in infrastructure, a massive investment! Today, much of our infrastructure is no longer the world's best, and is dramatically falling apart. Our private sector needs this foundation to rely on for economic growth for the future. While many believe that foreign outsourcing is entirely a function of lower costs of living in these developing nations, this is not entirely the case. Increasingly, we are seeing U.S. operations moving overseas owing to a more modern, enabled foundation for business; arguably, some areas of eastern China have better infrastructure than the United States! Increasingly, China and India are moving away from low-cost, low-tech to low-cost, high-tech. What is becoming lost on our leaders is that we must invest in our nation to compete for our future. How competitive will America be within the global market if we are higher-cost, lower-tech? Economic success can only occur with investments in our public infrastructure.

### SOLUTION 3: IMPROVE OUR EDUCATIONAL SYSTEM

In this section, I will discuss three primary "foundation for the future" objectives; our educational system, our public infrastructure (roads/rails/telecommunications/energy), and our inner cities. The first foundation item is the most important, to be competitive against India and China in the future. We will call this battle the *brain game*, and based on recent results, it is clear that we are not winning this battle. The industries that are important today, and will be so in the future—biotechnology, information technology, communications, engineering— all require highly educated and intelligent workers. Per the National Science Foundation, most high school students don't take advanced science, with only a quarter of them in physics and a quarter in chemistry.[11] It also concluded that U.S. students are "devastatingly far" from leading the world in science and math. While government programs like No Child Left Behind are focused to ensure primarily that all students meet certain levels of proficiency, no great focus has happened to determine how to make our students the best in the world. We're so focused on no student being left behind, and yet we're in jeopardy (if it hasn't already happened) of being left behind within the global *brain game* battle!By the start of the twentieth century, America started to gravitate toward a centrally planned, bureaucratic education system, seeking to replace local, allegedly tainted school programs with a predictable, standardized approach. In 1905, the National Association of Manufacturers editorialized that "the nation that wins and has success in competition with other nations must train its youths in the art of production and distribution." The German educational system at that point was the crown jewel of the world. American business, along with Labor, pressed Congress to expand federal spending on education, focusing on areas important to manufacturing. At this point in our history, all the way through the Second World War, our educational system had a purpose, and private and public enterprise were together, and behind this purpose. Today's level of productivity of education dollars is significantly below America's productivity in 1970,[12] not even comparing how far we are falling behind other nations.

After the Second World War, American business and national organizations continued to pressure our public administrators to make our educational system more competitive. With the "Sputnik Scare" of the 1950s, and other threats, business leaders always have successfully beaten the drum for change. We must understand the math and sciences, and as will be mentioned later in this chapter, we are deficient in comparison to world leaders in both of these.[13] In order for us to compete with India and China, we must invest in our educational system; we must sacrifice to do so.

Our new "Sputnik Scare" is the "Asian-Scare." School enrollment in India has increased up to 90% since 2000; in primary school alone, it has 202 million students being taught at a million schools. At the university level today, it will produce 3.1 million college graduates, which will double by 2010! Its top universities, such as the Indian Institute of Technology, are the best in the world bar none. China has a lot of catching up to do (given Mao's Cultural Revolution debacle), but it is now spending 3.2% of its GDP on education (United States' is at 5%), which is higher than ever before. With almost 220 million in grade to high school, it is as well a growing educational phenomenon.

Another *easy out* excuse for the United States is to consider our problems "a funding problem." From 1951 to 1991, the annual expenditure per student in U.S. public schools went from $1,189 to $5,237, a 350% increase! The average salary of a public school teacher rose by 45% in real wage terms from 1960 (the first year that data were available) to 1991; that is frequently another *easy out* rallying cry, regarding teachers' pay. Yet with dramatic increases in teachers' pay and funding per student, the average SAT scores fell 41 points between 1972 and 1991.[14] Having taught in an M.B.A. program, I was shocked how difficult it was for me to sometimes understand the content of a graduate student's ideas and answers due to poor basic grammar/vocabulary and quantitative analysis skills. At many universities, remedial instruction is provided for students, and not just for international students. Per Chester Finn, a former Reagan Administration official, "surely college ought to transport one's intellect well beyond factual knowledge and cultural literacy. But it's hard to add a second story to a house that lacks a solid foundation."

Why is our educational system failing us when we need it the most for this hypercompetitive global competition? First, look at the state of our school systems and administrators. Hardly to be considered as innovative and progressive, many of these organizations are saddled with bureaucracy, tenure focus, and a focus of compliance over quality. School boards are politically elected officials, and are either preoccupied in many cases with the political whims of their constituencies, or the mounds of rules that they must adhere to in order to not offend any group. In Denver, an old, historic high school that I work with, North High School, was saddled with poor CSAP scores, and was losing students rapidly to better-performing schools. However, being unable to hold individual teachers accountable for performance, the administrators were handcuffed. This school was heading for closure, when the community stepped up, and sought to keep it open. Being a largely Hispanic working-class neighborhood, this school was a critical landmark to the economics and psyche of the community. Through civic pressure, the school board ordered a dramatic reorganization that would have each teacher reapply for his or her job, as holding each teacher accountable for performance wasn't possible. The good news is that this reorganization will hopefully save this critical school. The bad news is that the principal and administrators should be able to make less transformational changes every year in order to ensure the success of the school. Denver is unfortunately one of the fifteen big cities with a high school graduation rate of 50% or lower.

Having spoken to high school administrators and teachers, it's clear that today's teacher is ill suited to drive world-class performance through his or her training and the class budgets. Not many schools have sufficient math, science, foreign-language, and geography programs to compete in this hypercompetitive world. Furthermore, with lower pay than the private sector, and no incentive/punishment program for student performance, why would we, the American public, expect anything to change? Mediocre teachers dominate teacher unions, top–down school administrators drain innovation from many good students, and elected school officials pander too much to special-interest groups. For a teacher trying to make a difference, what's the incentive? There aren't bonuses for better student results, and lesson planning is so centralized that it cannot be anything other than unimaginative. We are moving away from, not closer to being the best and most innovative school system in the world. There is no substantive rallying cry today like the one that surrounded manufacturing during the early twentieth century, up to the Second World War. There is no rallying cry today like the one that surrounded math and science after the "Sputnik Scare." But maybe there needs to be an "Asian Scare" rallying cry regarding the Indian and Chinese students who are studying a lot harder than our young are, and are squarely focused on stealing our jobs through a hypercompetitive global economy.

Such a rallying cry needs to exist today in the field of science. By the time that U.S. students reach their senior year of high school, they rank below their counterparts in seventeen other countries in math and science. U.S. high school students ranked last of sixteen countries tested in physics. Today, in our schools, we have a severe shortage of qualified science teachers, which is a real problem. An amazing 28% of those who teach at least one science class between seventh and twelfth grades don't have a major or minor in science.[15] Even those who have science degrees are often teaching out of their specific area of expertise. For our future, we must establish a farm system that allows us to win the *brain game* relative to science. What happens if we don't raise our students' levels of science closer to that of the competition? For the past decade, we have imported brainpower, but it appears as if this is slowing down. In 2000, people who were born abroad filled 38% of the jobs requiring a Ph.D. in science or technology.

In 1990, only 24% filled these jobs.[16] The worst part of this news isn't that more foreigners are filling in for our losing the *brain game*, but rather the fact that we are already seeing corporations respond by simply outsourcing the entire Ph.D. function to an overseas operation. After all, why relocate so many Indian engineers to the United States for software development when such development can be done in India? India has 520,000 IT engineers making about $5,000 a year. According to Eric A. Hunushek, a professor at Stanford University, if America raised its performance in science to that of Western Europe within a decade, our Gross Domestic Product growth would be 4% higher by 2025, and 10% higher in thirty years. Perhaps this is wishful thinking, because the real competition isn't Europe, but rather China and India. But we will most certainly lose market share and GDP growth if our test scores in math and science continue to fall as they have been.

Look at India's educational philosophy. Besides having some of the best post-secondary schools in the world (Indian Institutes of Technology and the Indian Institutes of Management), there are growing centers of excellence in science, engineering, medicine, and the liberal arts. Both the parents and the students are incredibly motivated toward success. That level of commitment between the parent and the student is almost impossible to realize as an expectation here in America. Competition for admittance of India's top students at the top schools is fierce, and only through strong secondary schools and very supportive family networks is admittance possible. In India the focus of innovation is in the private schools. There is a lot that we can learn from India when it comes to competition and driving success through a school system, and a family.

Another *difficult-in* solution that needs to be addressed is the typical lack of commitment of the American parent versus that of India or China. While the level of passion and commitment from an Indian parent is off the chart relative to other developed nations, such as the United States, we don't have this sort of passion. In general, parents are more focused on television at night than they are working with their child on its homework assignment.

One of the biggest barriers to change is the inability to imagine and execute upon something different. This is true for both the educational system and the corporations competing within a hypercompetitive global economy. What about different uses of the Internet in school? What about foreign languages, and innovative uses in ways to move forward without many accomplished language teachers (using the Internet and televisions, for example)? What about links via computers and videoconferencing to India and China? Computers for all uses in wonderful new, imaginative ways, using the technology to create and to sharpen minds.

What about math? Instead of using stale, mechanical approaches to teaching math, how about teaching mathematical concepts as applied to real-world problems, as opposed to having students simply memorize steps or tables. Why not use new types of teaching of today without abandoning the basics? Arguments against new concepts of teaching is precisely what's wrong with our education system; instead of using new innovations and techniques to complement foundation/existing ones, they are often silenced as being outside standard teaching approaches. This is an unfortunate *easy out* fallout to reform in our educational system.

One other interesting idea is the Individualized Education Plan (IEP); it is an individualized approach to understanding the child's skills and deficiencies. The argument in favor of real IEP's is that it is not possible for any teacher to teach a group of six-year-old children to read without understanding each of their unique differences. Today's lesson plans seek to have all students succeed through the same standard approach that was used the prior school year, and so on. This method simply identifies our educational approach to be a "cattle call," ushering the students through the system and out to society to become a productive worker. Again, this isn't a shot at the teachers being asked to do the work, or even possibly the administrators to conform their approach to the draconian rules of the school board, but is anyone paying attention? Are we paying attention, or fooling ourselves into thinking that this bland approach of conformance will work in our society?

Back in the beginning of the twentieth century, our educational system had a purpose to support the growing manufacturing arena of our economy. Through the Second World War and beyond, that was the same purpose of our educational system. Starting with the 1960s, a new purpose emerged with a need for our science and math to be strong enough to compete with the Soviets during the Cold War. As a result, some very critical innovations came about, including the Internet and mobile technology. Today, our educational system doesn't have a purpose. If you believe that it does, what is that purpose? Today, the purpose, if you were to consider it to have one, would be to comply with the bureaucratic rules, to ensure compliance and political correctness in the system, and to "leave no child behind." Yet there are two major rallying cries that our educational system could build a strategy around: one, the events of 9-11, and not truly understanding the world around us. If it wasn't clear before 9-11, it is certainly clear today that we must understand the world for them to understand us. The second rallying cry is the foundation of this book—to build our competitiveness in order to halt the massive impact on our national economic superpower status as a result of growing threats around the world, most notably those of China and India.

There are several *easy outs* related to our educational system. The first is that our educational system continues to practice the same teaching methodologies over and over, emphasizing compliance over innovation and world competitiveness. Despite America's dismal performance in our test scores compared with the rest of the world, there are few sweeping material changes being considered or implemented. Another *easy out* related to our educational system is the continuous cry of insufficient funding. Relative to the spending done in other nations, our educational system is well funded, and yet we're not competitive. And what about the *easy out* of parents? In India, the parents of many students are so dedicated to helping their children succeed that they won't accept any social invitations during the school year. Competition is steep, and the parents' first priority is to ensure that their children compete in this environment. In other developing nations, there are similar levels of commitment from parents. In America, our *easy out* is to expect the school system to educate your children, when in fact this is simply one leg of a three-legged stool. The child must have other tools for learning outside of the school and home, such as specific and even alternative methods of training. This second leg could be involvement within the Girl Scouts, camps, Sunday School, or whatever. The third leg, of course, is that of the home as the center for learning. Spending time with your children after a long day of work is truly the *difficult in*, but one of great necessity. Parents must get much more involved with their children for us to raise a new generation of workers who can compete against the India's and China's of this hypercompetitive world economy.

## SOLUTION 4: IMPROVE OUR NATION'S PHYSICAL INFRASTRUCTURE

As was noted in Chapter 7, both China and India are spending billions annually to improve their undeveloped national infrastructures. Today, it is obviously easier to travel both personally and commercially across the United States than it is to do so across China, India, or Russia. As a result, our economy has had significant advantages both from an import and an export standpoint that these developing nations do not. However, as a result of our lack of focus on physical infrastructure, for the most part, over the past decades, our system is on the decline at a time when we can least afford it to be failing us. The American Society of Civil Engineers (ASCE) gave our infrastructure a grade of D in its 2005 report.[17] Americans are spending more time stuck in traffic, including commercial drivers. Hurricane Katrina was a cautionary event regarding how inefficient attention to secure our infrastructure can lead to disastrous results. While the Department of Homeland Security and other agencies are rightfully concerned about the impact of a potential terrorist event, Hurricane Katrina presented a much scarier proposition; that our physical infrastructure will fail our economy and us if it is not upgraded as quickly as possible. According to the ASCE, an investment of $1.3 trillion over a five-year period is necessary from our public and private sector in order to improve conditions to acceptable levels. Such an investment is not just a matter of convenience, but is rather a dire need for interstate commerce and international trade.

The infrastructure needed for our commercial markets is either eroding, heavily congested, or both. Of the 12,000 miles of inland waterways operated by the Army Corp of Engineers, nearly 50% of the infrastructure is inoperable. By 2020, if nothing changes, that amount will increase to 80%. Obviously, the state of these waterways has, and will have a significant impact on our economy. There is today a lot of focus on our ports due to increased threats of terrorism, but even without this, the increased volume of 10% annually is log-jamming these facilities. While improvements are occurring, including automation and process improvements, the total effort seems well below the increases in commercial traffic. The growth of Chinese imports has really affected the large ports on the West Coast, particularly

Los Angeles and Long Beach, California. East Coast ports now have difficulties handling the new generation of supersized cargo ships, if some ports can handle them at all. There isn't much planned renovations or new port construction being undertaken to increase capacity, and the inland infrastructure to handle the freight once it's off the ship (cross-docking facilities, as an example) are shaky at best. Having been intimately involved in this business lately, I can tell you that finding reliable and available ports to handle your import or export requirements is difficult indeed, particularly during the peak consumer seasons. For America to improve its commerce capacity as a manufacturing power, it must review the viability of its seaports, beyond any critical Homeland Security concerns. Port capacity will be a significant underlying factor for America's ability to be competitive in the global marketplace of the future. As well, even with significant capacity, supporting business processes and productivity must support American competitiveness: some suggest today that our biggest problem at the ports isn't capacity, but rather productivity!

In the rail area, we have limited rail capacity in this country for the first time since the Second World War. This is because with a nation focused on highways and cars/trucks, little emphasis has been given to using rail as a transportation option. With the rising price of fuel and the increase of global trade, rail service increasingly becomes an important variable. First, the railroads are primarily focused on capacity, and not service. Second, many businesses seeking rail as a solution are not physically located close enough to a rail spur to be served by it. Even for those companies that are able to have service from the rail companies, congestion and inefficient operators have affected the level of service that they should expect. Rail intermodal traffic has quadrupled since 1988 (primarily due to international trade), rising from 5.9 million loads to 12.2 million in 2006, and will grow dramatically over the next ten years.[18]

Can our critical infrastructure situation allow us to win in this hypercompetitive global economy? In the *Supply Chain Digest's* annual logistics report, Rosalyn Wilson stated[19]:

We have not made sufficient investment to maintain and improve our aging transportation system and it can no longer meet the needs of the record setting growth in freight flows. We face capacity constraints at virtually all major freight gateways and congestion and bottlenecks throughout the system as it approaches full capacity.

Not only this, it is noted that Asian ports are six times more productive than American ports: as I mentioned earlier, many suggest that our biggest problem at the ports is productivity, not capacity. Who is taking responsibility for doing something about this: the ports, the cities, the states, the Feds, the Unions, the cargo carriers, who? Today, the answer is sadly, nobody. What about our clogged airways, or our overloaded highways? Per the ASCE report, it is noted that it will cost $9.4 billion a year for twenty years to eliminate all bridge deficiencies.[20] The underinvestment over a long period of time has occurred as a result of a lack of a strategic federal transportation program. But don't stop there, as virtually all aspects of our infrastructure are in bad shape. An oil pipeline supporting the largest U.S. oil field (8% of U.S. production) needed to be shut down in Alaska in August of 2006 due to "unexpectedly severe corrosion." This affected oil production seriously for months, sidelining hundreds of thousands of barrels of oil from out of the U.S. economy at a time when oil prices were already at record setting levels.

What about the rolling blackouts experienced on the East Coast in the summer of 2003? Electrical outages cut service east to New York, west to Detroit, and north to Toronto, affecting up to 50 million people. This power outage cost New York City alone half a billion dollars in lost revenue, according to estimates from the City Council. California as well has experienced electricity brownouts, although mostly due to improper energy management and scandal. However, with so much of the United States having faced, and potentially facing in the future, such energy issues, can we trust the reliability of our energy sources without significant upgrades in infrastructure? It is likely that such outages will happen again in some of the most populous areas in the United States.

For so many politicians, the *easy out* of these problems is to either blame another branch of government (states blame feds, and vice versa), or to manage them through crisis only, always waiting for the next disaster to take action. In addition, many transportation projects authorized by Congress are done with political gain in mind, not need. A recent large Highway Bill passed by Congress contained some 5,000 earmarks for projects by members of Congress seeking to court their constituents' favor. The most famous of these was the "Bridge to Nowhere" in Alaska, a bridge between two islands that will serve fifty people and cost the American taxpayers $200 million.[21] Unless our politicians start to look below the surface, infrastructure problems will continue to erode our competitiveness and create major impacts to our economy. Hurricane Katrina of 2005, the East Coast brownouts of 2003, and the Alaskan Oil Pipeline shutdown of 2006 are major warning signs of infrastructure that must be addressed. Are our politicians ready to take the *difficult-in* to address? Hopefully. If not, this will certainly have major impacts to how competitive we will become with the world economy in the future.

Sometimes, if we look to other countries for ideas, we will find solutions that can work in the United States. South Korea is a good example. Despite rapid economic growth during the 1980s, the country took a nosedive in 1989 amid the Asian financial crisis; growth rates were cut in half, and it appeared to look like an economy entering the mature stage, with slower development. Among other reforms, South Korea instituted a large government investment program in its infrastructure in an effort to keep up with regional competitors such as China and Japan. A bullet train system to serve the nation was developed, and investments in broadband infrastructure have taken place. Government investment and research in such critical fields as biotech and nanotech are occurring, and have been successful. The government had to take the lead with respect to these activities given the global nature of its local corporations. Only through public investments in new schools, communication systems, modes of transportation, and research facilities can South Korea become more competitive in this hypercompetitive global economy.

The last area of infrastructure that must be addressed is that of energy. The United States currently imports 50% of its oil, versus only a third during the 1973 crisis. With U.S. oil refining already at 97% capacity, there is little room for economic growth, which is largely dependent on oil. With estimates of imported oil in 2025 being 70%, and no programs in sight to increase our overstretched oil-refining capacity, our ability to grow as an economic world power must be an area of concern. New oilfields can be found, and efficiency levels of vehicles can and must be improved, but these actions won't be enough to offset what is becoming our greatest peril of outsourcing of how to solve for energy problems around the world. A 2000 U.S. Geological Survey estimated that there were three trillion barrels of recoverable oil worldwide. World petroleum reserves are finite, and the U.S. reserves are very small in comparison to OPEC and the rest of the world. With this natural resource in so much demand yet being so finite, and America's position so fragile, it is easy to see that our continued economic growth is dependent on solving this problem. In terms of motor vehicle use, China's fuel consumption is where the United States' was in the 1910s, and growing rapidly. With greater competition occurring for precious world resources, America must develop *difficult-in* strategies for oil use and production, rather than today's easy out of ignoring the problem. While a lot of discussion regarding outsourcing focuses on Chinese imports by Wal Mart, what about the gasoline you purchase everyday as an import of concern? We must improve the infrastructure of roads, airfields, waterways, and rails to reduce our dependence on foreign oil. We must have more efficient electrical utilities to reduce our dependence in that area. This battleground will be a key *Brain Game* for the world in the next couple of decades, offering many jobs to the winner, and outsourcing of brainpower to other nations for the losers.

## SOLUTION 5: FIX OUR INNER CITIES

Let's face it; we cannot expect today's corporate executives to spend their time focusing on domestic problems. They are too busy trying to compete in this hypercompetitive global economy. Most managers spend every minute simply trying to keep their heads above water, and cannot focus on much else. However, the corporate managers who have offices in the inner cities are reminded daily of these travails on their way to work. The homeless begging for money, and decay all around their polished office settings. As a native of Baltimore, and having spent much time in several of the largest cities of the East Coast, I view our largest cities as opportunities for solving the *easy out*. Instead of shipping jobs overseas to cheap labor, why not create innovative manufacturing solutions to render production costs competitive in some of our most economically depressed areas? If India can create innovative manufacturing solutions for low-income Indians, why can't America create manufacturing opportunities that are cost competitive in our inner cities? Look at some studies that suggest the net savings of some offshoring to be only 10–20%, and look at some of the "unexpected costs" associated with doing business in a developing nation thousands of miles away, and tell me that America can't find innovative solutions for utilizing our inner cities.

Others have already seen this as a viable suggestion, albeit on a small scale. In its seventh year, Inner City 100 is a list of the fastest-growing companies in America's inner cities. This program is in a partnership with the Initiative for a Competitive Inner City (ICIC) led by the well-known professor Michael Porter from Harvard.[22] Such grassroots programs are successful on the scale that it is started within; over five years, it has created more than 11,000 new jobs, all of them at a decent wage within the zone of employment. Of these companies, 88% of them rated the inner city location as good or excellent, and 72% rated their location as better than what it was three to five years ago. Of those who have participated, 75% have been in services, 15% in manufacturing, 5% in retail, and 4% in wholesale/distribution. While this is a good start, it is on such a small scale that it can only be viewed as a philanthropic effort in the private sector than it potentially could be a private–public joint venture on a much larger scale.

Instead of outsourcing, why not move toward making our inner cities manufacturing centers? If the net savings associated with outsourcing manufacturing to China can be as low as 10% benefit, why couldn't our public sector create enterprise zones in our most depressed cities? With a focus on scientific management, why couldn't BPO become the next big thing in Baltimore, Detroit, or Gary, Indiana? Such is the innovation that we need to bring forward for our foundation for the future.

## PUBLIC SERVICE

In considering possible solutions needed for American corporations to no longer take the *easy out*, I began by asking Americans to understand, as I believe that many of the business problems today exist as a result of a poor understanding of history and the world. Outsourcing and offshoring are symptoms of a larger problem, with the foundation of this problem being a lack of understanding of the world, and of history. Once we understand, we can craft a successful game plan. That successful game plan must start off with a *foundation for the future*. During the early part of the twentieth century, our nation looked forward, and its people sacrificed for a better life for its younger and future generations. In Asian cultures that share more of a focus on *we* versus *me*, this is happening today; investments in education, in their national infrastructure, and in their depressed regions are an investment in our future. It is ironic that these same three areas of investment that exist today by India and China are also critical to America today, and yet we aren't investing as much. American business needs to become more competitive, and to do so, it needs a stronger foundation for the future.

Even if we build the *foundation for the future*, what's next? In the next section, I will discuss solution areas that our politicians must focus on, and then the following section will be what our corporate leaders must do. What's important in these next sections are two things: one, the solutions must be achievable and action-oriented instead of platitudes and generalities. And second, these solutions must focus on the problems and not the symptoms, as many pundits seem to gravitate toward.

## SOLUTION 6: ESTABLISH A RELIABLE, VALID, AND INDEPENDENT FEDERAL STATISTICAL BUREAU

For our government to compete, we must have a statistical bureau that is reliable, valid, independent, and powerful enough to support innovation. In a competitive information-based world economy, the development of reliable and valid statistics is essential. Public servants must be able to make decisions based on the most accurate data from as much varied information as is available, and these data should be provided to American corporations as "competitive intelligence." Yet in looking at the fiscal year 2007 budget, a very disappointing picture is presented regarding the use of statistics in our federal government. The responsibility for the collection, analysis, and dissemination of statistics is spread throughout all departments, with each of the seventy or so agencies having at least $500,000 allocated for statistical analysis. On top of this, there are thirteen different agencies that are in place specifically for the collection, analysis, and dissemination of statistics. Obviously, statistical data should be a single source of truth, which is obviously difficult to achieve when so many interlinking government entities are capturing and analyzing the same information. Having such a decentralized approach to federal statistics appears to be in place as a bastardization of the importance of statistics in government. Consider the following 2007 budget (Table 10.1).[23]

Beltway politics is obviously more important than a credible statistical system. Compiling, analyzing, and interpreting all of the information that affects our nation is a massive task and, as such, needs a focused and extensive amount of financial resources associated with the task. None of these budgets on its own is able to achieve this purpose, or to provide the relevance needed for statistical analysis in today's hypercompetitive world economy. Turning information into data with today's technological advances can be a major competitive advantage for a government or corporation. Many of the data collection routines that exist today in both the public and the private sector are outdated, and useless, such as the use of voluntary surveys for data collection. Using RFID technology, for instance, has amazing potential for those who understand how to utilize this tool in today's fast-moving world economy. But establishing the infrastructure needed to make RFID and other latest technologies is not cheap. Therefore, the consolidation of our statistical activities into one statistical bureau that can focus on putting the infrastructure in place to accurately and objectively turn information to data makes a lot of sense. If we are serious about American competitiveness, we will demand this initiative immediately.

Asking our government to consolidate statistical bureau operations is not without precedent in our recent history. There have been functions of government that

**Table 10.1**
**2007 Federal Budget for Statistical Analysis**

|  | FY 2005 Actual | FY 2006 Estimate | FY 2007 Request |
|---|---|---|---|
| (All data in million dollars) |  |  |  |
| Bureau of the Census: Current Programs | 196.1 | 195.5 | 184.1 |
| —Periodic Programs | 548.7 | 606.4 | 694.1 |
| Bureau of Labor Statistics | 529.0 | 537.1 | 563.3 |
| Bureau of Economic Analysis | 72.6 | 75.3 | 76.5 |
| Statistics of Income, IRS | 38.5 | 40.5 | 41.5 |
| National Agricultural Statistics Service | 106.0 | 110.2 | 116.0 |
| —Census of Agriculture | 22.4 | 29.1 | 36.6 |
| Economic Research Service, USDA | 74.2 | 75.2 | 82.5 |
| Energy Information Administration | 83.8 | 85.3 | 89.8 |
| National Center for Health Statistics 1/, 2/ | 109.0 | 109.0 | 109.0 |
| National Center for Education Statistics 2/ | 90.9 | 90.0 | 93.0 |
| Bureau of Justice Statistics | 46.7 | 46.2 | 59.8 |
| Bureau of Transportation Statistics | 26.3 | 26.7 | 27.5 |
| Science Resources Statistics, NSF | 31.0 | 33.0 | 36.0 |

*Source:* White House, Office of Management and Budget, 2007.

have been consolidated for the public good, such as the consolidation that has occurred in Homeland Security. Statistics are important objective tools needed for the development of sound policy. With a consolidation of funding, which would follow the consolidation of function, the statistical component could establish a state of the art information technology system. A neutral, unbiased statistical system would make some of the bipartisan politics regarding whether outsourcing and offshoring is good or bad for our economy disappear. While statistical analysis certainly isn't a perfect science, the goal of a statistical component should be to make it as close to perfect as possible. The current government strategy doesn't even pretend to have this as a goal. It would be impossible to conclude that over seventy units in twelve separate cabinet departments performing government statistical analysis is an efficient and effective approach.

In the past, Congress has considered the consolidation of federal statistical bureaus into one Bureau of National Statistics (BNS), but such efforts have never materialized. Why? I have seen very few arguments proposing logically that statistical collection, analysis, and dissemination should be left in the hands of numerous government agencies. Much like corporate politics, a leader should only be willing to fight a political battle when the gain to be achieved is greater than the price to be paid for fighting the battle. It is likely that few politicians, or even corporate leaders, have pushed too hard on this issue, given the lack of a demand for scientifically managed government. This is where the understanding must take place, as there may not be a bigger cause today for our economic future than having reliable, valid, and objective statistics for the use and development of our future policies in the world economy. The *easy out* is for our leaders, both private and public, is to argue in favor of the status quo, weak, subjective statistics, or no statistics at all. The *difficult in* is for us to dedicate ourselves to making objective, logical decisions to be competitive in the future. Our politicians must take on this battle as a matter of priority.

One more point: in the old economy, reliable, valid, and objective statistical data were less important than they are today. Today, regulatory and trade policy is heavily dependent on government statistics. Many think that our government overstates and China's government understates the bilateral deficit between the two countries. The funny truth is that if you added together the balances of all of the governments of the world, there would be a world deficit, as if the Earth is trading with Mars! Despite all of the gamesmanship that goes on between and across countries, our citizens depend upon our government to establish the soundest economic policies possible within the world economy. An economic statistical bureau that is the best in the world would give us a competitive advantage in determining economic policy, and that's what's most important to us. Establishing the best national statistical bureau would be a major step for America to show its people and the rest of the world that it is serious about winning in the hypercompetitive world economy.

## SOLUTION 7: REFORM OUR FINANCIAL REPORTING SYSTEM

Let's say that our policy makers today decide to establish the finest statistical bureau in the world in the next five years. Imagine how much of an advantage our corporations would have in competing with foreign corporations that wouldn't have such a system. Now, think what would happen if we had government accounting rules in place to enable us to be more competitive, rather than preventing success through overregulation. I believe strongly that our public accounting system currently in place does more to discourage than enable competition. As a result, *easy outs* are taken quite frequently because of a financial reporting system that can present inefficiency as more efficient. Third parties understand the difference between adding accounting value versus adding economic value, focusing on the former as what the customer typically wants. Of course, most third party vendors would wish to start off trying to focus on economic value, but doing so is a difficult proposition for many Fortune 500 corporations. Instead, consulting firms and third parties take the *easy out*, which brings in revenue for them, and makes the corporate manager look good for one year, perhaps, before the wheels fall off on the deal. This happens so often in Corporate America that third parties and consulting firms are developing strategies based on accounting gimmicks rather than true productivity savings. This has formed the basis for the cottage industry that I have written so much about.

Therefore, the first solution regarding our public corporate accounting system is one that focuses on economic value versus accounting value. To understand the differences between the two, we need to think back to 1934 with the creation of the Securities and Exchange Commission. Prior to 1934, neither the Federal Trade Commission nor the New York Stock Exchange required companies to produce periodic reports. Since financial statements are the most widely used and comprehensive way of communicating financial information about a business enterprise, this reporting mechanism from the management to the stockholders has become somewhat controversial in the hypercompetitive global marketplace of today. For one, both investors and corporate managers feel that financial information and compliance factors provided to and from them is overload, and of very little use in their analysis. Only 3% of all investors actually use annual reports in their investment decisions, and the average investor spends 5 to 15 minutes reading the report. In addition, the format of these reports is becoming too complex and complicated for even the institutional investor to understand, or even care about. An external user may be presented with 100,000 characters of information whereas the company's operation explained in detail contains 100 billion characters, according to a study done in 1994. The public accounting system in place intends to wisely determine the parameters that a corporation must follow in providing the most accurate, reliable, and objective 100,000 characters out of 100 billion, but as you can see mathematically, it is a difficult endeavor, and must be handled efficiently.

It was noted in an earlier chapter that financial data are not objective, and we know this to be true, no matter what financial accounting system is in place. But the recent history of U.S. accounting has played out to have a means-to-an-end focus on accounting principles versus the measurement of true economic value. Enron's leaders used the complicated interpretations of our public accounting rules to establish a definition of accounting value that was much higher than was the company's economic value. They were able to accomplish this through playing around with interpretations of the subjective accounting rules that exist in our system. What was our response to this problem? To add additional accounting complexity into the corporate environment through the Sarbanes-Oxley Act of 2002. First, this *easy out* solution passed by Congress was done without a thorough understanding of what happened; Enron management was able to trick its investors as a result of too many rules, not because there were not enough rules. So when Congress added still more rules, they clearly showed the American public that they didn't understand that this was the problem. Financial reform must be implemented allowing for clarity and simplicity in the economic presentation of companies' performance. Today's U.S. accounting rules are too political and complex, and basically out of touch with what is needed for us to compete in the hypercompetitive global economy. The accounting system must provide clarity to investors in both the operational results and the shareholders' stake in the corporation. It must simplify, not confuse.

Finally, accounting rules should encourage corporate managers to build real wealth in the companies, and not make apparent wealth appear only as a function of accounting rules. The great benefit of capitalism is that it can be the ultimate win–win proposition; the ideal situation exists when the CEOs earn their bonuses based on real gains of shareholders, and even employees. Today, the wrong link exists, and CEOs can gain massive bonuses through showing paper gains (or no gains at all) versus true economic value. As a result, the concept of capitalism is tainted, and the wrong incentives are provided to leaders. When this occurs, leaders are provided with incentives to make unnatural decisions such as over-outsourcing or improper outsourcing.

Many Americans, politicians, and even some corporate executives don't really understand how our financial system can either be an enabling or disabling factor for us within a hypercompetitive global economy. It is truly sad when an Indian colleague compares some of our accounting "reform" (such as SARBOX) to some of the massive bureaucracy of his nation's socialist past. Or the casino mentality of our economy that rewards corporate managers and traders as a result of accounting scenarios versus wealth creation.

Who will oppose a reform of our current-day accounting system? Special interest groups like the American Institute of Certified Public Accountants (AICPA) will probably oppose it, as complexity in accounting rules means more revenue for accountants. However, with the Enron, World-Com, and other scandals fresh in our minds, shouldn't the American public truly demand reform versus *easy out* politics? In my opinion, the only true answer is to provide the American public with true reform, to link our accounting system with the true economic value of the corporation. If this true reform occurs, there will be immediate changes in policies at large corporations regarding their behaviors and policies. While not perfect, of course, at the very least, corporations won't be rewarded for making bad decisions and taking the *easy outs*.

Do our politicians have the guts to support the needed reform in the face of opposition by special interests, such as the AICPA? Do our politicians have the guts to take the necessary actions to reform statistical bureaus, agencies, and cabinets in the face of special interests? These are the *difficult in* decisions that must be made by our public servants. In my opinion, there is everything to gain from the difficult in versus the *easy out*. It is not an overstatement to suggest that our collective economic future hangs in the lurch, and trying to resolve these problems without reforms would be a futile exercise. Our citizens must take notice.

## SOLUTION 8: POLITICIANS WHO ARE POLICY MAKERS, NOT POLITICIANS

There are many examples of politicians making politically motivated and unsound policy. The Sarbanes Oxley Act of 2002 is the perfect example of a political response to a policy issue. Will SARBOX make the Enron problems go away? Yes, but its approach is such overkill that the policy makers who endorsed it don't understand how strangling it is to American competitiveness. Most companies of the Fortune 500 aren't Enron and World-Com, so why should greater than 99% of the corporations be burdened with rules to control the unethical less than 1%? We must ask our politicians for answers that don't solve one problem while creating another.

When most of our policy makers are lawyers versus business people, legislation becomes slanted toward compliance versus solutions. As evidence, how many policies have our legislators enacted to make America more competitive? Not much of any consequence. If we want our policy makers to promote American economic competitiveness, we must elect more business people to public office. Have political leaders who have a prerequisite of understanding the global economy, history, and the world. Have politicians who understand the importance of valid, reliable, and objective data in the middle of the Information Age, and new technologies. Have politicians who understand that confusing and overkill-type public accounting rules hurt our economic growth instead of encouraging it.

If we elect leaders who are more interested in executing policy versus legislating, can we be more competitive? I think so. One advantage that China's communist/capitalist system has over America's, or even India's democratic/capitalist system, is an ability to forgo politics that cloud innovation, reform, and decisive decision making. While that doesn't mean that we want to denounce democracy, it does mean that we need to add responsibilities to the democratic process to allow our politicians to be more of policy makers, and less of politicians. In business today, the marketplace is moving so quickly in this hypercompetitive global model that corporations that do not act quickly and decisively will either be acquired or even eliminated.

Americans must be more responsible in their civic practices to elect officials who are willing to respond as quickly and decisively on reform. For our congressmen and senators, we should focus more on their understanding of policy versus their canned views on matters. Do they understand the history of protectionism in the United States? Do they understand the state and challenges of the Chinese and Indian economies? Do they even know geographically where China and India are on a map? If they aren't qualified in their understanding of such basics of the world economy, and ours, they are not qualified to establish and vote on policy decisions that will affect our economy. The American public must do a better job of researching the understanding levels of our politicians, which will lead to more qualified people getting into office, regardless of what their political stance is. I am more concerned with an elected official's knowledge than I am with his stance because I believe that a knowledgeable leader will more likely make an informed decision than an uninformed one. If you go to an employment Web site, you will see "minimum requirements" for candidates who want to apply; shouldn't we have the same for our politicians, at least in principle?

## PRIVATE SECTOR—GAME-CHANGING IDEAS

The primary focus of changing the *easy out* must be on the private sector, but with a lot of help from the public sector in support of these efforts. Too many a solution on outsourcing has been focused on corporations, and I can tell you from being a corporate manager that it can't be done without support from our public institutions. While there is much work that our corporate leaders must undertake in order to be competitive, we need the help of the public sector, as is the case in India and China. If statistics are unreliable, our financial systems overly bureaucratic, our transportation system clogged, and our young poorly educated, how can we compete? As our nation invests in itself, our corporate leaders must step up and create a culture of innovation and game-changing ideas that existed during the early period of our Industrial Revolution. Today, for us to win in this evolving global marketplace, we need game-changing ideas from private industry.

Regardless of whether America invests in its foundation to the degree that is occurring in China and India, our private sector must reform itself. The *easy out* is for our corporations to believe what the statistics seem to be telling us, and conclude that they are competitive in the hypercompetitive economy. Courageous leaders in corporations will seek the *difficult ins* as a matter of understanding how to compete. The key word in this whole chapter is *competition*. Even though our CEOs and other executives may be rewarded handsomely for not competing, because of their short-term compensation packages, they must look beyond and understand the world economy. Competition is the key theme, like never before. Many of our leaders today have their heads buried in the sand, and are being rewarded for doing so. Leadership and courage cannot be regulated at these companies; it can only be instilled into the culture through an understanding and a willingness to compete. While maybe not deliberately and consciously, Chinese and Indian companies hope our leaders continue to be shortsighted so they can continue their astounding growth trends.

Naysayers will of course point to history, and note that Americans were deathly afraid of Japanese competition back in the eighties and nineties, and we're still the number one economy, hands down. Unfortunately, such a comparison ignores important future demographics. By the year 2025, China and India together will be larger in population than the no. 3 to no. 7 largest nations, and will equal 35% of the world's total population! Compare this to Japan, which will be the thirteenth most populous nation at that point, with having a declining growth rate (only Japan and Italy will be declining). Obviously, the economic superpower competitors of our future will represent a greater threat to our economic well-being than our competitors in the past.

Corporate leaders should look at these demographics as tremendous market opportunities. From an opportunity standpoint, the growing middle classes of China and India represent terrific market possibilities. From a threat standpoint, such markets represent terrific labor markets for national companies to blossom in place of the multinational corporation (MNC) and prominent United States–based companies. From a labor standpoint, the strategy of the MNC has been to focus more production where the markets are growing, and this is obviously bad for America's labor. But does this policy help or hurt the MNC? While these societies are welcoming the business opportunities of the MNC/U.S. corporation, they will eventually want to be independent from these global entities, and take on more of a national flavor. Today, their economies are growing primarily as manufacturing operations for foreign MNCs. As they build financial systems, an educated workforce, and national infrastructure, these nations would obviously like to build more of their own corporations rather than relying on MNCs. Any MNC that doesn't see this happening is fooling itself; as India and China grow in might, there may be less of a global economy than more of one, owing to nationalist needs of pride and security.

Therefore, my solution for game-changing ideas within the private sector must focus on three key factors: one, scientifically run companies; two, the need for a new era of worker/management/labor union relations; and lastly, a focus on key industries that will greatly assist us in being competitive.

## SOLUTION 9: SCIENTIFICALLY RUN COMPANIES

What I believe will happen in the future of an Asian-based world economy, is that well-established Western-based companies will outsource much of their labor to India and China, hoping that such efforts will provide an entrée into the massive and emerging Asian consumer markets. There are some United States–based companies that have already begun to manufacture in China, not simply to reduce labor costs but to gain a foothold into what will be the biggest consumer opportunity over the next few decades. The Chief Supply Chain Officer of one of the largest medical supply providers in the world told me that this is his strategy. This strategy is obviously logical given the size of these populations, but we are not seeing a sweeping opening of China's and India's consumer markets to a lassiez faire opportunity for our companies. And I believe that the reasoning behind this is more complex than simple protectionism. I believe that China and India allow foreign companies into their nations in a guarded, controlled manner to prevent foreign domination of the consumer markets until their own companies can be developed. Currently, Wal-Mart has sixty-six stores in China, hardly a dominant market. With the purchase of Taiwan-based Trust-Mart, Wal-Mart gains another 108 stores, this still is hardly a major market for the world's largest retailer. I believe that an MNC seeking to enter and control China and India markets will be thwarted as local companies sprout up after having learned and copied Western management and operational practices.

A game-changing idea that our corporations must adopt is to learn to operate in a scientific (yet innovative) manner. With the phenomenal proliferation of information technology in business today, there is a level of information available unmatched by any other era. But these data must be accumulated, managed, and analyzed. Today's average American corporation does not understand how to harness this emerging tool. Much like our government bureaus, the American corporations don't give enough focus to a national treasure of technology and standard formats that would give the organization an objective, reliable, and valid foundation from which to make decisions. Many companies have data for only regulatory reporting purposes. If they have databases, the data are often invalid, fragmented, and incomplete. As a result, companies spend a lot of time accumulating reports, scorecards, and the like and take very little time to analyze or interpret the reports.

How important are information and data to the U.S. Corporation in our hyper-competitive global economy? It is the difference between a company being able to be a scientifically run company versus one that makes decisions based solely on leader experience, or tribal knowledge. CEOs cannot rely on scattered and unreliable federal statistical bureaus or, in many instances, their own databases, so they must rely on their staff's experiences, or information points in the company's culture. To quote Professor P.M.S. Blackett (Nobel Prize winner, 1948): "The scientist can encourage numerical thinking on operational matters, and so can help to avoid running the war on gusts of emotion."[24]

There has never been a better time in history for a scientifically run corporation. The knowledge and information that is needed in a corporation is all around, but rarely ever harnessed. Typically, the information of a company that exists in a database might be 5% of the total knowledge within the company. The rest is either on the hard drives of employees' computers; in file cabinets; on pads of paper floating around warehouses, plants, and processing centers; at retail; or in the most difficult spot to harness, the brain of the employee. Today, much of that 95% of raw information can be harnessed into data and processed into a corporate database that will allow the corporation to make rational decisions. Technologies are emerging today such as RFID that show tremendous promise in formalizing this 95% of the data that are informal today. The companies that figure this out for the future and have powerful databases able to process the information will have a tremendous competitive advantage over other companies, including those in China and India. I really wonder why more American corporations and third parties don't understand this untapped opportunity to be such a global competitive advantage!

The scientifically run company must have valid, reliable, and now a thorough percentage of the company's information in its database. Just like how Frederick Taylor simplified the notion of blue-collar labor in a manufacturing setting in the early twentieth century, there is an opportunity to implement management science to the leadership of a corporation. Just like when blue-collar workers back in the 1900s resisted (some still do today) the notion of the one right way of conducting a business process, the proper use of company information being turned into data could standardize how U.S. companies are led. Why not? Why should not the standardization and rationalization of management be a rallying cry for American competitiveness? The key for this to happen is the harvesting of 95% of the information that exists in corporations today but is not captured, and the proper database management of the remaining 5% that is conventional data in business today. Imagine the BPO opportunities that America would take back from India if it led the world in information gathering and analyzing!

This is a game-changing idea—the semistandardization of executive leadership within a Fortune 500 corporation! This is truly Scientific Management, part two. Are American corporations ready for this? As a corporate manager, I can tell you that the market opportunity possible if a company was able to get to this lost ark would be absolutely enormous. Today, the lines of distinction between one company and another from a manufacturing and distribution standpoint is very minor; in fact, in some industries, there are manufacturing/copacking third parties that produce the same product for competitive companies! Many of the clothing and apparel retailers have the same or similar manufacturing facilities in China and elsewhere. Pension programs are administered by Fidelity for many companies, IT is outsourced to EDS, and the three or four companies do auditing for most of the Fortune 500. Almost all of the manufacturers in the world use SAP for their enterprise resource planning (ERP) software, and so on. Today, it is very difficult for a leader to create game-changing ideas given the same tribal knowledge that exists from one company to the next. Once in a while, a corporation emerges as an innovator, such as Wal-Mart, Apple, and Microsoft, but these situations are becoming rarer. How do game-changing ideas get implemented? It has been demonstrated that the answer isn't through the Messiah CEO walking through the door, although companies continue to search for this cult of personality to come aboard and change everything.

The answer of innovation is in the past, and in the detail. Any day of the week, I will place my bet on an average corporate manager running a company with well-harvested and managed data that equals 50–75% of the company's knowledge versus a perceived superstar CEO with 5% of the company's knowledge at his or her disposal. Process flows, time studies, engineered standards, presentations, rates, benchmarking, competitive intelligence, market demographics, employee opinions, and so on are all standardized and presented for executives to make the right decisions, encouraging innovation and leadership. CEOs then are able to build a culture around these data, around making decisions based on well-executed and timely information turned into data for use. This is the scientifically run company of the future.

How will the scientifically run company of the future approach outsourcing? The answer is that it will be a winner in the game of outsourcing. American companies have a foundation of information technology that is not matched in India or China. In any endogenous (economic) growth model, there are labor, capital, and technological advancement factors to be considered. Today, the scale tilts toward India and China in the area of labor. While these developing nations have made significant progress in technological advancement, the United States still has a significant lead in this area, and will maintain that lead for the foreseeable future. The American corporation can leverage its technological superiority (and infrastructure) by developing a cutting edge, completely optimal approach to management and leadership that was never possible before. In the 1990s, information technology began to proliferate. Now in the 00s, it is becoming increasingly easy to capture the 95% of information that is nonstandard, through tools such as standard data formats (XML) and RFID. Innovative corporate executives could gain a competitive advantage over not only domestic but also foreign competition by implementing a scientifically run company. Yet doing so is a *difficult in*, and it will take courage; no longer would the executive and his or her staff be the cult of personality. Instead of placing the decision making of the corporation in the hands of pure experience and little data, decisions will be based on knowledge translated into usable data and the appropriate, not dominant, use of executive management experience.

Imagine if American corporations became the most scientifically run organizations as a result of the world's best data/information, with executives who have the discipline and insight to make decisions based on objective analysis. I believe that *creative destruction* would occur, and we would finally have growth industries that would fairly and adequately replace disappearing jobs.

## SOLUTION 10: IMPLEMENT A NEW ERA OF WORKER–MANAGER–LABOR UNION RELATIONS

What is your opinion on the state of worker–manager relations in America today? If you believe our federal statistical bureaus, you must feel very good about the current state of worker relations. Unemployment is low and productivity is high, which on the face of it would appear to be a sign of strong worker relations. But should we believe the federal statistics indicating that the state of employee relations is good today? If you are an employee at a Fortune 500 corporation and are a manager, you may be torn between a desire to establish humanistic policies involving loyalty and employee entitlement and pressures to achieve productivity by the elimination of jobs. More than ever, there is friction between managers who want to drive results through a process of job elimination versus those who want to value their employees at all costs, no matter what the national statistical bodies might conclude. Outsourcing often comes into play as a tool for driving employees out of the company and lowering wages. Obviously, neither action is endearing to the workforce. As a corporate manager, I can tell you that I myself struggle over the question of loyalty versus driving results, and have concluded that there is a better approach than either, as I will discuss later in this section.

Not only is there a split today within the managerial ranks over approach but the work ethic of our workers has suffered after decades of an overly humanistic approach to the question of worker relations. In trying to create a loyal environment, American corporations have successfully created a family environment. A family corporate environment was acceptable when the world wasn't competitive, but has become very much problematic in today's hypercompetitive environment. After decades of being treated as family, the worker felt pride and develop some sense of loyalty about working at the corporation, and he became a living part of the corporation. In the recent movie *Rocky Balboa*, Paulie (Rocky's brother-in-law) tells Rocky, "If you stay at a place for a long period of time, you become that place. This job is all that I have." Later in the movie, Paulie is pink-slipped, and his whole identity is lost. This picture still exists today, even after two decades of layoffs in corporate America.

Those of us who grew up in times of massive corporate layoffs don't identify strongly with the concept of corporate–worker loyalty. While corporate managers have been trained to believe that loyalty in the workplace is a dying concept, many of us haven't been taught that at the same time options exist between pure loyalty and pure apathy. As a result of this, the modern corporate manager either turns it on or turns it off, and the worker feels betrayed and confused. As well, there are workers smart enough to understand outsourcing strategies that make sense for the company, and those who do not. I've always thought that the average worker will understand an outsourcing situation well before the manager acts upon it. Conversely, when a poorly thought or irrational outsourcing arrangement happens, the worker is angry not about being betrayed but rather from losing a job due to poor management.

Given these dynamics that exist across such a large percentage of corporations today, it is difficult to conclude that worker relations are solid, despite what the report numbers state. Having spoken to so many of my peers at other corporations, I am told that the number one issue in their workforces is that of *trust*. I think the reason for this is that while a workforce can understand and rationalize an outsourcing strategy when appropriate, it struggles significantly when outsourcing is handled inappropriately or as an answer for everything. I have seen outsourcing implemented in a manner that the workforce supported, even though it affected their employment because they respected the decision and the process. Yet more often than not, workers are increasingly disgruntled by the outsourcing and offshoring of jobs as a substitute for poor management practices in the corporation.

The foundation for my thinking on this matter is that the strain of worker–manager relations is a fight for America's middle class. The future success of China, India, and Russia will be a direct result of these countries' being able to build and sustain a viable middle class. The *American Dream* suggests that anyone can become middle class if they choose to work for it. The loss of any jobs to India or China creates a psychic insecurity that is greater than the net loss of jobs. Much like in Taylor's day, but for different reasons today, our worker–manager relations must promote a vision for the middle class where everybody profits. The worker–manager relations cannot be positive when the workers feel like management is seeking to destroy gains made within the middle class. Outsourcing and offshoring have led workers to conclude that this is happening to them.

The relationship between the worker and the manager must be focused on mutual respect, not collegiality. In today's environment, the worker can see right through the insincerity of collegiality, as the hypercompetitive global economy leads to results over loyalty. Therefore, the manager must lean on scientific management rather than friendship and loyalty in running the department. When the manager uses data, process flows, time studies, and other scientific management approaches in making decisions, the worker will end up winning, in many cases. Contrary to what our economists tell us, China and India aren't impossible to compete against because of their lower labor costs. Scientific managers who can use data and process to win have a better chance of improving the lot of our workforce than the people-person manager, or the Chainsaw Al Dunlap types.

Restoring worker–manager relations must be done in polishing an old concept (Scientific Management) for today's twenty-first-century economy. No longer relying on loyalty to win, or even slash and burn, but rather objective, empirical evidence contributing to what decisions should be made. In the early twentieth century, Frederick Taylor reasoned with the workforce and, as a result, the workforce prospered. Getting management and the workforce to agree on a rational, scientific approach to decision making is perhaps the most important initiative that a corporation can make in the new economy. Both sides of the relations have their own irrational human natures, but only through rational thinking and execution can the middle class be restored and all parties allowed to prosper.

Contentious behavior is the *easy out* for managers today when their self-interests are not aligned with the best interests of the employees, or the corporation. Entitlement is the *easy out* for today's worker who believes that he or she is owed more than a paycheck in today's hypercompetitive global economy. The *difficult in* for both parties is to take a leap of faith to trust one another through a scientifically managed approach. In some cases, this will lead to workers' jobs being outsourced or offshored for rational reasons. However, if outsourcing decisions are made based on rational analysis and respect between managers and workers, there is no question in my mind that less outsourcing will occur from America to other nations, and more insourcing to America from other nations will occur. The new era of worker–manager relations, if implemented properly, will be the primary reason for overturning this easy out that has been affecting the workforce in a way that hasn't shown up in the employment numbers.

This also needs to be a new era for labor unions in American business today. While I wouldn't go as far as some others and suggest that labor unions are no longer needed in business today, I would say that the unions need to redefine their purpose to convince others of the value they add to the process. Today's workers don't need advocates as they did during the early twentieth century in Frederick Taylor's day. Instead, the labor union of the twenty-first century could become the Frederick Taylor of our era, seeking to enhance relations between workers and managers. This is ironic, as many contend that labor unions were Taylor's greatest nemesis. Yet as a functional middleman between management and workers, couldn't that kind of role be possible? Responsible labor leaders realize that today's labor union cannot use the same argumentative, combative approach for highly educated, primarily middle class workers today as it did one hundred years ago for uneducated, lower class immigrants. Declining union membership in recent years show some unions that they need to change, and redefine their roles. Instead of mainly spouting rhetoric of the evils of outsourcing, why would they not build programs between workers and managers for harmony and productivity? Why not support efforts that outsource workers when appropriate, and add jobs when necessary as well? Wouldn't the concept of a labor union that fights for true corporate productivity be the best friend of the worker, of the middle class? Yes, if the labor unions can think out of the box and implement such game-changing ideas they might well become more relevant in today's competitive marketplace. Labor unions either need to add value in today's hypercompetitive global economy or need to fade away. Perhaps they can help America understand this new definition of productivity (that isn't only a "labor productivity" factor).

It is so important for workers and managers in America to begin a new era of relations that neither the workforce nor the management, nor even the labor unions, can afford to wait for the other side to step forward. Escalation occurs in attempts at problem resolution when neither side will back down. Mitigation of tensions and inefficiency happens when one or both of the sides understand that working together is always better than choosing separate paths. We should not be fooled into thinking that a combative worker–manager relationship, even when labor unions are involved, is capitalism at work. Wealth creation is the foundation for capitalism, and all parties must have equal opportunity to create their own wealth. Developing public and private sector rules that skew the benefits of capitalism primarily into one camp is not good for anyone in the long run. Suggesting better harmony through greater opportunities for wealth creation for all is not socialism at all. It is simply the smartest approach to winning in the hypercompetitive global economy.

## SOLUTION 11: BUILD A STRONG MANUFACTURING FOCUS AS A BASE FOR THE INDUSTRIES OF THE FUTURE

In a 2003 study, Jeremy Leonard found that U.S. manufacturers had a 22.4% structural cost disadvantage compared to its nine largest trading partners.[25] These high structural costs include the following:

1. High marginal corporate tax rates
2. Employee benefit costs
3. Tort litigation
4. Regulatory compliance costs (environmental, workplace, tax)

Interestingly enough, America's competitive position in the world manufacturing market has more factors than the labor rates of our employees. Generalizations suggesting that our workers must become "knowledge workers" has led to misconceptions that America is too high priced to be manufacturers and that all of our citizens should be knowledge, white-collar workers instead of blue-collar. It is also due to the misconception that all innovative, higher paying white-collar management work would go to us, the Americans.

As a result of the generalizations that categorized and associated the knowledge worker with white-collar work, it became quite easy for our popular theorists to conclude that Americans no longer needed to consider manufacturing work as viable, and that we weren't competitive in it anyways. The blue-collar workers of Detroit encouraged their sons and daughters to break the chain of assembly-line work, go to college, and become engineers, IT programmers, or research scientists. The *American Dream* went hand in hand with a move from blue-collar to white-collar. All of these generalizations weren't fatal twenty years ago before the proliferation of Asian tigers (primarily India) on America's white-collar jobs. Once India Inc. provided a legitimate challenge to Americans and their white-collar jobs, the picture became very clear how much of a mistake it was to conclude that America doesn't need blue-collar work often associated with a strong manufacturing base. Yet today, we're fighting to keep our white-collar jobs away from India, and assuming that a viable manufacturing base is not possible in direct competition with China and other Asian manufacturers. Why does it make sense to dig in our heels and fight for white-collar jobs but not blue-collar ones? Why does America believe that it shouldn't and can't compete in manufacturing? And an even more troubling question, what is our plan to replace these jobs (creative destruction)?

Manufacturing and much of industrial work is viewed from a productivity standpoint much more so than most white-collar and service work. If one concludes that there is a productivity culture in the United States, then there would be no question but that America can be competitive in industrial work. A nation with a culture of strong productivity and higher wages should be able to compete against nations with low productivity and low wages. In much of white-collar work, however, it isn't as easy to measure and manage productivity, given our poor statistical public and private data systems. An inability to effectively measure productivity in an industry that emphasizes 60% of our workforce should make us wonder if we really understand the term. We can't suggest that manufacturing productivity has improved dramatically because hours worked (which doesn't include outsourcing) decreased, and output has stayed the same or increased.

Not only must America focus on manufacturing in the twenty-first century, it must replace its tired old thinking that manufacturing is not strategic for a knowledge society. It must also replace the ridiculous thinking that America can't compete in manufacturing without similar $1 an hour labor rates. The days of Asian countries with low-tech, low-wage manufacturing is over; the future will be high-tech manufacturing as the norm for all nations. With high-tech manufacturing comes high-tech ideas, in areas such as biotechnology, alternative energies, and other emerging future markets. The production of sweaters and socks should no longer define manufacturing. Americans have images of Asians working in sweatshops, and these do exist. But the future holds a much different view of Chinese manufacturing. And without an eye toward manufacturing, America will lose very profitable, innovative markets of the future.

In America's old world, our innovators would develop and create new products, trademark or patent them, build a company, and then ship the product to far away lands in to gain more profit from the effort. But in the future, if India and China become the innovators, the knowledge workers, and they manufacture, and even manage the finance aspects of a company to sell and profit, what do these nations need from America? Not much is the answer. America must develop its own supply chain to compete against these national forces that are using offshoring (legitimately) as an opportunity to gain more wealth. When America offshores the manufacturing by default (without trying), they are offshoring ideas that will turn into future innovators in China and India. Do you think that China will be content with being America's manufacturing center forever?

Just like China and India want to compete by having more knowledge workers to develop and research products on their own and cut us out of the process, America must want to compete through efficient and cost-competitive manufacturing, addressing these structural cost disadvantages as well. Any proper economic equation would suggest that if America were a hypercompetitive manufacturing market, it would own more of the world market, no matter the current wage differential. It doesn't make sense that America isn't a growing manufacturing power instead of one losing steam.

In the Second World War, manufacturing was a vital interest of the United States. In the postwar recovery for the United States and the world, manufacturing was also an interest vital to the United States. In today's world, energy and biotechnology will either lead to lasting economic prosperity or lasting malaise and war. It will be up to an economic superpower to steer the world in the right direction. The future of all of this is manufacturing. Manufacturing will take the next economic superpower into the lead, as it has done time after time in recorded history. There is no such thing as an economic superpower that wasn't a manufacturing superpower, and we must question whether there ever will be.

American corporations must change their course. Their natural reliance on the *easy out* of outsourcing and offshoring has strategic ramifications for our economic future. While I don't expect the average U.S. corporation, mired down by short-term profitability goals, to be concerned over strategic ramifications for our economy, I do expect them to understand what's possible for them to achieve relative to economic growth. In too many markets, corporations aren't versed in how to grow their top line; they are just focused on a reduction of costs contributing to a profitable bottom line. The addition by subtraction method may appear to be attractive from a short-term accounting standpoint, but it is bound to catch up to a company without a growing top line. Innovation will help American corporations grow its top line. If anything, manufacturing will be the future battleground for innovation and intelligence, and therefore the greater need for knowledge workers. Therefore, our de facto national strategy on manufacturing and knowledge workers is all wrong, and dangerous to our economic health.

So what is a corporation to do about this? How and why should these companies seek to innovate via manufacturing? For one, through a scientifically run company. These companies cannot outsource thinking by outsourcing manufacturing. In many cases, these companies are actually outsourcing thinking by outsourcing manufacturing, and they don't even understand.

History repeats itself again; new innovations require a strong manufacturing foundation to fulfill them. Forget the weak association between the knowledge worker and white-collar work. A big opportunity for America's knowledge worker also exists in manufacturing. Blue-collar workers who can manufacture and think are the future growth for the world. America needs to make this link and become the world leader, as it is positioned to do if it can wake from its sleep.

# Conclusion: Get Involved

> The discipline of living in truth is urgent today because modern life reduces community and accountability to its thinnest, thereby tempting us to live in a shadow world of anonymity and nonresponsibility where all cats are gray. In such a world, becoming people of truth is the deepest secret of integrity and the highest form of taking responsibility for ourselves and our own lives.
>
> —Os Guinness, "A Time for Truth" (2000)

The term *truth* often becomes a ticket for those who think that they own it to use it to preach to others. But as Thoreau noted, "It takes two to speak the truth—one to speak, and another to hear." Today in our public debate, there is too much supposed truth in the form of preaching, and too little truth in the form of listening. Truth cannot exist without both, and as such, not much can exist today within the public discourse on such topics as outsourcing, offshoring, temporary workers, and American competitiveness.

I truly believe that the escalation of global competitiveness has only begun in the last two years, and is more of a threat to our economic well-being than we have ever faced in our history. However, I believe that we, not they (China and India), are the problem, and citizens must focus more on civic issues than we ever have in order to solve them. To do so, we must both speak and hear. And we must get involved.

If this book has inspired you to get involved, start by going to www.iaprod.org, and check out the "Institute for American Productivity." This policy institute is dedicated to providing understanding and solutions to America's sliding competitiveness in our hypercompetitive global economy. You'll find articles and data on American competitiveness, debate and links to different places where you can get more intimately involved in this important topic. The website and the Institute is a grassroots effort intended to make the issue of American competitiveness an important one for the 2008 elections.

I also encourage you to do your own research on America's economic history, and to learn more about the cultures and history of our world. How can we expect to compete against China and India if we don't understand their cultures and history, or even our own history? There is a significant amount of information available at your library or on the Web regarding these topics. Please take the time to learn more about them, and to use this information to make informed decisions as either a citizen or a worker. The solution of understanding applies to you, the reader as well.

Another suggestion is for you to learn a foreign language. I have formally learned Russian, and am learning Mandarin Chinese and Spanish on my own. Remember that millions of Chinese students are learning English, while Americans are learning Mandarin in the thousands; which society will have an advantage in the future?

Getting involved in your community is critical as well. How many of you are parents, and aren't involved in your child's educational system? Even if you're not a parent, there's no doubt an underdeveloped school system in your area that could use your assistance as a volunteer. Also, get to understand the specifics of the by-laws of your local school board program. Take a tour of the school facilities, and ask questions as to why our educational methods haven't changed for decades. Really understand and act upon the importance of education to our economic future.

If you are a parent, please dedicate your life to being an active parent in the education process of your child. It is not the school's sole responsibility to educate your child. Reduce your television watching, or quit your bowling or softball league, or whatever, and dedicate yourself to your child and his or her education process. It is one of the most important things that you'll do in your life.

As a worker, be less of a spectator and more of a player in the success of your company. I frequently use the phrase "get the spectators off the field" in my job as a call to action for workers at all levels to participate in making our company more competitive. Challenge your boss, your bosses' boss, and his or her boss. Be assertive in ensuring that competition and scientific management are part and parcel of the mainstream operations at your company. You spend too many hours at your place of employment to not try to stand up and make a difference.

If you are a manager or a leader of a company, remember that the conduct of your function affects the lives of your workers and investors in the company. As a result, these people are counting on you to make effective, efficient, and objective decisions. Consider using scientific management principles at work, including formalizing the 95% of untapped knowledge into data. Consider a data-driven, analytical approach as the gateway to both efficiency and innovation.

Remember that outsourcing is not something that our competitors are doing to U.S. workers, it is something that U.S. citizens are doing to ourselves. It is not too late for managers and workers to reinvent their relationship in a conducive way to achieve productivity. Both managers and workers must also speak out in the public forum for much-needed infrastructure and policy makers to help them succeed in this hypercompetitive global economy. Now it is time for you to act, to get involved!

# Notes

## CHAPTER ONE

1. Center for American Progress, *Outsourcing Statistics in Perspective*, cited on March 16, 2004, http://www.americanprogress.org/issues/2004/03/b38081.html.

2. For a review of outsourcing surveys and responses from its respondents, visit www.deloitte.com/us. This study that I am referring to was conducted in 2004 by Deloitte Touche Tomatsu, entitled "Calling a Change in the Outsourcing Market."

3. Peter S. Goodman, and Phillip P. Pan, Chinese Workers Pay for Wal-Mart's Low Prices, *WashingtonPost.com*, http://www.momandpopnyc.com/campaigns/walmart/articles/Labor%20Practices_Unions/ChineseWorkers,%20WaPost,%202.23.04.pdf.

4. Charles Fishman, The Wal-Mart You Don't Know, *Fast Company*, December 2003 (Issue 77), 68.

5. AFL-CIO.org, *More Than 70% of Wal-Mart's Inventory Made in China*, cited on May 3, 2007, http://www.aflcio.org/corporatewatch/ns05062005.cfm?RenderForPrint=1.

6. See, e.g., Peter Drucker, *The New Realities*, to understand how he believed the Information Age was going to transform America away from manufacturing.

7. *Economic Report of the President*, 2006, 3, http://www.gpoaccess.gov/eop/download.html.

8. In 1990, C. K. Prahalad and Gary Hamel introduced the term *core competency* in a *Harvard Business Review* article entitled "The Core Competence of a Corporation," May–June 1990, 79–93.

9. Boston Logistics Group, *The Asian Sourcing Boom: How Long Will It Last?* cited on May 17, 2006, http://www.bostonlogistics.com/images/BLG_Asian_Sourcing_Boom_Excerpt.pdf.

10. Daniel W. Drezner, *Differentiating between Outsourcing and Offshoring*, cited on February 2, 2004, http://www.danieldrezner.com/archives/001060.html.

11. Data regarding "temporary labor growth" came from the Bureau of Labor Statistics (BLS) Web site www.bls.gov, which is the best place to get this data, but as is noted in my book, it is questionable, at best, as a source of data. Another source for me was American Staffing Association. *Staffing Statistics*, cited in 2007, http://www.americanstaffing.net/statistics/employee_survey_download_figures.cfm.

## CHAPTER TWO

1. Much research on "The History of Outsourcing" starts in the 20th century. See, e.g., Thomas Friedman, *The World Is Flat* (New York: Farrar, Straus, and Giroux, 2005) for a more historical definition.

2. Joseph A. Schumpeter, *The Process of Creative Destruction* (1942).

3. Trade Partnership Worldwide, LLC. *Impact of Imports from China on US Employment*, cited in November 2005, http://www.tradepartnership.com/pdf_files/2005_China_imports.pdf#search='U.S.%20imports%20to%20China.

4. International Monetary Fund (IMF). *World Economic Outlook*, September 2006.

5. Pete Engardio, *Chindia* (New York: McGraw-Hill, 2007).

6. International balance of trade statistics are available at the U.S. Census Bureau (http://www.census.gov/foreign-trade/balance/), but the reader must question the validity of this data.

7. Toyota 2005 and 2006 Annual Report data.

8. Eric Schlosser, *Fast Food Nation* (New York: Harper, 2005), 160–163.

9. Friedman, *The World Is Flat*, 9–11.

10. See, e.g., http://www.doubletongued.org/index.php/citations/china_price_1, for a definition of the term *China Price*.

11. BLS data regarding unemployment. www.bls.gov.

12. Edward Iwata and Barbara Hansen, Pay, Performance Don't Always Add Up, *USA Today*, cited on April 20, 2004, http://www.usatoday.com/money/companies/management/2004-04-30-exec-pay_x.htm.

13. Peter Drucker, *The New Realities* (New York: Harper & Row, 1989), 25–26.

14. Engardio, *Chindia*, 52, 234, 240.

## CHAPTER THREE

1. Gross Domestic Product (GDP) Data Gathered from Bureau of Economic Analysis Web site, www.bea.gov/.

2. Staffing Data Gathered from Staffing Industry Analysts, Inc., http://www.staffingindustry.com/research_data/.

3. Frederick W. Taylor, *Principles of Scientific Management* (New York: Norton, 1967).

4. Peter Drucker, *The New Realities* (New York: Harper & Row, 1989), 225.

5. See, e.g., Wikipedia's "Management Consulting" (http://en.wikipedia.org/wiki/Management_consulting) for a brief history of the origins of Management Consulting.

6. Robert H. Waterman Jr. and Thomas J. Peters, *In Search of Excellence: Lessons from America's Best Run Companies* (New York: Warner Books, 1988 [reissue date]).

7. Steel Maker Sees a Long-Term Threat from China Nucor Sets Out to Bolster Support for U.S. factories Nucor's Norfolk Plant at a Glance Meeting Tonight, *Red Orbit*, http://www.redorbit.com/news/science/225199/steel_maker_sees_a_longterm_threat_from_china_nucor_sets/index.html.

8. See, e.g., the American Staffing Association (http://www.americanstaffing.net/index.cfm) for information on temporary labor.

9. OhmyNews. *Nearly 50,000 Workers Take Buyouts, Early Retirements at GM*, cited on June 27, 2006, http://english.ohmynews.com/ArticleView/article_view.asp?no=301454&rel_no=1.

10. Linda Levine, Offshoring (a.k.a. Offshore Outsourcing) and Job Insecurity among U.S. Workers., CRS Report for Congress, June 18, 2004, 1–17.

## CHAPTER FOUR

1. John Buffington, *Measuring the Differential between Economic and Accounting Performance of a Public Corporation* (Naples, FL: Walden University, 1996).

2. Michael Jacobs, *Short-Term America* (Boston: Harvard Business School Press, 1991).

3. World Bank, *Accounting Standards in China*, October–December 2001, 19–20.

4. Hackett Group Research Confirms Companies Are Responding to Sarbanes-Oxley. *DM Review*, http://www.dmreview.com/editorial/dmreview/print_action.cfm?articleId=1006860.

5. New Accounting Rules Raise Price of Audits, *USA Today*, cited on April 12, 2005, http://www.usatoday.com/money/companies/regulation/2005-04-12-audits_x.htm.

6. IT Business Edge, Hackett: Sarbox Drives Biggest Finance Cost Rise in 13 Years, cited on September 22, 2005, http://www.itbusinessedge.com/item/?ci=6888.

7. First use of the term *casino capitalism*, by John Bogle, 2003 National Investor Relations Institute Conference, June 11, 2003.

8. CEO Compensation, Forbes.com, cited on April 21, 2005 and Yahoo News, June 12, 2007, http://www.forbes.com/2005/04/20/05ceoland.html and http://news.yahoo.com/s/ap/20070609/ap_on_bi_ge/executive_compensation.

## CHAPTER FIVE

1. *Economic Report of the President*, 2006, 2007. http://www.gpoaccess.gov/eop/download.html.

2. U.S. Current Account Deficit Causes Concern Around the Globe, *Global Insights*, cited on September 25, 2006, http://www.globalenvision.org/library/3/1265/1/.

3. U.S. Department of Labor, A Chartbook of International Labor Comparisons, cited in June 2006, http://www.dol.gov/asp/media/reports/chartbook/index.htm.

4. Mark Wilson, *Accuracy, Accountability, and Public Trust: Why Congress Must Reform the Federal Statistical System*, Heritage Foundation, Backgrounder #1138, September 16, 1997.

5. My Years at the BLS by Shawn Ritenour, cited on October 21, 2000, http://www.lewrockwell.com/orig/ritenour1.html.

6. John Williams publishes a monthly newsletter discussing the "analysis behind government reporting," at http://www.shadowstats.com/cgi-bin/sgs?

7. Murray Rothbard, *Statistics: Achilles Heel of Government* (Naples, FL: Walden University, 2004).

8. Mark Brandly, *Don't Believe Those Inflation Numbers* (Naples, FL: Walden University, September 1, 2006), http://www.mises.org/story/2302.

9. See, e.g., Paul Strassmann, Five Steps to Improve Your Information Productivity, *Baseline Magazine*, October 15, 2006.

10. Robert Gordon, *Exploding Productivity Growth: Context, Causes, and Implications*, Brookings Papers on Economic Activity, cited on February 2003, http://faculty-web.at.northwestern.edu/economics/gordon/Productivity-Brookings.pdf.

11.  Patrick J. Buchanan, Death of Manufacturing, *The American Conservative*, August 11, 2003.

12.  See, e.g., surveys on the economy at http://americanresearchgroup.com/economy/, http://brain.gallup.com/, and www.pewresearch.org.

## CHAPTER SIX

1.  Frederick W. Taylor, *Principles of Scientific Management* (New York: Norton, 1967).

2.  Building Blue-Collar . . . Burgers? cbsnews.com, cited on February 20, 2004, http://www.cbsnews.com/stories/2004/02/20/politics/main601336.shtml.

3.  Patrick J. Buchanan, Death of Manufacturing, *The American Conservative*, August 11, 2003.

4.  National Association of Manufacturers, *A Case for a Strong Manufacturing Base*, Cited in September 2006, http://www.nam.org/s_nam/sec.asp?CID=201720&DID=230272.

5.  Peter Drucker, *Post Capitalist Society* (New York: Collins, 1994).

## CHAPTER SEVEN

1.  Frederick W. Taylor, *Principles of Scientific Management* (New York: Norton, 1967).

2.  John C. Bogle, Owners Capitalism vs. Managers Capitalism. 2003 National Investor Relations Institute Conference, June 11, 2003, http://www.vanguard.com/bogle_site/sp20030611.html.

3.  R. M. Bushman, J. D. Piotroski, and A. J. Smith, *What Determines Corporate Transparency?* Journal of Accounting Research, 2004, 42, 207–252.

## CHAPTER EIGHT

1.  Mike Shedlock, *Paulson, Bernanke Strike Out*, cited on December 17, 2006, www.safehaven.com.

2.  The Analects of Confucius Are Records of His Words and Acts, see, e.g., *English Translation of the Analects* by Charles Muller, http://www.hm.tyg.jp/~acmuller/contao/analects.html.

3.  Pete Engardio, *Chindia* (New York: McGraw-Hill, 2007).

4.  Ministry of Communication, People's Republic of China, http://english.gov.cn/about.htm.

5.  United Nations, Infrastructure Development in the People's Republic of China, Cited on November 15, 2006, http://www.unescap.org/ttdw/common/TPT/ReviewofPlanning/CountryPapers/China.pdf.

6.  China Builds Strong Infrastructure, *Xinhua NewsAgency*, October 16, 2002.

7.  Ministry of Communication, People's Republic of China, http://english.gov.cn/about.htm.

8.  People's Republic of China—Infrastructure, *GlobalSecurity.org*, http://www.globalsecurity.org/military/world/china/infras.htm.

9.  Urumqi, Wikipedia, http://en.wikipedia.org/wiki/Urumqi.

10.  United Nations, Infrastructure Development.

11. India Economic Summit: Meeting New Expectations, cited on November 27, 2006, http://www.weforum.org/pdf/summitreports/india2006.pdf.

12. World Bank Economic Data, http://www.worldbank.org/.

13. Andrei Roudoi, Sustainability of Russian Growth, *Global Insights*, cited on November 1, 2005, http://www.chass.utoronto.ca/link/meeting/papers/1101am_ar.pdf.

14. Red China's Pollution Problem, *The Distributist*, cited on June 6, 2007, http://distributism.blogspot.com/2007/02/red-chinas-pollution-puzzle.html.

15. A Stand against China's Pollution Tide, *Washington Post*, January 12, 2006.

## CHAPTER NINE

1. Big City Schools Struggle with Graduation Rates, *USA Today*, June 20, 2007.

2. Wall $t Bonuses Balloon to New Record, CNNMoney.com, cited on January 11, 2006, http://money.cnn.com/2006/01/11/markets/job_bonuses/index.htm.

3. How the BPO Industry will Change Our Lives, *Rediff.com*, cited on July 23, 2004, http://www.rediff.com/money/2004/jul/23bpo1.htm.

4. Pete Engardio, *Chindia* (New York: McGraw-Hill, 2007).

5. The "Confederation of Indian Industry" is a nonprofit organization in place to provide leadership for Indian companies. Its Web site is http://www.ciionline.org/.

6. Iran Oil Revenue Could Disappear by 2015, *Associated Press*, December 25, 2006.

## CHAPTER TEN

1. Robert Cowley, *What If?: The World's Foremost MILITARY Historians Imagine What Might Have Been* (New York: Berkley Trade, 2000).

2. Two US Senators Seek Trade Sanctions on China Over Lack of Yuan Reform, Forbes.com, cited on September 15, 2006, http://www.forbes.com/markets/feeds/afx/2006/09/14/afx3019070.html.

3. AFL-CIO, *Bill Would Require Tariffs on Chinese Goods if Currency Manipulation Continues*, cited on September 26, 2006, http://blog.aflcio.org/2006/09/26/bill-would-require-tariffs-on-chinese-goods-if-currency-manipulation-continues/.

4. Labor Unrest Is Growing in China, *China Labor Watch*, http://www.chinalaborwatch.org/en/web/article.php?article_id=50209.

5. China and the Hong Kong WTO Meetings, *American Thinker*, cited on November 29, 2005, http://www.americanthinker.com/2005/11/china_and_the_hong_kong_wto_me.html.

6. A Chat with David Crystal, *Wordsmith.org*, cited on February 26, 2001, http://www.wordsmith.org/chat/dc.html.

7. David Crystal is a wonderful resource for understanding the role of English as a world language. See, e.g., Roles and Impact of English as a Global Language, http://www.cels.bham.ac.uk/resources/essays/Doms6.pdf.

8. Consulate General of the United States, Remarks by Ambassador Karan k Bhatia, cited on October 25, 2006, http://shenyang.usembassy-china.org.cn/programs_events.html.

9. Committee for Economic Development. *Education for Global Leadership: The Importance of International Studies and Foreign Language Education for U.S. Economic and National Security*, 2006, http://www.ced.org/docs/report/report_foreignlanguages.pdf.

10. Committee for Economic Development, *CED Urges Increased Investment in International Education and Foreign Language Studies,* cited on February 6, 2006, http://www.ced.org/newsroom/press/press_foreignlanguages.pdf.

11. Committee for Economic Development, *Learning for the Future: Changing the Culture of Math and Science Education to Ensure a Competitive Workforce,* 2006, http://www.ced.org/docs/report/report_scientists.pdf.

12. George A. Clowes, U.S. Productivity Soars in Business, Slumps in Education. *School Reform News,* cited on September 1, 2004, http://www.heartland.org/Article.cfm?artId=15601.

13. Robert Reich, Education Key to Solving America's "Real Jobs" Problem. Northwestern University, Institute for Public Research, Fall 2005, Number 1.

14. Clowes, U.S. Productivity Soars in Business, Slumps in Education.

15. William C. Symonds, America's Failure in Science Education, *Business Week,* March 16, 2004.

16. Ibid.

17. American Society of Civil Engineers, *America's Crumbling Infrastructure Eroding Quality,* cited on March 9, 2005, http://www.asce.org/reportcard/2005.

18. American Association of Railroads, *Intermodalism: The Transportation Imperative for the 21st Century,* cited on June 15, 2006, http://www.aar.org/government_affairs/cong_testimony_intermodalism_june_2006_sherry.pdf.

19. Supply Chain Digest's 2006 Annual Logistics Report, http://www.cscmp.org/.

20. Dan Gilmore, Transportation Infrastructure—Should You Care? *Supply Chain Digest.* July 21, 2006.

21. Reason Foundation, *Funding Our Crumbling Roads,* cited on February 6, 2006, http://reason.org/commentaries/staley_20060206.shtml.

22. News about the "Initiative for a Competitive Inner City" is available on http://www.icic.org/vsm/bin/smRenderFS.php?PHPSESSID=2b9231c76ee5ce80abf017a b4104c793&cerror=.

23. Edward J. Spar, Federal Statistics in the FY 2007 Budget, Council of Professional Associations on Federal Statistics, AAAS Report, Chapter Twenty-one, 2007.

24. Mary Jo Nye, *Physics, War, and Politics of the 20th Century* (Harvard University Press, 2004), http://www.hup.harvard.edu/pdf/NYEBLA_excerpt.pdf.

25. Jeremy A. Leonard, *How Structural Costs Imposed on U.S. Manufacturers Harm Workers and Threaten Competitiveness,* report prepared by the Manufacturers Alliance/MAPI and The Manufacturing Institute, NAM, December 2003.

# Bibliography

AFL-CIO. Bill Would Require Tariffs on Chinese Goods if Currency Manipulation Continues. Cited on September 26, 2006. Available from http://blog.aflcio.org/2006/09/26/bill-would-require-tariffs-on-chinese-goods-if-currency-manipulation-continues/.

AFL-CIO. Policy Solutions to Shipping Jobs Overseas. Cited in September 15, 2006. Available from http://www.aflcio.org/issues/jobseconomy/exportingamerica/outsourcing_solutions.cfm.

American Competitiveness Institute. President's Letter on Competitiveness. Cited in October 15, 2006. Available from http://www.whitehouse.gov/stateoftheunion/2006/aci/print/index.htl.

American Enterprise Institute. Is Productivity for Real? Presented by Brent R. Moulton. Cited on August 15, 2006. Available from http://www.aei.org/include/pub_print.asp.

American Enterprise Institute. The Advantages of High Productivity Growth. Cited on November 3, 2006. Available from http://www.aei.org/events/filter.,eventID.749/summary.asp.

American Enterprise Institute. The Benefits of Increased Productivity Growth for Workers. Cited on November 15, 2006. Available from http://www.aei.org/include/pub_print.asp.

American Prospect. Productivity Tanks, No One Notices. Cited in November 2006. Available from http://www.prospect.org/deanbaker/2006/11/productivity_tanks_no_one_noti.html.

American Prospect. Republicans Insist that Productivity Is Lower than the Data Show. Cited in November 2006. Available from http://www.prospect.org/deanbaker/2006/11/republicans_insist_that_produc.html.

American Society of Civil Engineers. America's Crumbling Infrastructure Eroding Quality. Cited on March 9, 2005. Available from http://www.asce.org/reportcard/2005.

American Staffing Association. Staffing Statistics. Cited in December 2006. Available from http://www.americanstaffing.net/statistics/employee_survey_download_figures.cfm.

Angus, Jeff. Offshoring: The Self-Inflicted Wound. *CIO Insights*, May 24, 2005. Available from http://www.cioinsight.com/article2/0,1540,1820148,00.asp.

Baker, Dean. Republicans Insist That Productivity Is Lower Than the Data Show. *The American Prospect.* Cited in November 2006. Available from http://www.prospect. org/deanbaker/2006/11/republicans_insist_that_produc.html.

Balaker, Ted, and Moore, Adrian. Outsourcing and Public Fear. Reason. Policy Summary of Study 333. Cited September 2006. Available from http://www.reason.org/ ps333polsum.pdf#search='america%27s%20policy%20on%20outsourcing.

Bardhan, Deo, and Kroll, Cynthia A. The New Wave of Outsourcing. University of California, Berkeley, Fisher School for Real Estate and Urban Economics. Fall 2003, 1–12.

Bogle, John C. Owners Capitalism vs. Managers Capitalism. *2003 National Investor Relations Institute Conference.* June 11, 2003. Available from http://www.vanguard.com/ bogle_site/sp20030611.html.

Boskin, Michael. Some Thoughts on Improving Economic Statistics. Available from http:// www.hoover.org/publications/epp/2846506.html?show=essay.

Boston Logistics Group. The Asian Sourcing Boom: How Long Will It Last? Cited on May 17, 2006. Available from http://www.bostonlogistics.com/images/BLG_Asian_ Sourcing_Boom_Excerpt.pdf.

Botelho, Greg. Power Returns to Most Areas Hit by Blackout. CNN.com. Cited on August 16, 2003. Available from http://edition.cnn.com/2003/US/08/15/power.outage/index. html.

Breaking Records. *The Economist.* February 10, 2005.

Buchanan, Patrick J. Death of Manufacturing. *The American Conservative.* August 11, 2003.

Bureau of Labor Statistics (BLS). The Effect of Outsourcing and Offshoring on BLS Productivity Measures. March 26, 2004.

Business Prophet. Cited on January 23, 2006. *Business Week Online.* Available from http:// www.businessweek.com/magazine/content/06_04/b3968089.htm.

Caplan, S. J. Think China, Inc. The Motley Fool. August 12, 2005. Available from http:// www.fool.com/investing/high-growth/2005/08/12/think-china-inc.aspx.

Center for American Progress. Outsourcing Statistics in Perspective. Cited on March 16, 2004. Available from http://www.americanprogress.org/issues/2004/03/b38081.html.

Center for American Progress. The Offshoring Numbers Game. Cited on July 2006. Available from http://www.americanprogress.org/issues/2004/06/b100515.html.

Clowes, George A. U.S. Productivity Soars in Business, Slumps in Education. *School Reform News.* Cited on October 2006. Available from http://www.heartland.org/Article. cfm?artId=15601.

Committee for Economic Development. CED Urges Increased Investment in International Education and Foreign Language Studies. Cited on February 6, 2006. Available from http://www.ced.org/newsroom/press/press_foreignlanguages.pdf.

Committee for Economic Development. Education for Global Leadership: The Importance of International Studies and Foreign Language Education for U.S. Economic and National Security. Cited in November 2006. Available from http://www.ced.org/docs/ report/report_foreignlanguages.pdf.

Committee for Economic Development. Learning for the Future: Changing the Culture of Math and Science Education to Ensure a Competitive Workforce. Cited in November 2006. Available from http://www.ced.org/docs/report/report_scientists.pdf.

Committee for Economic Development. Making Trade Work: Straight Talk on Jobs, Trade, and Adjustment. Cited in March 15, 2006. Available from http://www.ced.org/docs/ report/report_trade2005.pdf.

Communications Workers of America. Outsourcing America's Future. Cited in February 2006. Available from http://www.outsourceoutrage.com/facts/.

Congressional Budget Office. CBO Testimony: Economic Relationship between United States and China. Cited on April 2006. Available from http://www.cbo.gov/ftpdocs/62xx/doc6274/04-14-ChinaTestimony.pdf.

Consulate General of the United States. Remarks by Ambassador Karan K. Bhatia. Cited on October 25, 2006. Available from http://shenyang.usembassy-china.org.cn/programs_events.html.

Cooper, Caroline. The Politics of Outsourcing. *Asian Times*. Cited on August 2006. Available from http://www.atimes.com/atimes/Global_Economy/FH20Dj01.html.

Cooper, James C., and Madigan Kathleen. U.S. Doubts about the Productivity Slowdown. *Business Week*. August 22, 2005.

Das, Gurcharan. India's Education Boom. *Newsweek International*. March 6, 2006.

Deloitte. Business in China, the Next Stage. Cited on March 7, 2004. Available from http://www.deloitte.com/dtt/cda/doc/content/dtt_wef_Business%20in%20China_030704.pdf.

Deloitte Research. The Macroeconomic Case for Outsourcing. Cited in July 2006. Available from http://www.deloitte.com/dtt/cda/doc/content/DTT_DR_MacroOutsourcing.pdf.

Drezner, Daniel W. Differentiating between Outsourcing and Offshoring. Cited on February 2, 2004. Available from http://www.danieldrezner.com/archives/001060.html.

Drucker, Peter. *The New Realities*. New York: Harper & Row, 1989.

Drucker, Peter. Peter Drucker Sets Us Straight. *CNN/Money*. Cited on January 12, 2004. Available from http://money.cnn.com/magazines/fortune/fortune_archive/2004/01/12/357916/index.htm.

Economic Report of the President, 2006. Cited in August 2006. Available from http://www.gpoaccess.gov/eop/download.html.

Economic Statistics and Macro Econometrics: The Figures Lie. Future Casts On-line Magazine. Cited on July 1, 2001. Available from http://www.futurecasts.com/Economic_statistics.html.

Engardio, Pete. *Chindia*. New York: MacGraw-Hill, 2007.

Engardio, Pete. The Future of Outsourcing. *Business Week*. Cited on January 30, 2006. Available from http://www.businessweek.com/magazine/content/06_05/b3969401.htm.

Federal Reserve Bank of Dallas. Free Enterprise: Measures of Productivity. Cited in April 2006. Available from http://www.dallasfed.org/eyi/free/0406product.html.

Fishman, Charles. The Wal-Mart You Don't Know. *Fast Company*. December 2003 (Issue 77), 68.

Friedman, Thomas. The World Is Flat. New York: Farrar, Straus, and Giroux, 2005.

Feffer, John. America's Real Achilles Heel. *ZDNET*. Cited on December 31, 2005. Available from http://www.zmag.org/Sustainers/Content/2005-12/31feffer.cfm.

Gartner: Look to China for Outsourcing Services. IT World.com. Cited on January 18, 2002. http://www.itworld.com/Man/2701/IDG020118chinaoutsourcing/.

George, Tana. Why Outsourcing Fails. *IT Manager's Journal*. Cited on February 6, 2006. Available from http://www.itmanagersjournal.com/articles/10536?tid=88&amp;amp;tid=86.

Getronics. Outsourcing Improves Productivity. Cited on June 30, 2005. Available from http://www.getronics.com/NR/rdonlyres/ejqpyxvcvtkwhgandidxim7af7an2t3osaqt52oibr35f4hxmavmogrtz7xlkgc5duuv25gwn7yalo6ibk2v6cad6me/wp_outsourcing_gartner.pdf.

Gilmore, Dan. Transportation Infrastructure—Should You Care? *Supply Chain Digest.* July 21, 2006.

Global Envision. A Brief History of Outsourcing. Cited on December 7, 2004. Available from http://www.globalenvision.org/library/3/702.

Goodman, Peter S., and Pan, Phillip P. Chinese Workers Pay for Wal-Mart's Low Prices. *WashingtonPost.com.* Cited in February 2006. Available from http://www.momandpopnyc.com/campaigns/walmart/articles/Labor%20Practices_Unions/ChineseWorkers,%20WaPost,%202.23.04.pdf.

Griswold, Daniel T., and Buss, Dale D. "Outsourcing Benefits Michigan Economy and Taxpayers." Mackinac Center for Public Policy. September 16, 2004. 1–8.

Homeshoring: Outsourcing to America's Living Rooms. IT World.com. Cited on July 6, 2006. http://www.itworld.com/Man/2701/nls_itinsights_homeshore060705/.

House of Representatives, Joint Economic Committee Report. "Faulty Wage Data from Labor Department." Cited in August 1995. Available from http://www.house.gov/jec/middle/cookbook/cooks.htm.

Isidore, Chris. New Worry for Drivers: BP Shuts Down Oilfield. *CNN Money.* Cited on August 8, 2006. Available from http://money.cnn.com/2006/08/07/news/international/oil_alaska/index.htm?cnn=yes.

IT Business Edge. Hackett: Sarbox Drives Biggest Finance Cost Rise in 13 Years. Cited on September 22, 2005. Available from http://www.itbusinessedge.com/item/?ci=6888.

Iwata, Edward and Hansen, Barbara. Pay, Performance Don't Always Add Up. *USA Today.* Cited on April 20, 2004. Available from http://www.usatoday.com/money/companies/management/2004-04-30-exec-pay_x.htm.

Jacobs, Michael. *Short-Term America.* Boston: Harvard Business School Press, 1991.

Johnson, Alex. A Textbook Case in Failure. MSNBC.com. Cited on May 16, 2006. Available from http://www.msnbc.com/id/12705167/print/displaymode/1098.

Jorgenson, Dale W., Ho, Mun S., and Stiroh, Kevin J. Will the U.S. Productivity Resurgence Continue? *Federal Reserve Bank of New York.* December 2004, Volume 10, Number 13.

Kane, Tim, Schafer, Brett D., and Fraser, Alison. Ten Myths about Jobs and Outsourcing. *The Heritage Foundation* (Web Memo #467). Cited on April 1, 2004. Available from http://www.heritage.org/Research/TradeandForeignAid/wm467.cfm.

Kedrova, Julia. Measuring Productivity. Federal Reserve Bank of Dallas. *Expand Your Insight.* June 2004.

Kemp, Graham. The ITO/BPO Connection. Outsourcing.com. Cited in Summer 2004, Volume 2, Number 2. Available from http://www.outsourcing.com/content.asp?page=01b/other/oe/q204/kemp.html.

Klein, Noami. Outsourcing the Friedman. *The Nation.* Cited on March 4, 2004. Available from http://www.thenation.com/doc/20040322/klein.

Levine, Linda. Offshoring (a.k.a Offshore Outsourcing) and Job Insecurity Among U.S. Workers. CRS Report for Congress. June 18, 2004. 1–17.

The Maverick Management Guru. FT.com. Cited on June 4, 2006. Available from http://www.ft.com/cms/s/57cb97bc-f3db-11da-9dab-0000779e2340.html.

Maybe Everyone Is Worried about Outsourcing. Computerworld Blogs. Cited on May 30, 2006. Available from http://www.computerworld.com/blogs/node/2639.

McCormack, Richard. China Replaces U.S. as World's Largest Exporter. *Manufacturing and Technology News.* Cited on September 5, 2006. Available from http://www.manufacturingnews.com/news/06/0905/art1.html.

Mehlman, Bruce. Offshoring Outsourcing and the Future of American Competitiveness. Harvard University, Kennedy School of Government. Cited on October 1, 2003. 1–15. Available from http://www.technology.gov/Speeches/BPM_2003-Outsourcing. pdf#search='america%27s%20policy%20on%20outsourcing.

Mintzer, Sydney. China's Industrial Policy—Not Its Currency Policy—Threatens American Competitiveness. *The China Trade Law Report*. Cited in August 2006. Available from http://www.ljnonline.com/issues/ljn_international/1_5/news/147081-1.html.

Mishel, Lawrence. Manufacturing Numbers: How Inaccurate Statistics Conceal U.S. Industrial Decline. *Economic Policy Institute*. April 1988. 1–11.

Mitchell, Anthony. Blowing It with China. *E-Commerce Times*. Cited on August 2, 2005. Available from http://www.ecommercetimes.com/story/45131.html.

Mooney, Paul. Undue Fears of China, Inc. *YaleGlobal*. Cited on September 29, 2005. Available from http://yaleglobal.yale.edu/display.article?id=6320.

Morici, Peter: U.S. Trade Deficit Exceeds 6 Percent of GDP. FinFacts.com. Cited on January 12, 2006. Available from http://www.finfacts.com/irelandbusinessnews/publish/printer_1000article_10004497.shtml.

National Association of Manufacturers. A Case for a Strong Manufacturing Base. Cited September 2006. Available from http://www.nam.org/s_nam/sec.asp?CID= 201720&DID=230272.

National Center for Policy Analysis. How Outsourcing Creates Jobs for Americans. Cited on July 27, 2004. Available from http://www.ncpa.org/pub/ba/ba480/.

National Center for Policy Analysis. Outsourcing Talk Is Seriously Overblown. Cited on October 13, 2004. Available from http://www.ncpa.org/edo/bb/2004/20041013bb. htm.

Nearly 50,000 Workers Take Buyouts, Early Retirements at GM. *OhmyNews*. Cited on June 27, 2006. Available from http://english.ohmynews.com/ArticleView/article_view.asp? no=301454&rel_no=1.

Olsen, Karsten Bjerring. Productivity Impacts of Offshoring and Outsourcing: A Review. Organisation for OECD Directorate for Science, Technology and Industry (STI). March 2006. 1–33.

Outsourcing Guide. *CIO Magazine*. Cited on July 15, 2006. Available from http://www. cio.com/archive/071506/2006_global_outsourcing_guide.pdf.

Outsourcing Major Driver of Productivity: Study. *Hindustan Times*. Cited on December 7, 2005. Available from http://www.hindustantimes.in/news/181_1535029,00020021. htm.

Outsourcing Offshoring World. Outsourcing: What Goes Around Comes Around. Cited on October 28, 2005. Available from http://www.offshoreoutsourcingworld.com/blog/ SoftwareOutsourcingbenefits/_archives/2005/10.

Overby, Stephanie. It's Cheaper in China. *CIO*. September 15, 2005.

Overby, Stephanie. The China Gambit. *CIO*. June 15, 2006.

Palley, Thomas. Economics of Outsourcing. *CounterPunch*. March 4, 2006.

Palley, Thomas. 2006. Pressure China to Change. *TomPane.com*. Cited on April 13, 2006. Available from http://www.tompaine.com/articles/2006/04/13/pressure_china_to_ change.php.

PBS. Frontline: Is Wal-Mart Good for America? Cited on September 9, 2004. Available from http://www.pbs.org/wgbh/pages/frontline/shows/walmart/interviews/gereffi.html.

Power, Carla. Not the Queen's English. *Newsweek Online Edition*. Cited on March 7, 2007. Available from http://www.msnbc.msn.com/id/7038031/site/newsweek/.

Prince, C. J. Just Say No? More Big Companies Are Refusing to Give Wall Street Quarterly Earnings Guidance. *Entrepreneur.* Cited in August 2005. Available from http://www. findarticles.com/p/articles/mi_m0DTI/is_8_33/ai_n14871916.

Productivity versus Outsourcing. *The Hindu.* Cited on June 7, 2004. Available from http:// www.hindu.com/2004/06/07/stories/2004060700771400.htm.

Reason Foundation. Funding Our Crumbling Roads. Cited on February 6, 2006. Available from http://reason.org/commentaries/staley_20060206.shtml.

Reich, Robert. Education Key to Solving America's 'Real Jobs' Problem. Northwestern University, Institute for Public Research. Fall 2005, Number 1.

Richman, Louis. Why the Economic Data Mislead Us. CNNMoney.com. Cited on March 8, 1993. Available from http://money.cnn.com/magazines/fortune/fortune_archive/1993/03/08/77578/index.htm.

Riedl, Richard E. The Failure of American Schools to Change: Innovations That Didn't Take. *The Newsletter of Western Center for Microcomputers in Special Education, Inc.* Cited in December 2006. Available from http://www.thecatalyst.us/zDoneArticles/19_1_Riedl.pdf.

Roudoi, Andrei. Sustainability of Russian Growth. *Global Insights.* Cited on November 1, 2005. Available from http://www.chass.utoronto.ca/link/meeting/papers/1101am_ar.pdf.

Russian Stocks Hit Record as Economy Booms. *Yahoo.* Cited on December 28, 2006. Available from http://asia.news.yahoo.com/061228/3/2v06y.html.

Saxena, Puru. Fantasy Land! *Safe Haven.* May 27, 2005. Available from http://www.safehaven.com/showarticle.cfm?id=3130.

Schlosser, Eric. *Fast Food Nation.* New York: Harper, 2005.

Sender, Isabelle. Building Roads to Riches. *Business Week Online.* Cited on May 25, 2006. Available from http://businessweek.com/print/inventor/content/may2006.

Sharpe, Andrew. What Have We Learned about Productivity in the Last Two Decades? Centre for the Study of Living Standards. Spring 2002 (Number 4). 53–63.

Shin, Annys. Is Wal-Mart's U.S. Growth Nearing Its Limit? *Washington Post.* Cited on December 2, 2006. Available from http://reclaimdemocracy.org/walmart/2006/us_growth_slows.php.

Sowell, Thomas. Outsourcing and Saving Jobs. *Capitalism Magazine.* Cited on March 16, 2004. Available from http://capmag.com/article.asp?ID=3565.

Spar, Edward J. Federal Statistics in the FY 2007 Budget. Council of Professional Associations on Federal Statistics. AAAS Report, Chapter 21. 2007.

State Institute on International Education in the Schools. Meeting the Need for World Languages, Remarks by Michael Lemmon. Cited on November 16, 2004. Available from http://www.internationaled.org/statesinstitute2004/MichaelLemmon.pdf.

Steelmakers Urge US Act against Chinese Subsidies. *Yahoo.* Cited on July 14, 2006. Available from http://asia.news.yahoo.com/060713/3/2n4hw.html.

Stein, Charles. Good Corporate Times Haven't Trickled Down to Employee. Boston.com. January 11, 2004.

Strassmann, Paul. Five Steps to Improve Your Information Productivity. *Baseline Magazine.* October 15, 2006.

Symonds, William C. America's Failure in Science Education. *Business Week.* March 16, 2004.

Taylor, Frederick W. *Principles of Scientific Management.* New York: W. W. Norton & Company, 1967.

Tech Policy. Outsourcing: White Collar Protectionists. Cited on February 2, 2004. Available from http://techpolicy.typepad.com/tpp/2004/02/outsourcing_whi.html.

Teixeira, Ruy. How Americans View the Economy. *The Century Foundation*. Cited on October 27, 2006. Available from http://www.tcf.org/list.asp?type=TN&pubid=1424.

Thornton, Mark. How Outsourcing Creates Jobs. LewThornton.com. Cited in February 2006. Available from http://www.lewrockwell.com/thornton/thornton20.html.

Trade Partnership Worldwide, LLC. Impact of Imports from China on US Employment. Cited on November 2005. Available from http://www.tradepartnership.com/pdf_files/2005_China_imports.pdf#search='U.S.%20imports%20to%20China.

Trade Wins, LLC. Chinese Subsidies and US Responses. Cited on April 5, 2006. Available from http://www.worldtradelaw.net/articles/magnuschinesesubsidies.pdf#search='chinese%20subsidies.

Triplett, Jack E., and Bosworth, Barry E. Productivity in the U.S. Services Sector. Brookings Institutional Press. Cited in March 2006. Available from http://www.brook.edu/PRESS/books/chapter_1/productivityintheusservicessector.pdf.

United Nations. Infrastructure Development in the People's Republic of China. Cited on November 15, 2006. Available from http://www.unescap.org/ttdw/common/TPT/ReviewofPlanning/CountryPapers/China.pdf.

U.S. Congress. Kennedy Puts Forth Plan to Jumpstart American Competitiveness. Cited in August 2006. Available from http://www.masstech.org/institute/clips/2_22_06kennedy-MTC.html.

U.S. Department of Labor. A Chartbook of International Labor Comparisons. Cited in June 2006. Available from http://www.dol.gov/asp/media/reports/chartbook/index.htm.

U.S. Department of Labor, Bureau of Labor Statistics. Productivity and Costs. Cited on November 4, 2004. Available from http://www.bls.gov/lpc/peoplebox.htm.

U.S. Doubts About the Productivity Slowdown. *Business Week Online*. Cited on August 22, 2005. Available from http://www.businessweek.com/magazine/content/05_34/b3948017_mz010.htm?campaign_id=rss_magzn.

U.S. State Department. U.S.-China Labor Issues Generate Strong Emotions. Cited on March 29, 2005. Available from http://usinfo.state.gov/eap/Archive/2005/Mar/29-848102.html.

US Will Collapse without Outsourcing. *Sify News*. Cited on August 31, 2004. Available from http://sify.com/news/nri/fullstory.php?id=13555966.

Ventoro. Offshore 2005 Research, Preliminary Findings and Conclusions. Cited on January 22, 2005. Available from http://www.ventoro.com/Offshore2005ResearchFindings.pdf.

Vieth, Warren, and Chen, Edwin. Bush Economic Report Praises Outsourcing Jobs. Cited on February 10, 2004. Available from http://www.post-gazette.com/pg/04041/271362.stm.

Waldman, Cliff. MAPI Quarterly Forecast of U.S. Export, Global Growth, and the Dollar. Manufacturers Alliance/MAPI. January 2007. 1–10.

Wallis, Claudia, and Steptoe, Sonya. How to Bring Our Schools out of the 20th Century. *Time*. Cited on December 10, 2006. Available from http://www.time.com/time/magazine/article/0,9171,1568480,00.html.

Weidenbaum, Murray. Outsourcing and American Jobs. Weidenbaum Center on the Economy, Government, and Public Policy. Cited on June 24, 2004. Available from http://wc.

wustl.edu/Breakfast_Programs_Transcripts/Weidenbaum_Outsourcing.pdf#search=
'outsourcing%20and%20jobs.

The White House. President Participates in Panel on the American Competitiveness Initiative. Cited on April 21, 2006. Available from http://whitehouse.gov/news/releases/2006/02/20060421ml.

The White House. Press Briefing by Administration Officials on American Competitiveness. Cited on February 01, 2006. Available from http://whitehouse.gov/news/releases/2006/02/20060201.html.

Williams, Matt, and Cohen, Jerome. To Strengthen Ties with China, Speak the Language First. *Christian Science Monitor*. Cited on September 30, 2005. Available from http://www.csmonitor.com/2005/0930/p09s02-coop.html.

Williams, Walter. Disappearing Manufacturing Jobs. *CNS News*. Cited on May 3, 2006. Available from http://www.cnsnews.com/ViewCommentary.asp?Page=/Commentary/archive/200605/COM20060503a.html.

World Bank. Accounting Standards in China. October–December 2001. 19–20.

Wu, Friedrich. China, Inc. International: How Chinese Companies Have Discretely Internationalized Their Operations. *The International Economy*. Fall 2005. Journal on-line. Available from http://findarticles.com/p/articles/mi_m2633/is_4_19/ai_n16031488/pg_1.

# Index

## About the Author

JACK BUFFINGTON, currently Director of Supply Chain Logistics for Molson Coors Brewing Company, has been a corporate executive, professor, academic researcher, Big Five consultant, and even a blue-collar hourly worker. He has taught at the University of Denver, where he serves on the Board of its MBA Program. He has studied Russian, Mandarin Chinese, and Spanish.